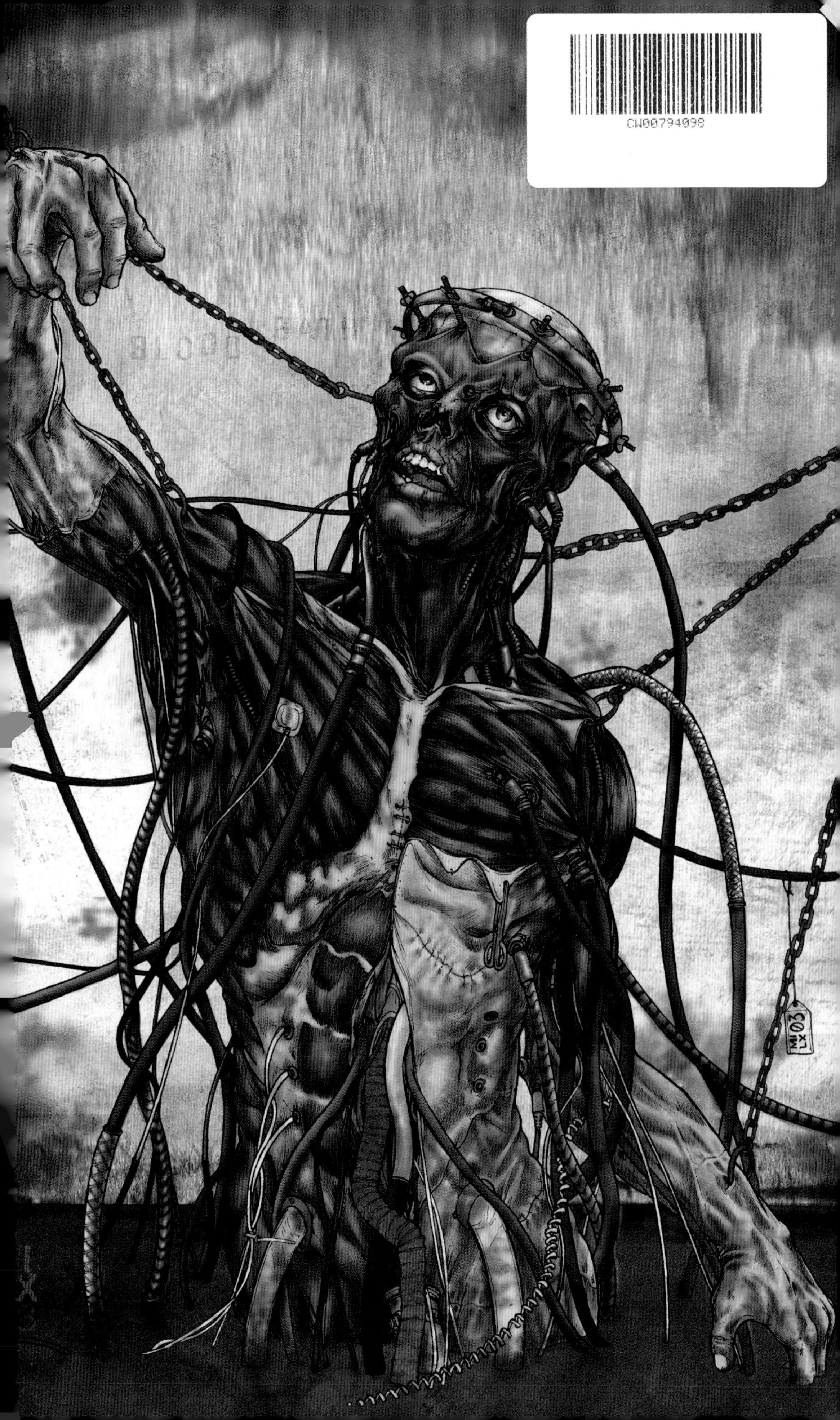

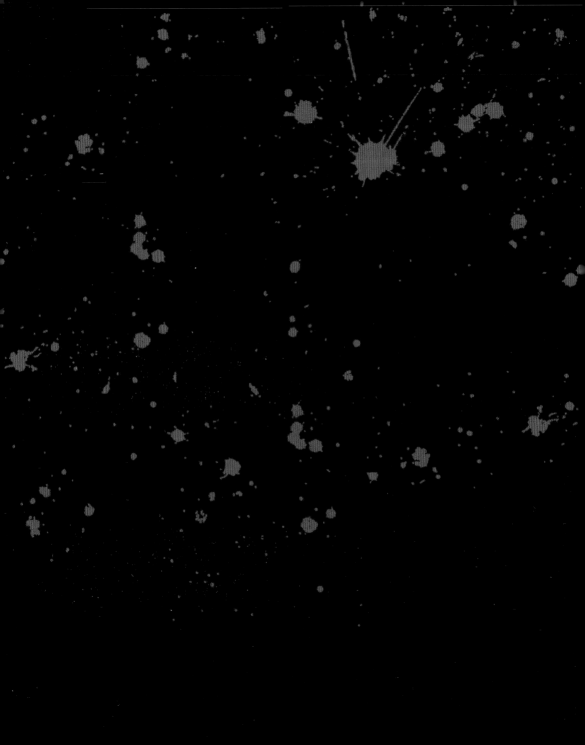

WAKE THE DEAD

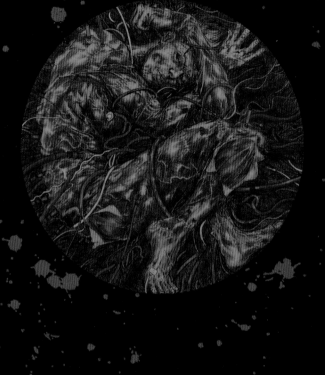

Steve Niles   Chee   Travis Walton

Dedicated to:

Misunderstood Monsters Everywhere.

Thanks everybody at IDW, Nikki, Jon Levin, Michael Dougherty and very special thanks to Chee for saving the day!

-Steve Niles

Wake the Dead

Story: Steve Niles

Art: Chee

Additional pages: Milx

Coloring: Travis Walton and Milx

Lettering and design: Robbie Robbins

Cover art: Milx

Editor: Jeff Mariotte

IDW PUBLISHING:

Ted Adams, Publisher
Jeff Mariotte, Editor-in-Chief
Robbie Robbins, Design Director
Kris Oprisko, Vice President
Alex Garner, Art Director
Cindy Chapman, Designer
Beau Smith, Sales & Marketing
Chance Boren, Editorial Assistant
Yumiko Miyano, Business Development
Rick Privman, Business Development

www.idwpublishing.com

ISBN: 1-932382-22-4
07 06 05 04 1 2 3 4 5

WAKE THE DEAD. June 2004. FIRST PRINTING. IDW Publishing, a division of Idea + Design Works, LLC. Editorial offices: 4411 Morena Blvd., Suite 106, San Diego, CA 92117.

Introduction
by Michael Dougherty

Growing up, a lot of people experienced the embarrassment of parents finding a stack of "unsavory" magazines tucked under the mattress. When we came home from school, the evidence would be found sitting on a countertop, while the scolding parent sat at the kitchen table, arms folded and ready to lecture. For most, the offending material was usually a pile of dirty magazines stolen from dad's own secret stash in his closet. But for me, the crime wasn't pornography. It was horror comics.

For whatever reason, pages of hand-drawn zombies, vampires, and dismembered limbs were considered just as distasteful as full-color photos of bouncing jugs and juicy spread eagles. Even worse, the fate of these publications was the same: the fireplace. So after a few repeat offenses where I watched *Creepy*, *Eerie*, and *Cycle of the Werewolf* go up in smoke, I stopped trying to find horror books. They became nostalgic memories while I started spending my allowance on more parent-approved comics like *Spider-Man* and *X-Men*.

As I got older, and superhero comics got lamer, I'd occasionally snoop around for new horror titles, but other than a few memorable years of *Clive Barker's Hellraiser* books, it seemed like raw and blood-splattered panels were a thing of the past. No more cannibal families. No more mad scientists performing experiments in their basements. No more fun. But recently, that's all changed.

While superheroes still dominate the comic shop, more aisles are slowly being claimed by horror titles not so different than the books of yesteryear. The twisted glee of Jhonen Vasquez's blood-soaked *Johnny the Homicidal Maniac* and *Squee* were the first rays of hope, but the past two years have become a true "scarlet age of horror" as the red ink started flowing by the gallon.

Steve Niles' *30 Days of Night* was like a warm rush of putrid air escaping from a freshly opened crypt, and I mean that as a compliment. It was the type of story that could've been ripped from a classic issue of *Eerie*: a remote Alaskan town besieged by vampires during an entire month of darkness. No pop-culture references. No tongue-in-cheek attitude. Just straightforward blood and guts. It was a series that brought back memories of secretly reading comics with a flashlight when I was supposed to be asleep, and when the series ended it only left me wanting more. Luckily, I didn't have to wait very long.

While *30 Days* put a fresh twist on the often overused vampire lore, *Wake The Dead* reintroduced us to another creature from our collective unconscious: Frankenstein's monster. Mary Shelley's story of science run amok has been told hundreds of times in almost every form of media, so hearing it would be told yet again as a comic book stirred feelings of both intrigue and skepticism. But after a few pages of exploding pigs and dismembered limbs, I had a twisted grin stretched across my face, and once again felt like that ten-year-old reading forbidden comics during the witching hour.

Wake The Dead felt like an old school horror comic even more than *30 Days* did. From the first page with its gothic house on a dark and rainy night, to the exaggerated and intricately rendered panels of ripped flesh and fountains of bright red blood, it was obvious that the book wasn't going to pull punches. If anything, it was going to hit you hard and fast, tear you open, then bitch slap you with your own large intestine. And that it did. Each book seemed to be filled with so much blood and bone that the pages felt moist, and I couldn't help but feel the need to wipe my hands after turning them. Even more interesting was the nagging feeling that I shouldn't leave the comics sitting on my bed in plain view, that the proper place for them was tucked under the mattress, away from prying eyes. For even though I was in my twenties and living on my own, I couldn't help but wonder if I might come home to find my mother sitting at the kitchen table, arms folded and ready to lecture, while more horror comics once again went up in smoke in the fireplace.

Michael Dougherty
April 2004

Michael Dougherty is a screenwriter and animator whose credits include *X-MEN 2* and the adaptation of *WAKE THE DEAD* for Dimension Films

chapter one

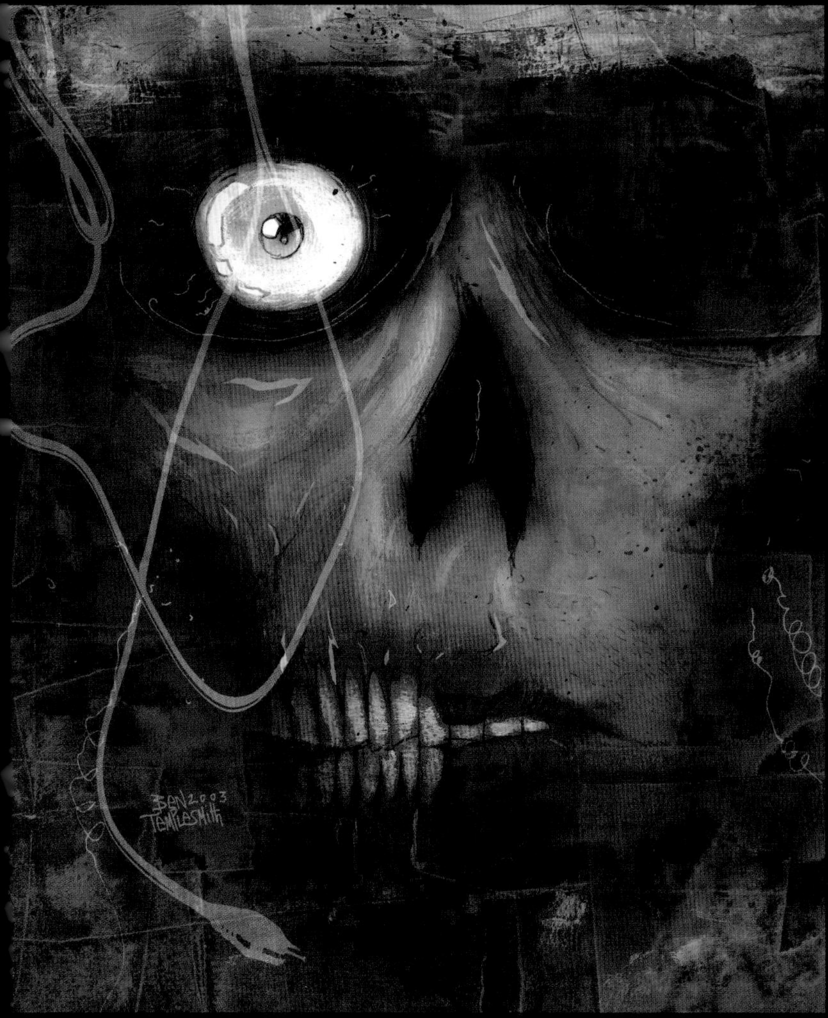
BEN 2003
TEMPLESMITH

Wake the Dead no.1 mini-series alternate cover by Ben Templesmith

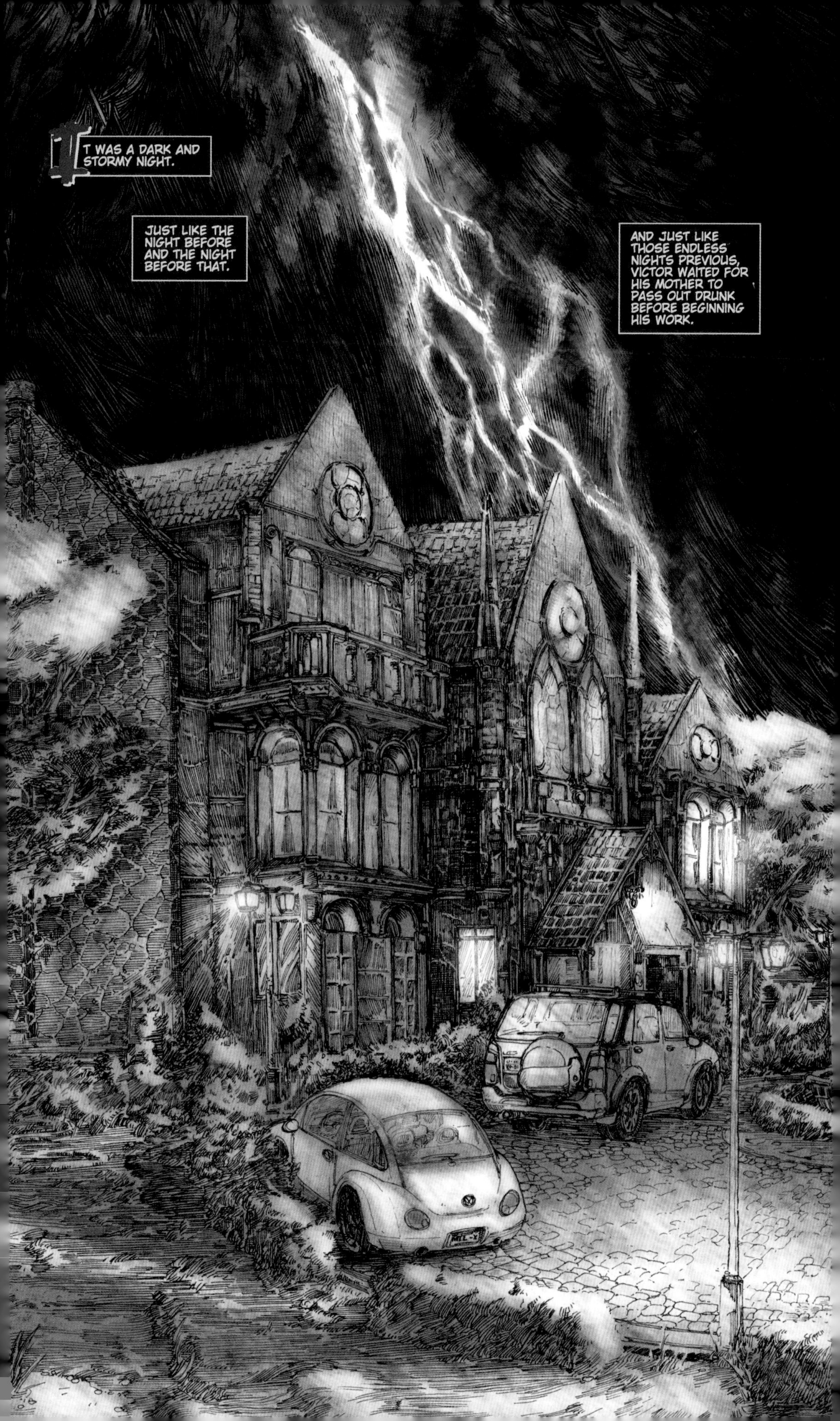
IT WAS A DARK AND STORMY NIGHT.
JUST LIKE THE NIGHT BEFORE AND THE NIGHT BEFORE THAT.
AND JUST LIKE THOSE ENDLESS NIGHTS PREVIOUS, VICTOR WAITED FOR HIS MOTHER TO PASS OUT DRUNK BEFORE BEGINNING HIS WORK.

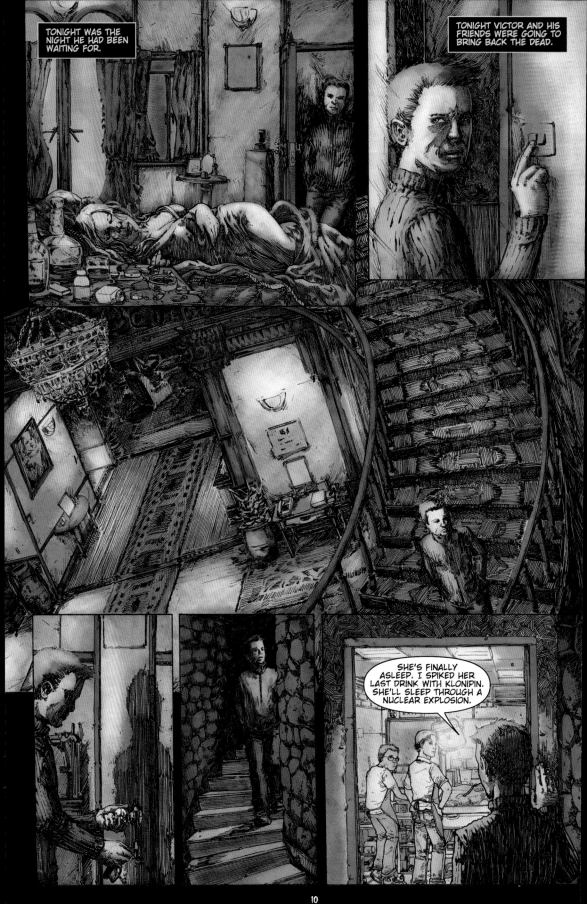

TONIGHT WAS THE NIGHT HE HAD BEEN WAITING FOR.

TONIGHT VICTOR AND HIS FRIENDS WERE GOING TO BRING BACK THE DEAD.

SHE'S FINALLY ASLEEP. I SPIKED HER LAST DRINK WITH KLONIPIN. SHE'LL SLEEP THROUGH A NUCLEAR EXPLOSION.

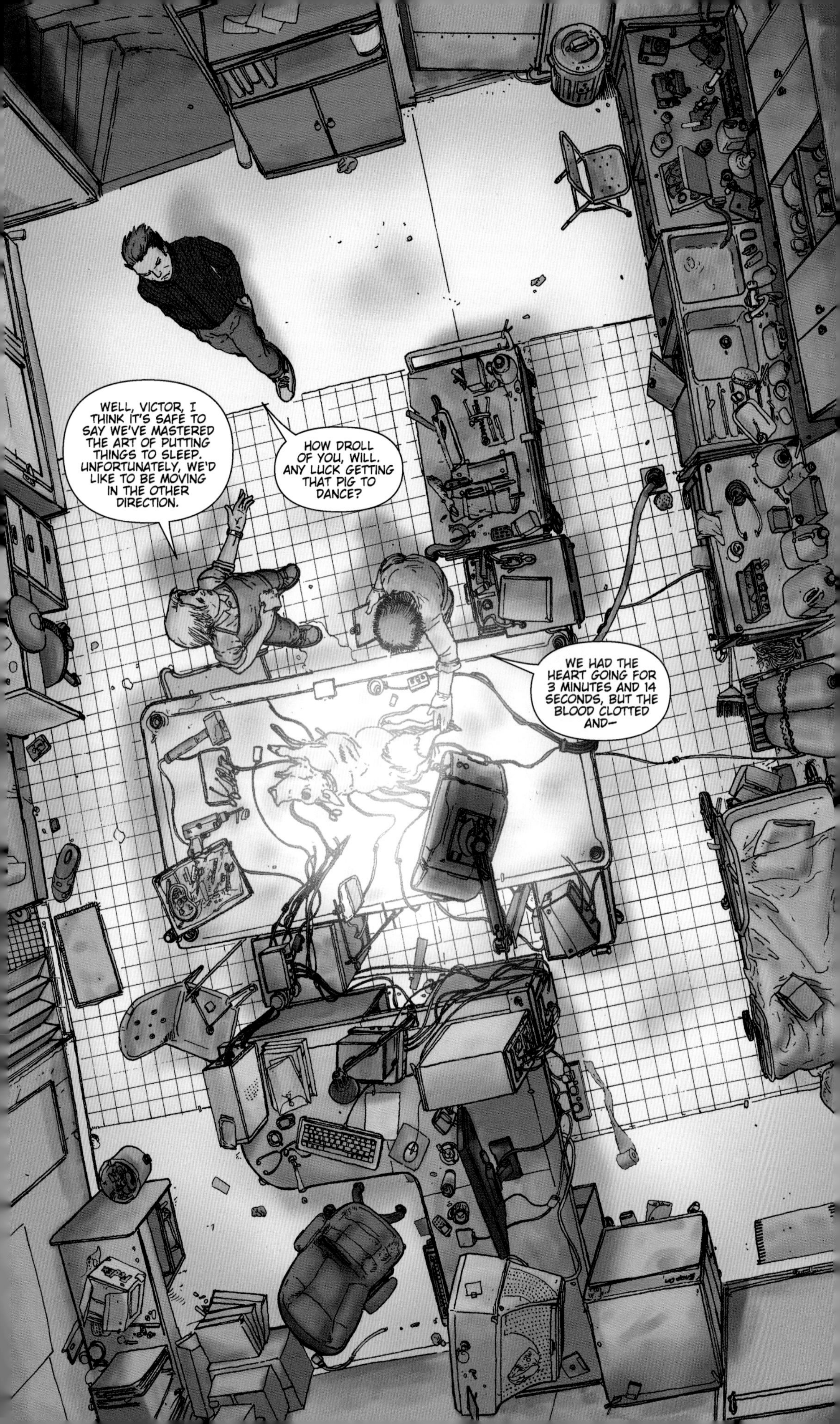
WELL, VICTOR, I THINK IT'S SAFE TO SAY WE'VE MASTERED THE ART OF PUTTING THINGS TO SLEEP. UNFORTUNATELY, WE'D LIKE TO BE MOVING IN THE OTHER DIRECTION.
HOW DROLL OF YOU, WILL. ANY LUCK GETTING THAT PIG TO DANCE?
WE HAD THE HEART GOING FOR 3 MINUTES AND 14 SECONDS, BUT THE BLOOD CLOTTED AND—

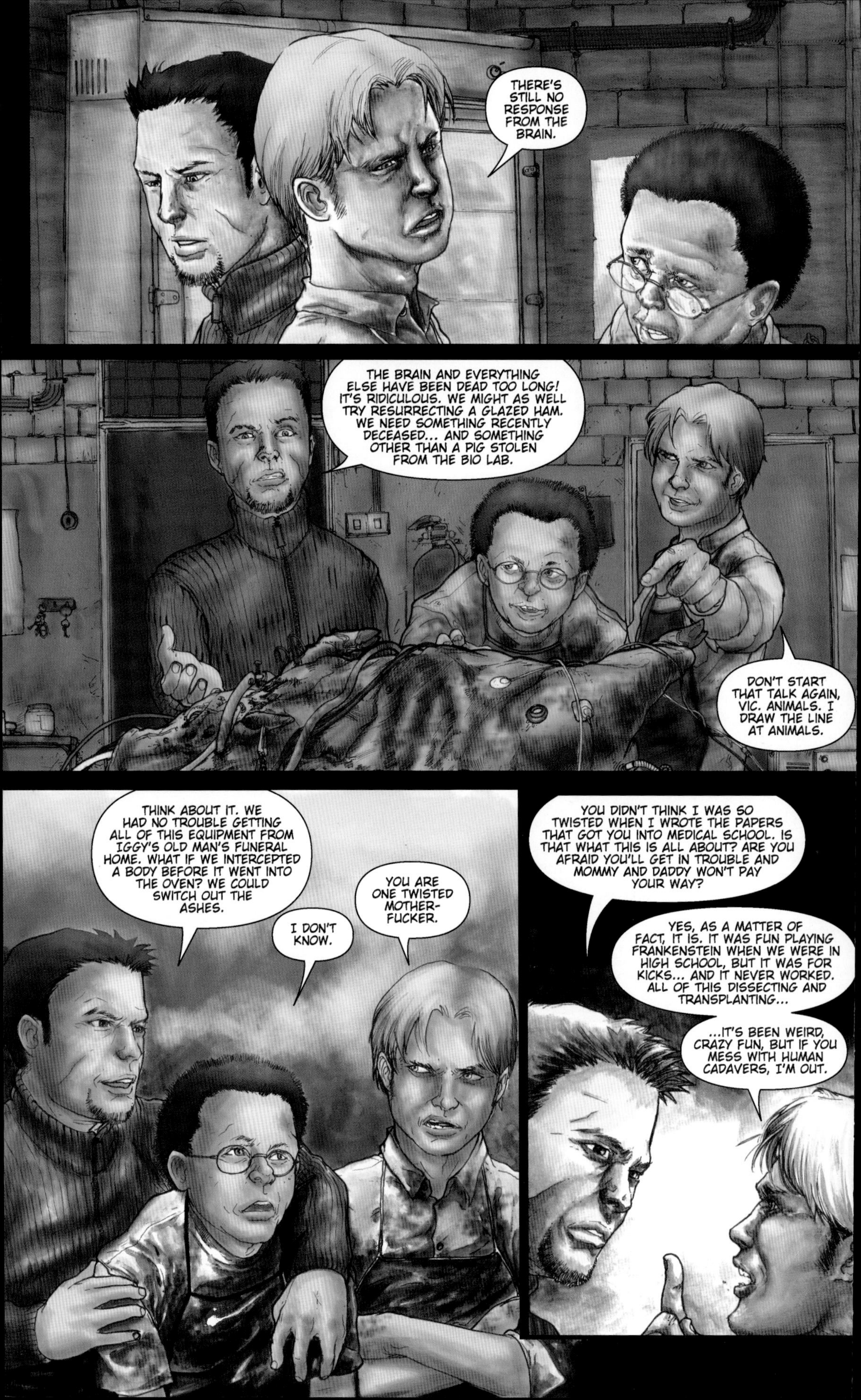
THERE'S STILL NO RESPONSE FROM THE BRAIN.
THE BRAIN AND EVERYTHING ELSE HAVE BEEN DEAD TOO LONG! IT'S RIDICULOUS. WE MIGHT AS WELL TRY RESURRECTING A GLAZED HAM. WE NEED SOMETHING RECENTLY DECEASED... AND SOMETHING OTHER THAN A PIG STOLEN FROM THE BIO LAB.
DON'T START THAT TALK AGAIN, VIC. ANIMALS. I DRAW THE LINE AT ANIMALS.
THINK ABOUT IT. WE HAD NO TROUBLE GETTING ALL OF THIS EQUIPMENT FROM IGGY'S OLD MAN'S FUNERAL HOME. WHAT IF WE INTERCEPTED A BODY BEFORE IT WENT INTO THE OVEN? WE COULD SWITCH OUT THE ASHES.
I DON'T KNOW.
YOU ARE ONE TWISTED MOTHER-FUCKER.
YOU DIDN'T THINK I WAS SO TWISTED WHEN I WROTE THE PAPERS THAT GOT YOU INTO MEDICAL SCHOOL. IS THAT WHAT THIS IS ALL ABOUT? ARE YOU AFRAID YOU'LL GET IN TROUBLE AND MOMMY AND DADDY WON'T PAY YOUR WAY?
YES, AS A MATTER OF FACT, IT IS. IT WAS FUN PLAYING FRANKENSTEIN WHEN WE WERE IN HIGH SCHOOL, BUT IT WAS FOR KICKS... AND IT NEVER WORKED. ALL OF THIS DISSECTING AND TRANSPLANTING...
...IT'S BEEN WEIRD, CRAZY FUN, BUT IF YOU MESS WITH HUMAN CADAVERS, I'M OUT.

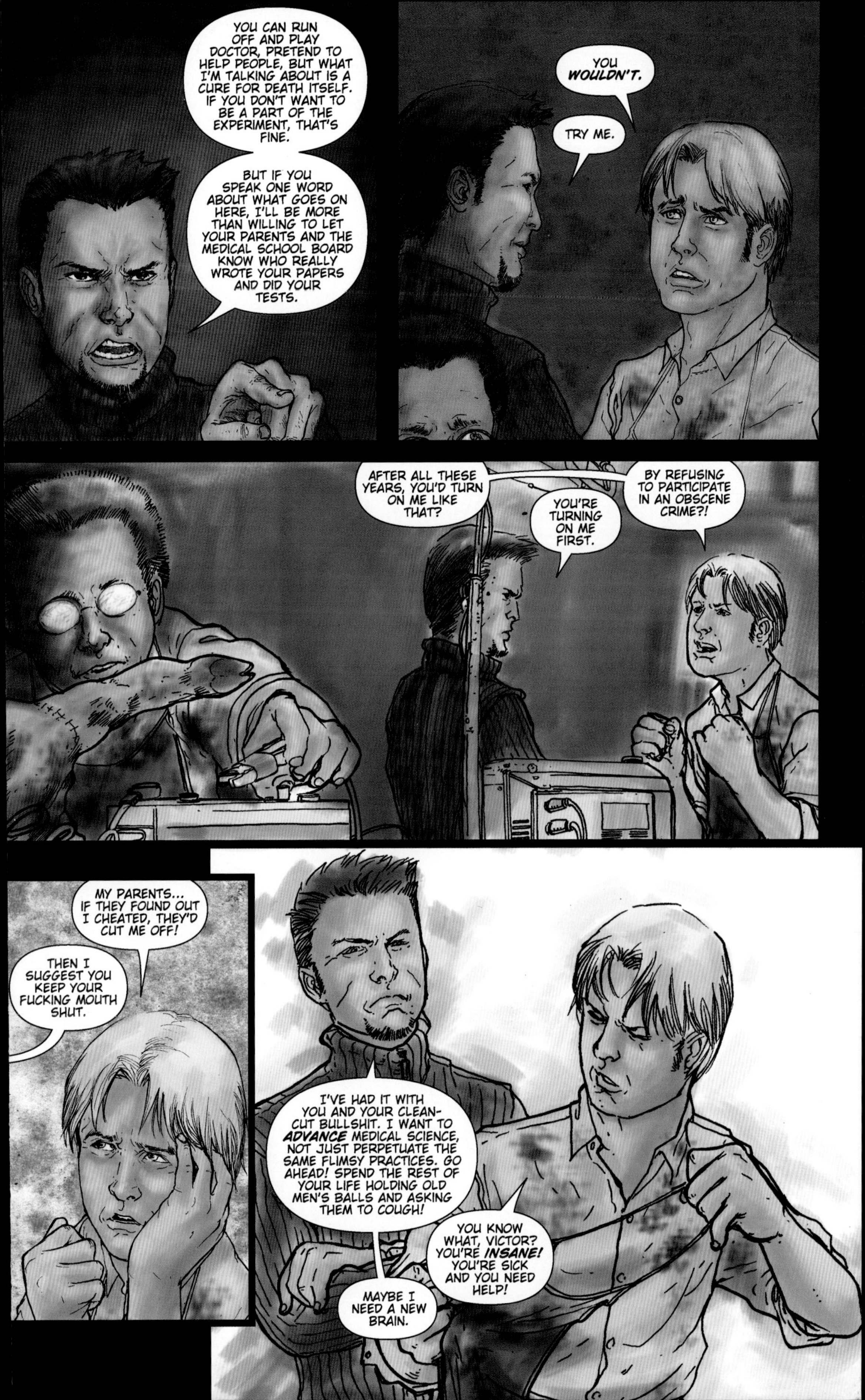

YOU CAN RUN OFF AND PLAY DOCTOR, PRETEND TO HELP PEOPLE, BUT WHAT I'M TALKING ABOUT IS A CURE FOR DEATH ITSELF. IF YOU DON'T WANT TO BE A PART OF THE EXPERIMENT, THAT'S FINE.
BUT IF YOU SPEAK ONE WORD ABOUT WHAT GOES ON HERE, I'LL BE MORE THAN WILLING TO LET YOUR PARENTS AND THE MEDICAL SCHOOL BOARD KNOW WHO REALLY WROTE YOUR PAPERS AND DID YOUR TESTS.
YOU *WOULDN'T.*
TRY ME.
AFTER ALL THESE YEARS, YOU'D TURN ON ME LIKE THAT?
YOU'RE TURNING ON ME FIRST.
BY REFUSING TO PARTICIPATE IN AN OBSCENE CRIME?!
MY PARENTS... IF THEY FOUND OUT I CHEATED, THEY'D CUT ME OFF!
THEN I SUGGEST YOU KEEP YOUR FUCKING MOUTH SHUT.
I'VE HAD IT WITH YOU AND YOUR CLEAN-CUT BULLSHIT. I WANT TO *ADVANCE* MEDICAL SCIENCE, NOT JUST PERPETUATE THE SAME FLIMSY PRACTICES. GO AHEAD! SPEND THE REST OF YOUR LIFE HOLDING OLD MEN'S BALLS AND ASKING THEM TO COUGH!
YOU KNOW WHAT, VICTOR? YOU'RE *INSANE!* YOU'RE SICK AND YOU NEED HELP!
MAYBE I NEED A NEW BRAIN.

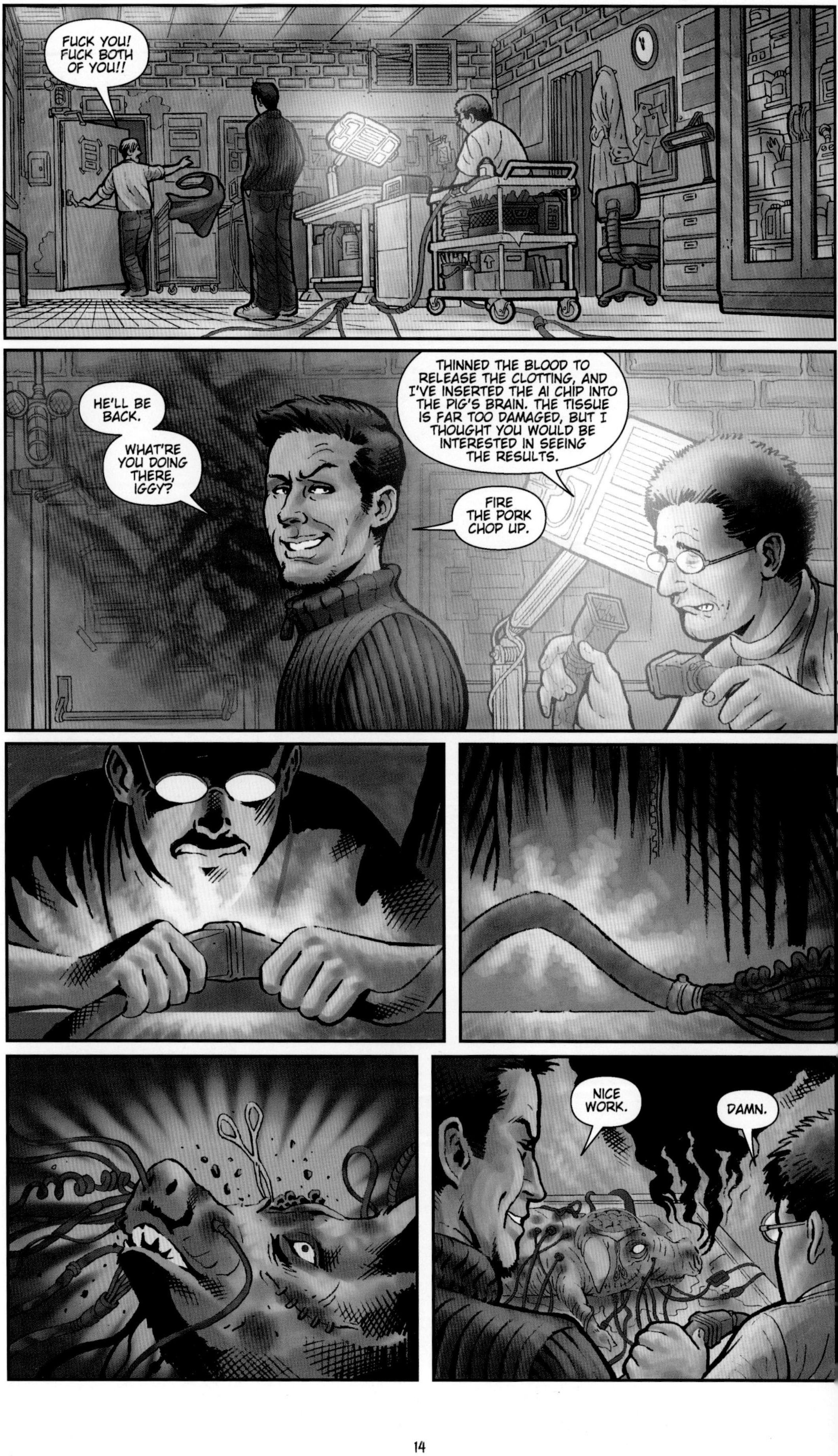
FUCK YOU! FUCK BOTH OF YOU!!
HE'LL BE BACK.
WHAT'RE YOU DOING THERE, IGGY?
THINNED THE BLOOD TO RELEASE THE CLOTTING, AND I'VE INSERTED THE AI CHIP INTO THE PIG'S BRAIN. THE TISSUE IS FAR TOO DAMAGED, BUT I THOUGHT YOU WOULD BE INTERESTED IN SEEING THE RESULTS.
FIRE THE PORK CHOP UP.
NICE WORK.
DAMN.

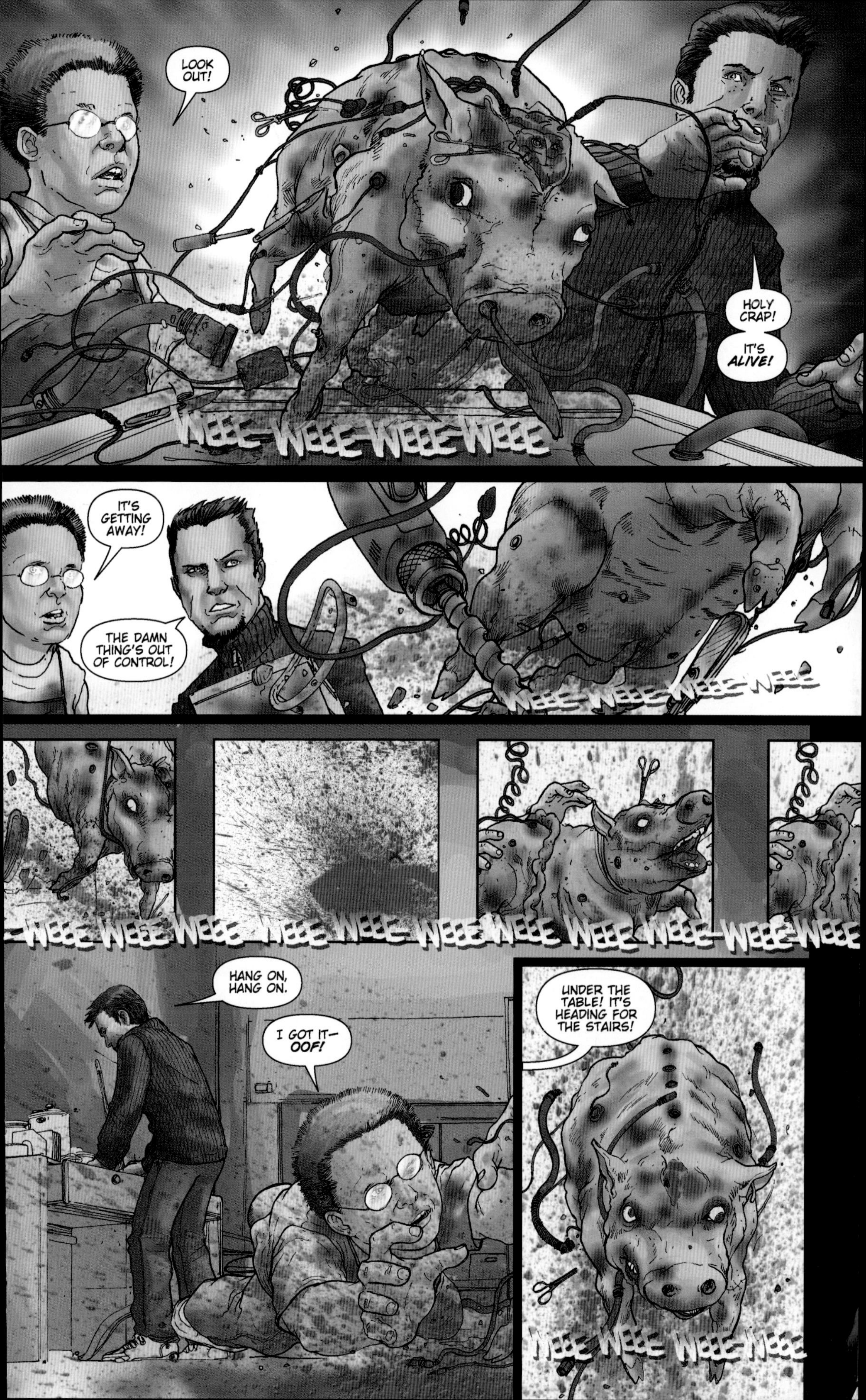

LOOK OUT!
HOLY CRAP!
IT'S *ALIVE!*
WEEE-WEEE-WEEE-WEEE
IT'S GETTING AWAY!
THE DAMN THING'S OUT OF CONTROL!
WEEE-WEEE-WEEE
WEEE WEEE WEEE WEEE WEEE-WEEE WEEE WEEE-WEEE
HANG ON, HANG ON.
I GOT IT— *OOF!*
UNDER THE TABLE! IT'S HEADING FOR THE STAIRS!
WEEE WEEE WEEE-WEEE

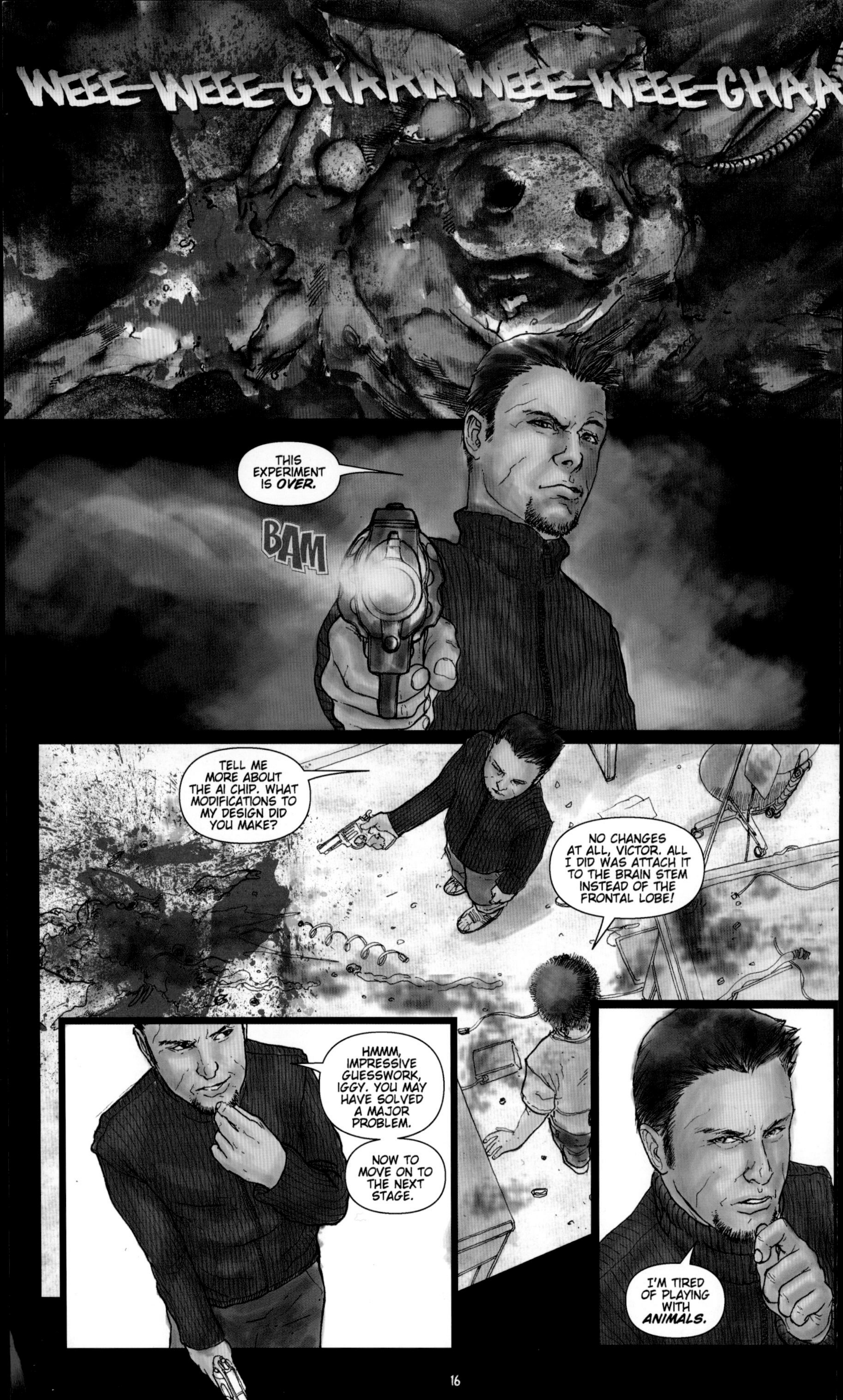
WEEE-WEEE-CHAAN WEEE-WEEE-CHAA
THIS EXPERIMENT IS *OVER.*
BAM
TELL ME MORE ABOUT THE AI CHIP. WHAT MODIFICATIONS TO MY DESIGN DID YOU MAKE?
NO CHANGES AT ALL, VICTOR. ALL I DID WAS ATTACH IT TO THE BRAIN STEM INSTEAD OF THE FRONTAL LOBE!
HMMM, IMPRESSIVE GUESSWORK, IGGY. YOU MAY HAVE SOLVED A MAJOR PROBLEM.
NOW TO MOVE ON TO THE NEXT STAGE.
I'M TIRED OF PLAYING WITH *ANIMALS.*

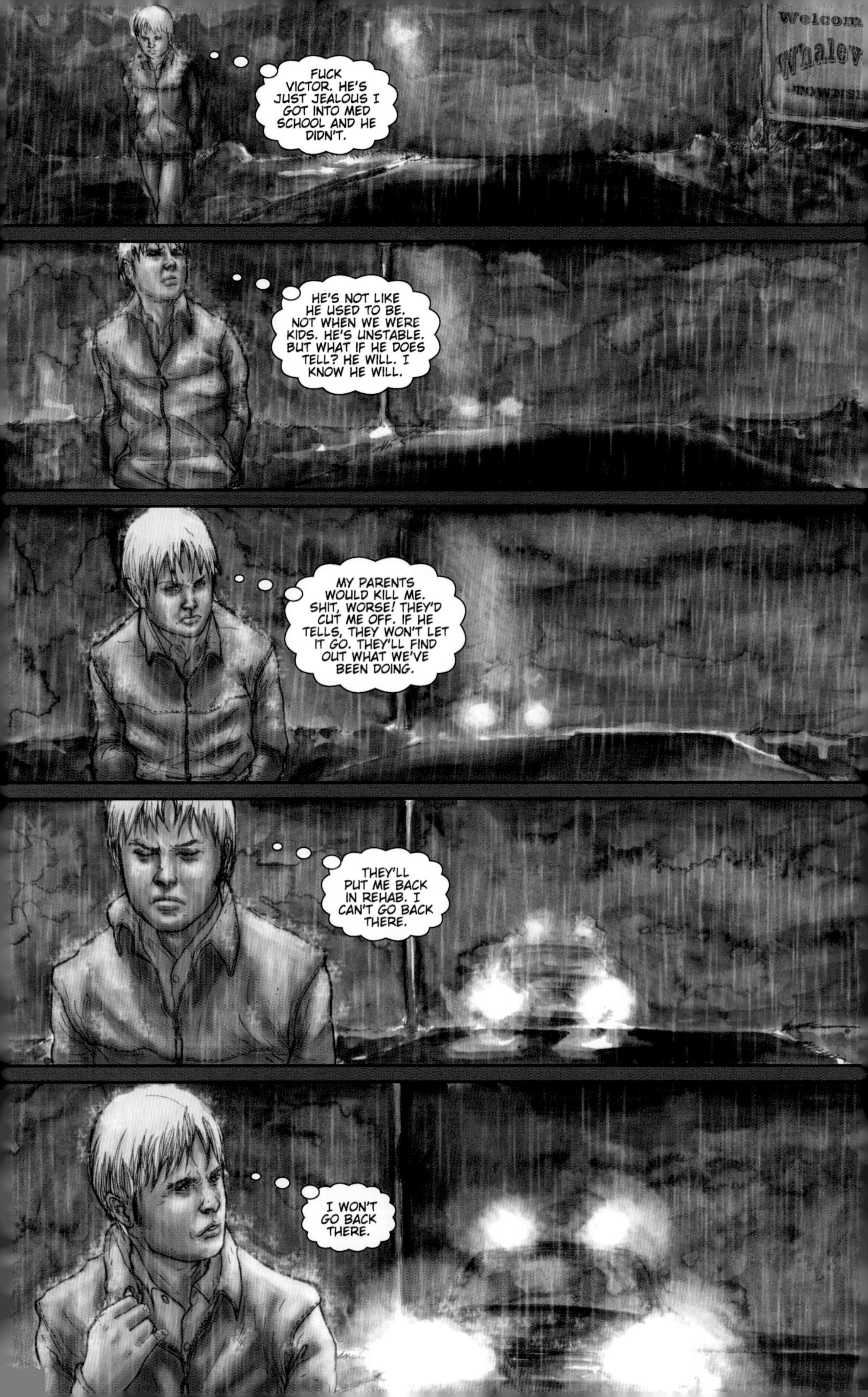
FUCK VICTOR. HE'S JUST JEALOUS I GOT INTO MED SCHOOL AND HE DIDN'T.
HE'S NOT LIKE HE USED TO BE. NOT WHEN WE WERE KIDS. HE'S UNSTABLE. BUT WHAT IF HE DOES TELL? HE WILL. I KNOW HE WILL.
MY PARENTS WOULD KILL ME. SHIT, WORSE! THEY'D CUT ME OFF. IF HE TELLS, THEY WON'T LET IT GO. THEY'LL FIND OUT WHAT WE'VE BEEN DOING.
THEY'LL PUT ME BACK IN REHAB. I CAN'T GO BACK THERE.
I WON'T GO BACK THERE.

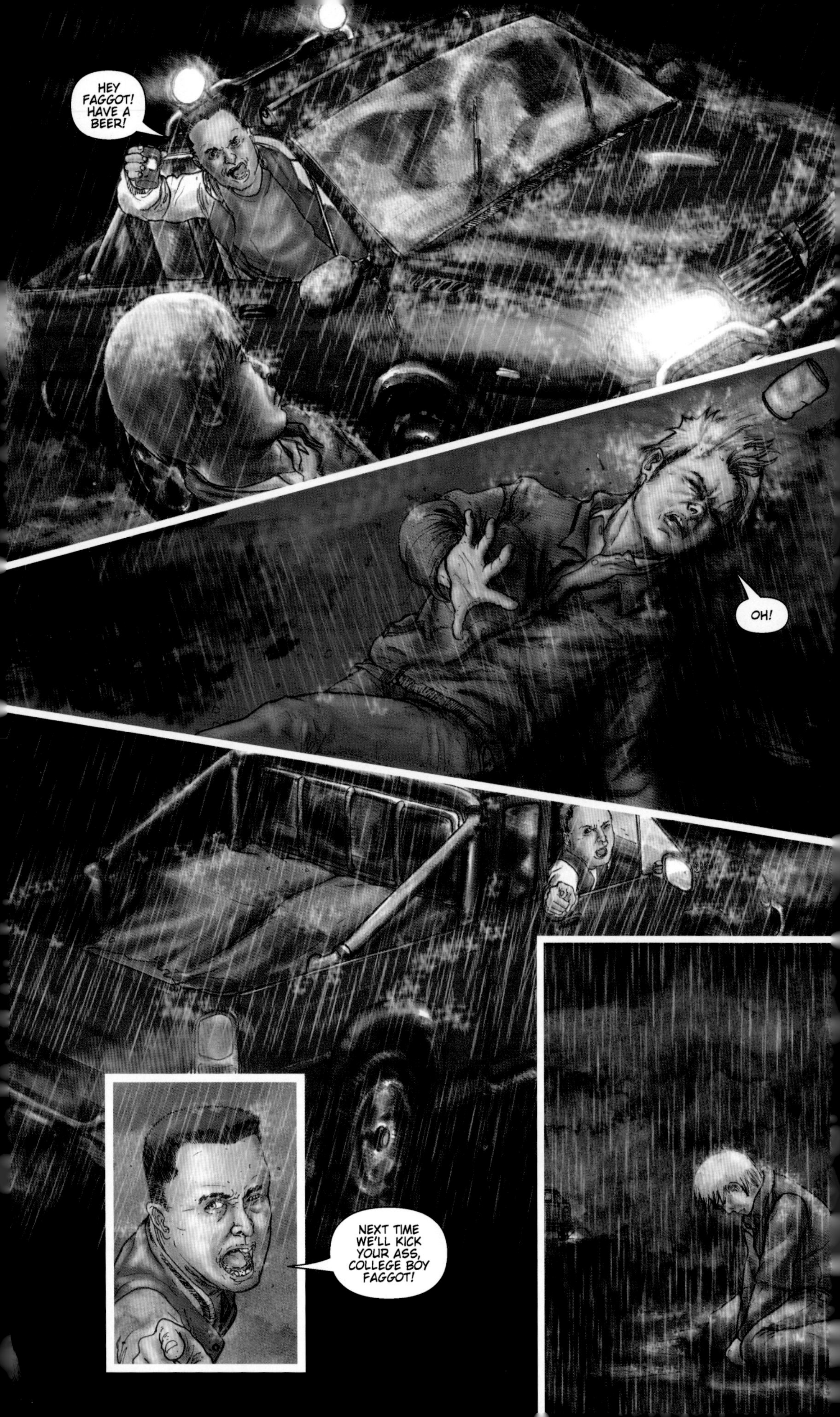
HEY FAGGOT! HAVE A BEER!
OH!
NEXT TIME WE'LL KICK YOUR ASS, COLLEGE BOY FAGGOT!

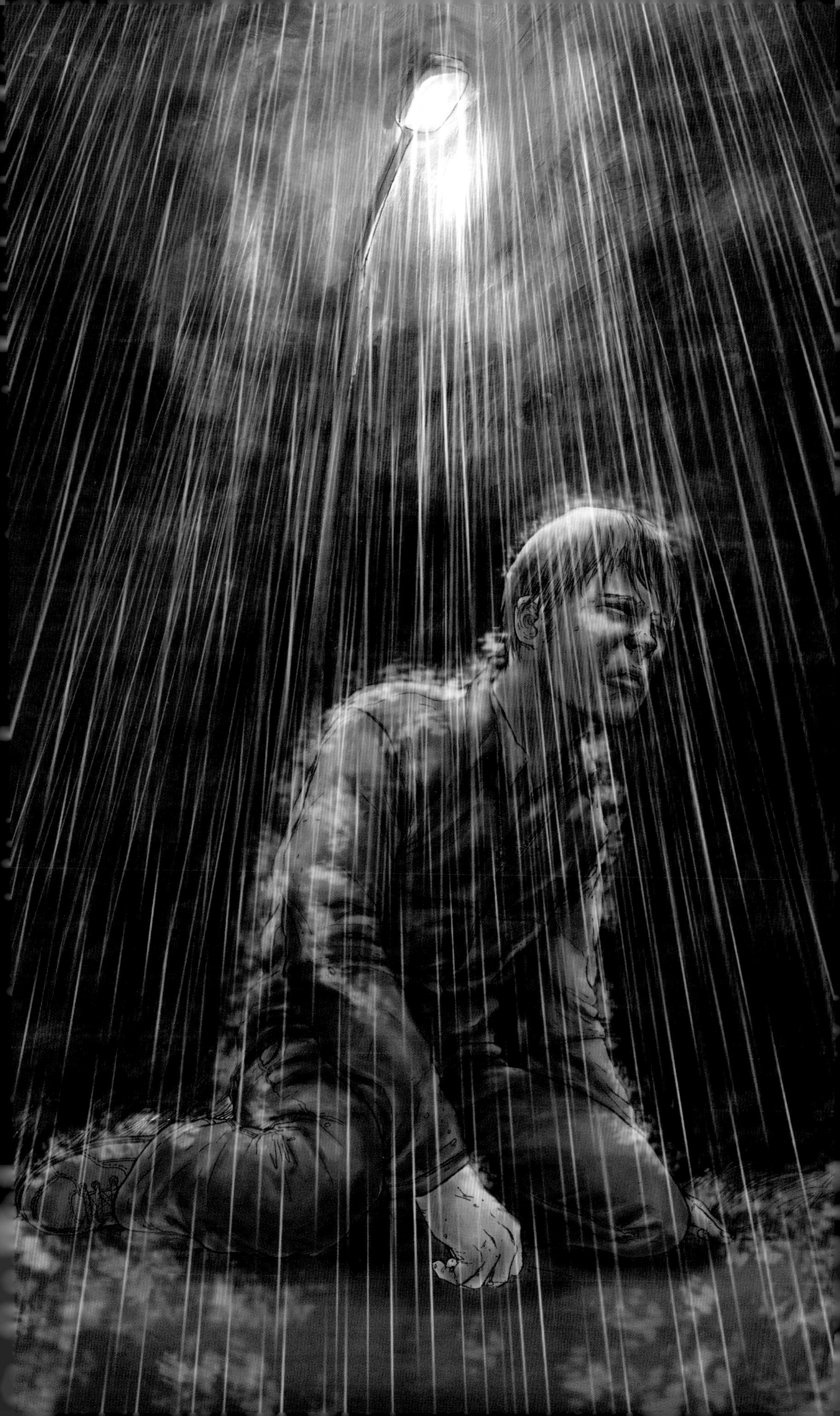

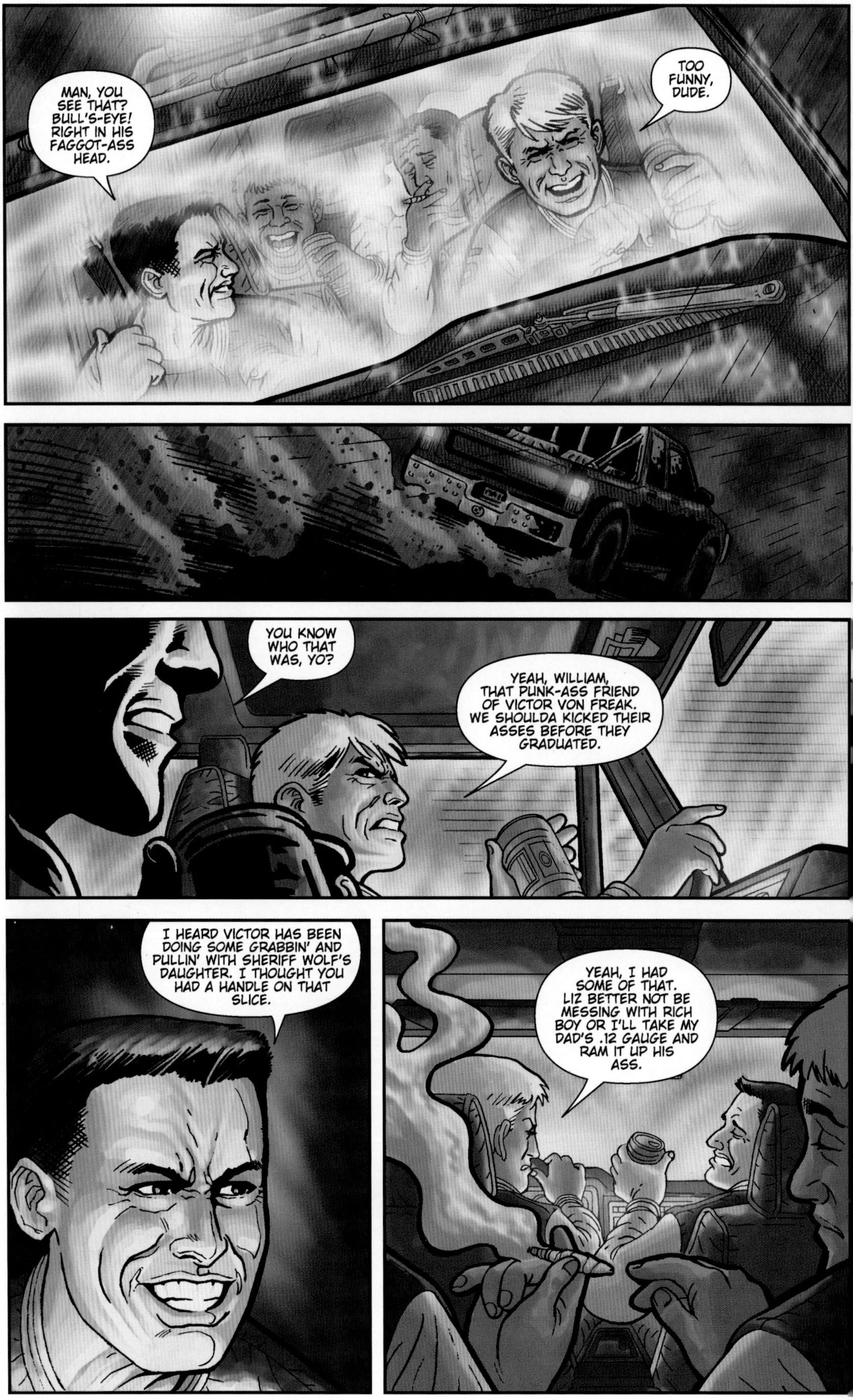
MAN, YOU SEE THAT? BULL'S-EYE! RIGHT IN HIS FAGGOT-ASS HEAD.
TOO FUNNY, DUDE.
YOU KNOW WHO THAT WAS, YO?
YEAH, WILLIAM, THAT PUNK-ASS FRIEND OF VICTOR VON FREAK. WE SHOULDA KICKED THEIR ASSES BEFORE THEY GRADUATED.
I HEARD VICTOR HAS BEEN DOING SOME GRABBIN' AND PULLIN' WITH SHERIFF WOLF'S DAUGHTER. I THOUGHT YOU HAD A HANDLE ON THAT SLICE.
YEAH, I HAD SOME OF THAT. LIZ BETTER NOT BE MESSING WITH RICH BOY OR I'LL TAKE MY DAD'S .12 GAUGE AND RAM IT UP HIS ASS.

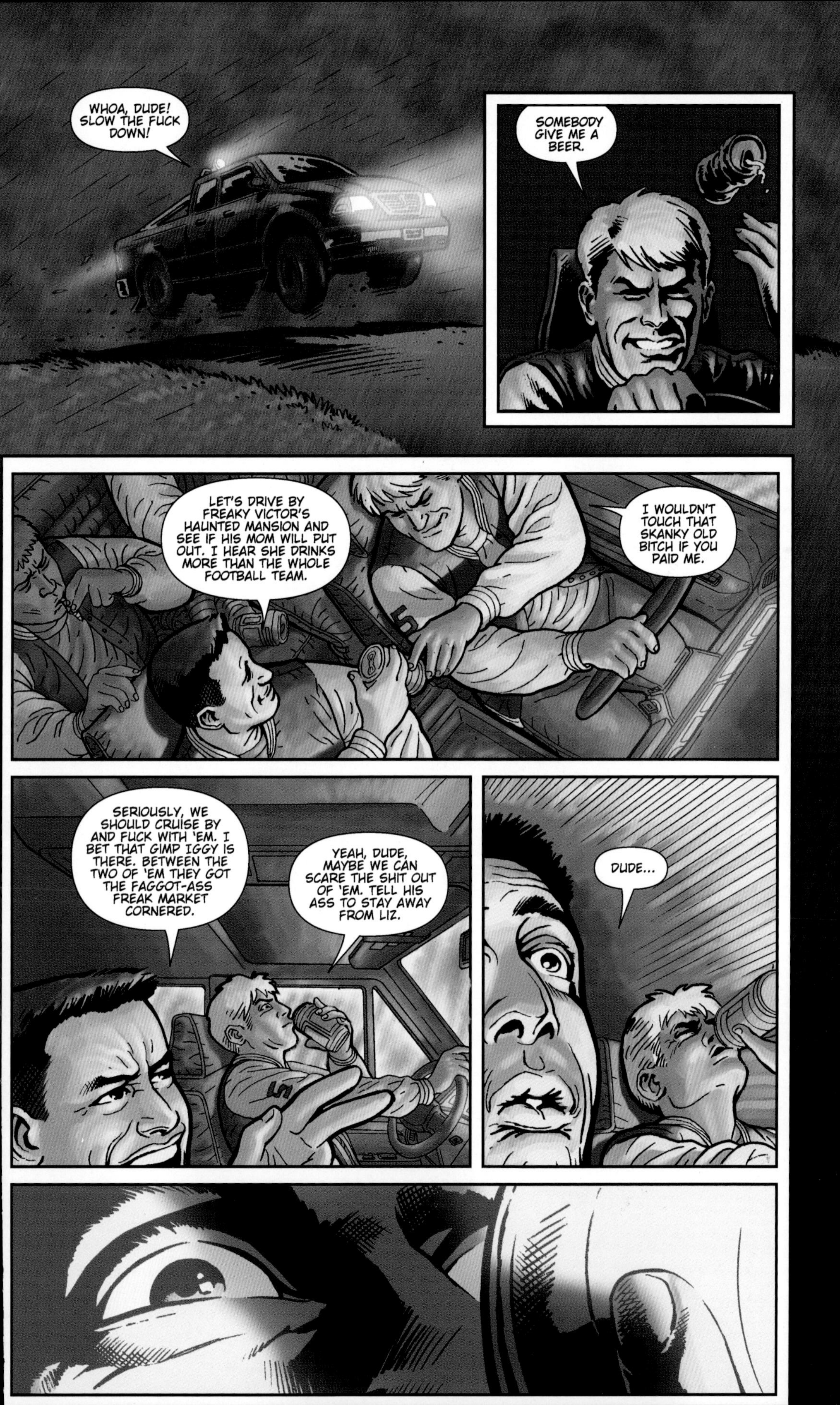
WHOA, DUDE! SLOW THE FUCK DOWN!
SOMEBODY GIVE ME A BEER.
LET'S DRIVE BY FREAKY VICTOR'S HAUNTED MANSION AND SEE IF HIS MOM WILL PUT OUT. I HEAR SHE DRINKS MORE THAN THE WHOLE FOOTBALL TEAM.
I WOULDN'T TOUCH THAT SKANKY OLD BITCH IF YOU PAID ME.
SERIOUSLY, WE SHOULD CRUISE BY AND FUCK WITH 'EM. I BET THAT GIMP IGGY IS THERE. BETWEEN THE TWO OF 'EM THEY GOT THE FAGGOT-ASS FREAK MARKET CORNERED.
YEAH, DUDE, MAYBE WE CAN SCARE THE SHIT OUT OF 'EM. TELL HIS ASS TO STAY AWAY FROM LIZ.
DUDE...

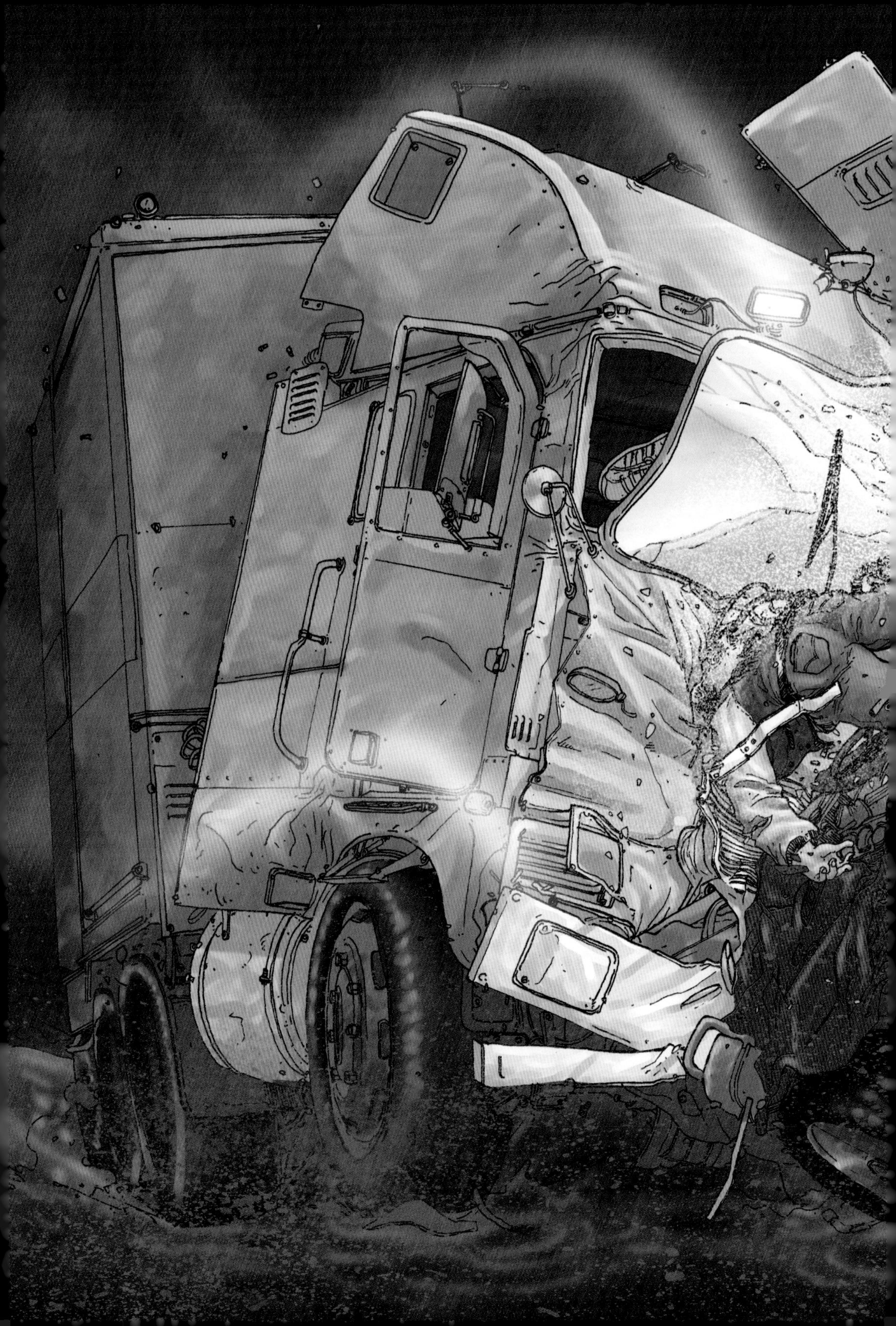

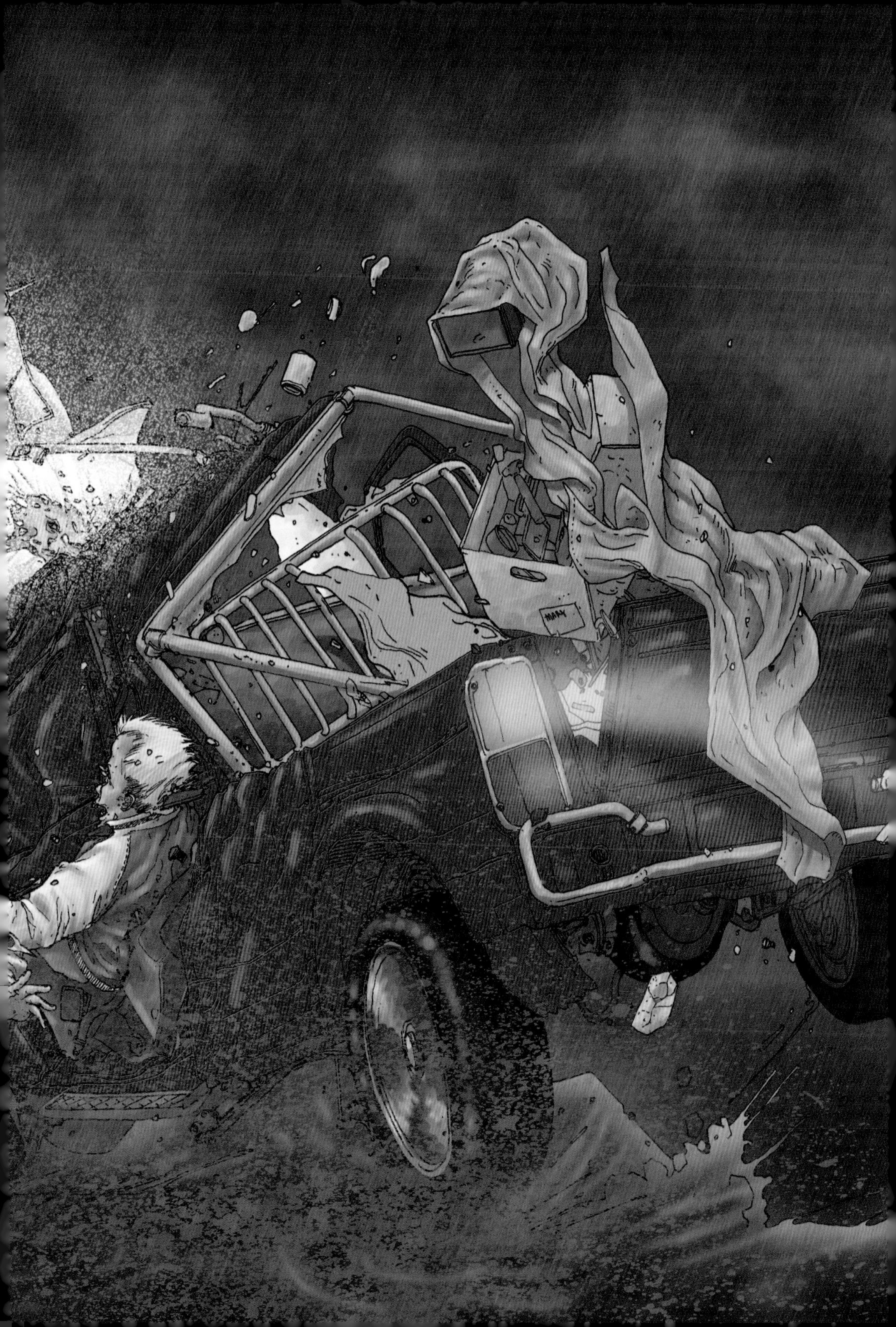

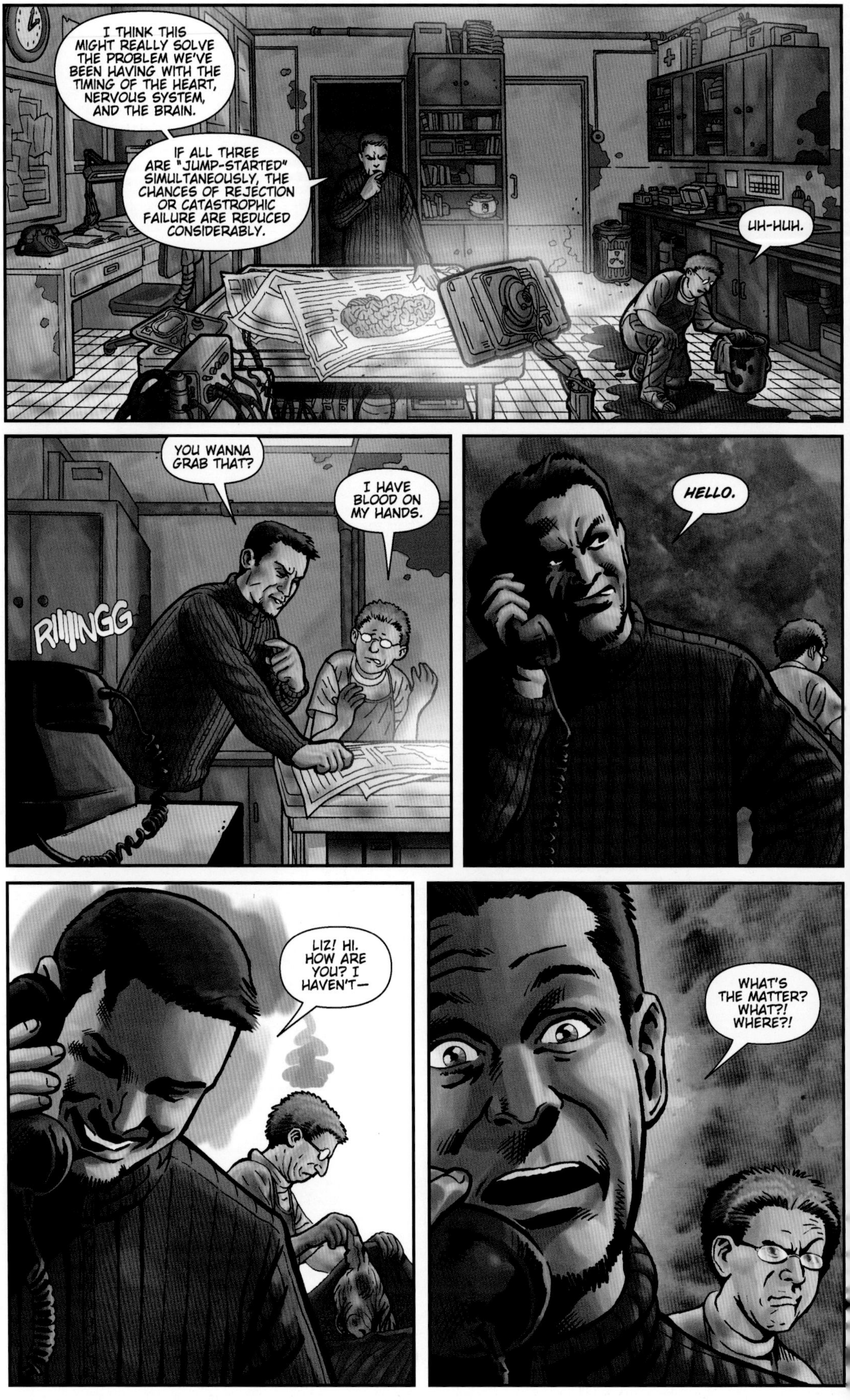
I THINK THIS MIGHT REALLY SOLVE THE PROBLEM WE'VE BEEN HAVING WITH THE TIMING OF THE HEART, NERVOUS SYSTEM, AND THE BRAIN.
IF ALL THREE ARE "JUMP-STARTED" SIMULTANEOUSLY, THE CHANCES OF REJECTION OR CATASTROPHIC FAILURE ARE REDUCED CONSIDERABLY.
UH-HUH.
YOU WANNA GRAB THAT?
RIIIINGG
I HAVE BLOOD ON MY HANDS.
HELLO.
LIZ! HI. HOW ARE YOU? I HAVEN'T—
WHAT'S THE MATTER? WHAT?! WHERE?!

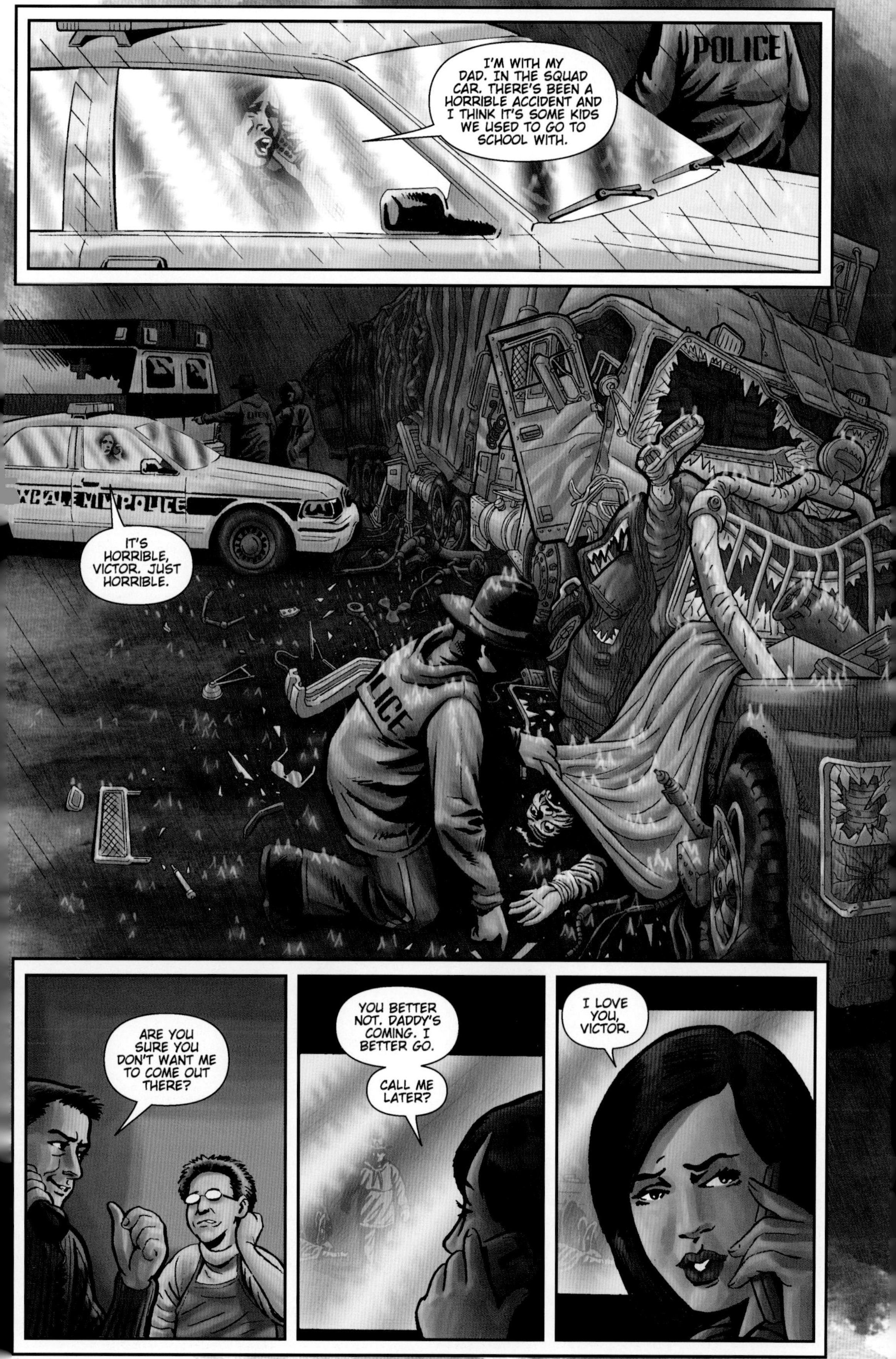

I'M WITH MY DAD. IN THE SQUAD CAR. THERE'S BEEN A HORRIBLE ACCIDENT AND I THINK IT'S SOME KIDS WE USED TO GO TO SCHOOL WITH.
POLICE
POLICE
IT'S HORRIBLE, VICTOR. JUST HORRIBLE.
ARE YOU SURE YOU DON'T WANT ME TO COME OUT THERE?
YOU BETTER NOT. DADDY'S COMING. I BETTER GO.
CALL ME LATER?
I LOVE YOU, VICTOR.

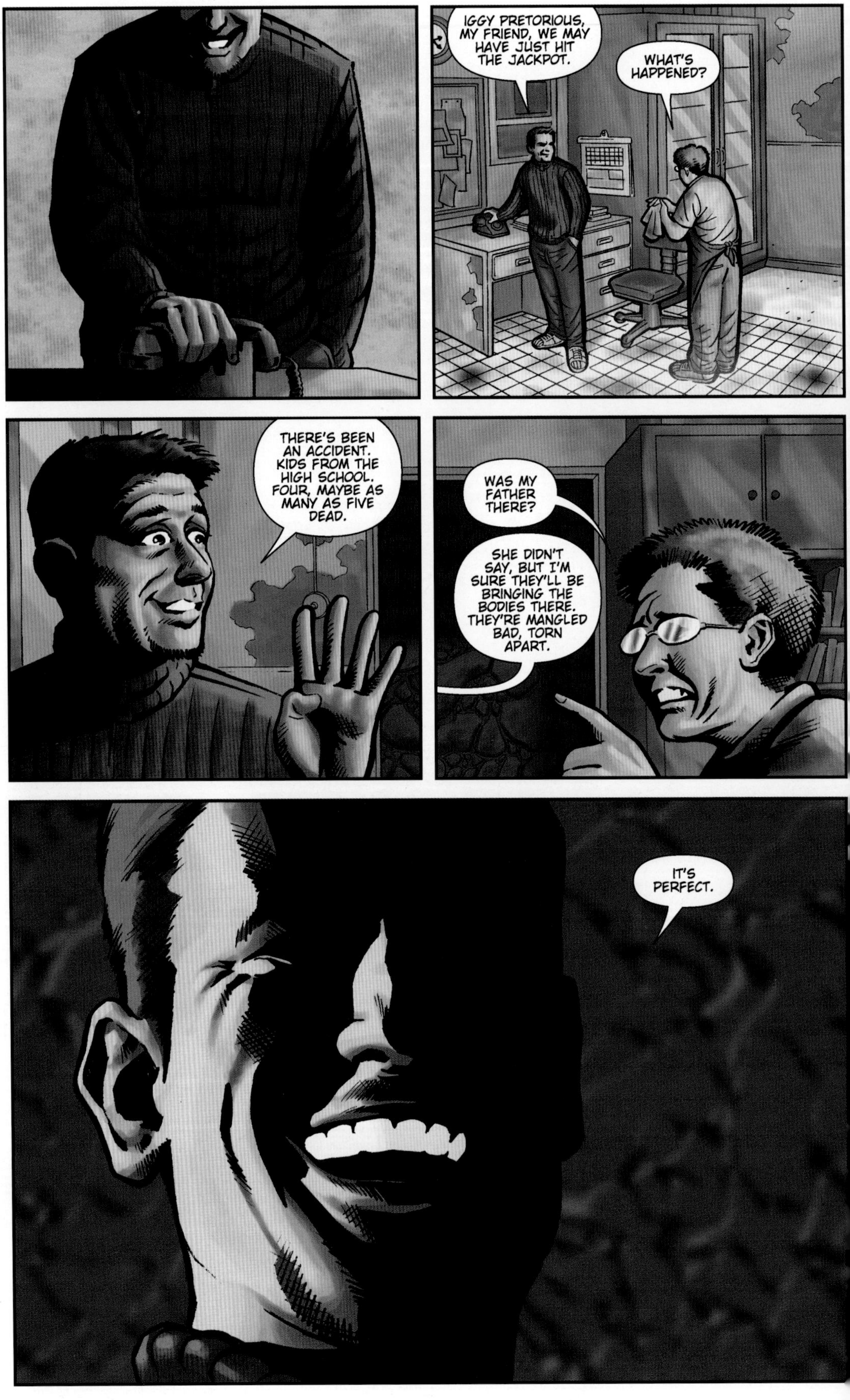

IGGY PRETORIOUS, MY FRIEND, WE MAY HAVE JUST HIT THE JACKPOT.
WHAT'S HAPPENED?
THERE'S BEEN AN ACCIDENT. KIDS FROM THE HIGH SCHOOL. FOUR, MAYBE AS MANY AS FIVE DEAD.
WAS MY FATHER THERE?
SHE DIDN'T SAY, BUT I'M SURE THEY'LL BE BRINGING THE BODIES THERE. THEY'RE MANGLED BAD, TORN APART.
IT'S PERFECT.

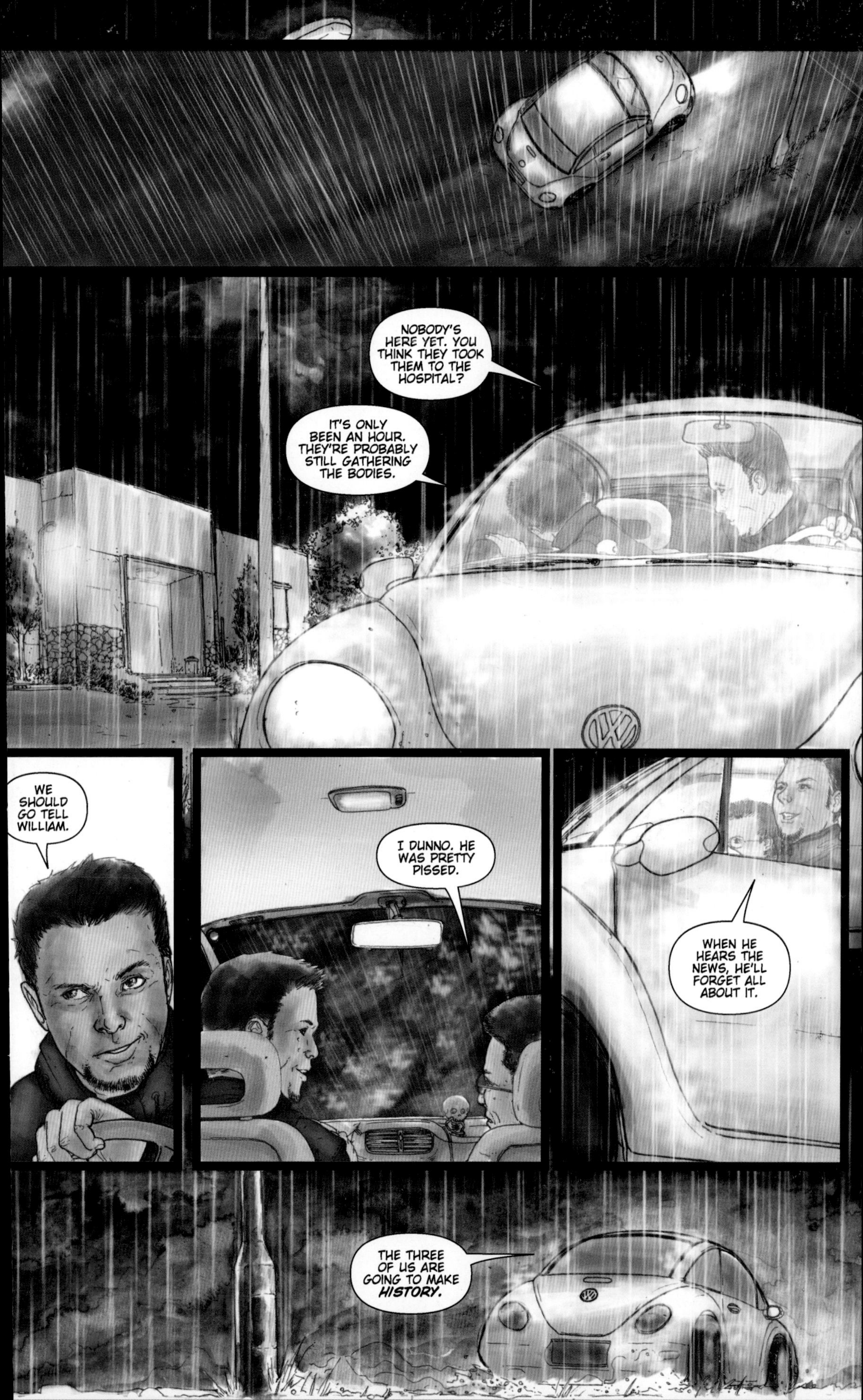

NOBODY'S HERE YET. YOU THINK THEY TOOK THEM TO THE HOSPITAL?
IT'S ONLY BEEN AN HOUR. THEY'RE PROBABLY STILL GATHERING THE BODIES.
WE SHOULD GO TELL WILLIAM.
I DUNNO. HE WAS PRETTY PISSED.
WHEN HE HEARS THE NEWS, HE'LL FORGET ALL ABOUT IT.
THE THREE OF US ARE GOING TO MAKE *HISTORY*.

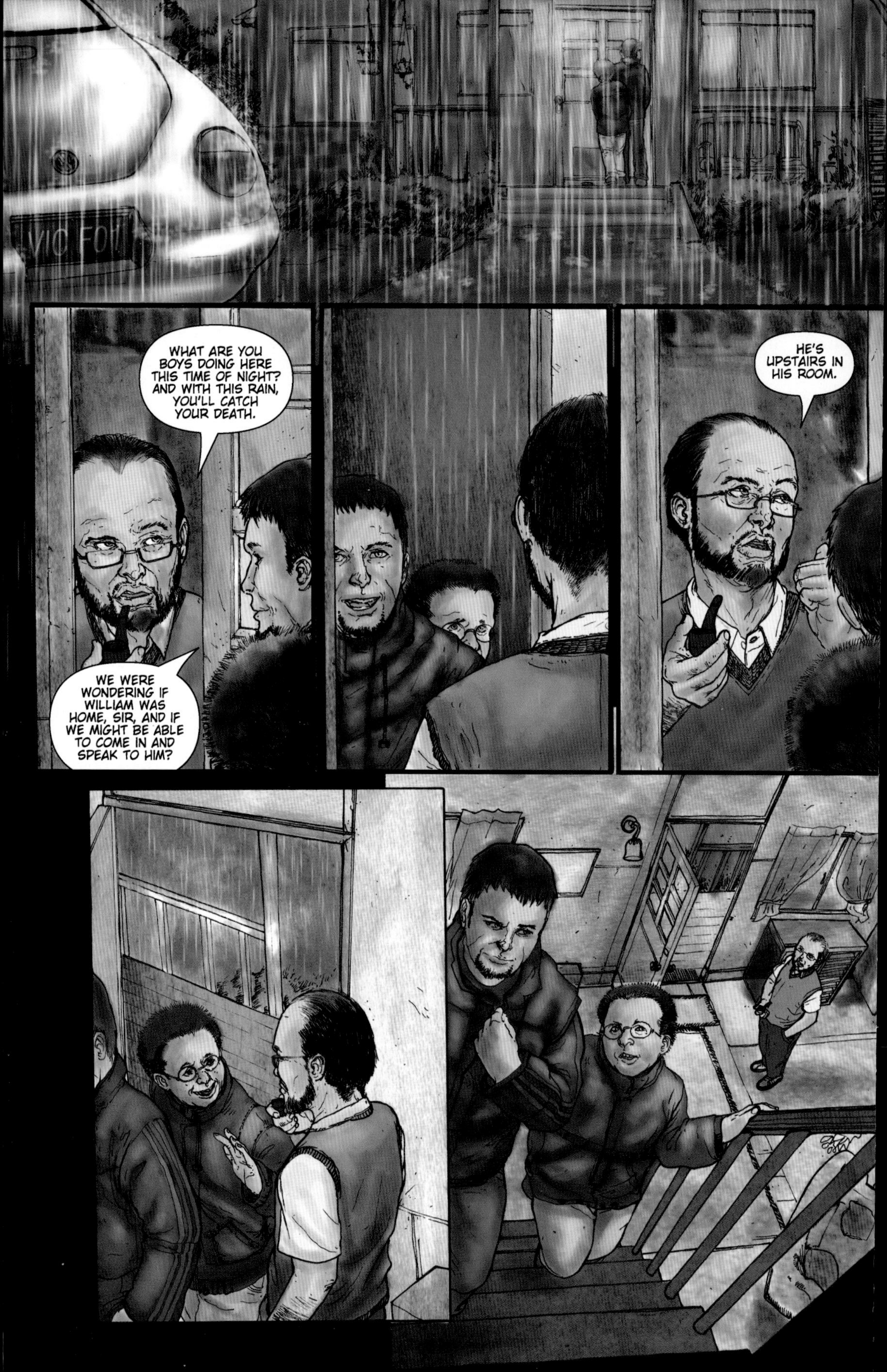
WHAT ARE YOU BOYS DOING HERE THIS TIME OF NIGHT? AND WITH THIS RAIN, YOU'LL CATCH YOUR DEATH.
WE WERE WONDERING IF WILLIAM WAS HOME, SIR, AND IF WE MIGHT BE ABLE TO COME IN AND SPEAK TO HIM?
HE'S UPSTAIRS IN HIS ROOM.

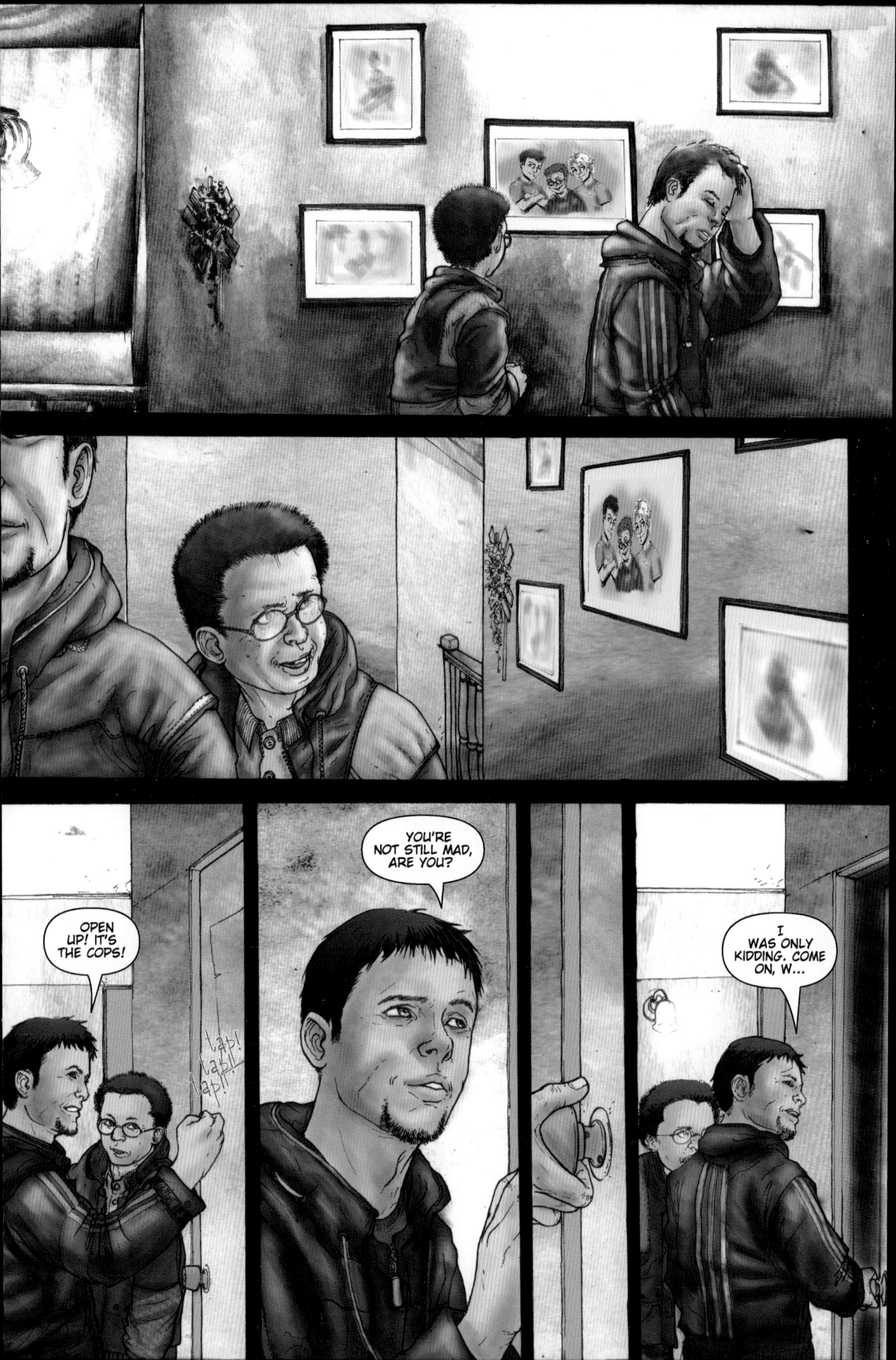
OPEN UP! IT'S THE COPS!
tap! tap! tap!
YOU'RE NOT STILL MAD, ARE YOU?
I WAS ONLY KIDDING. COME ON, W...

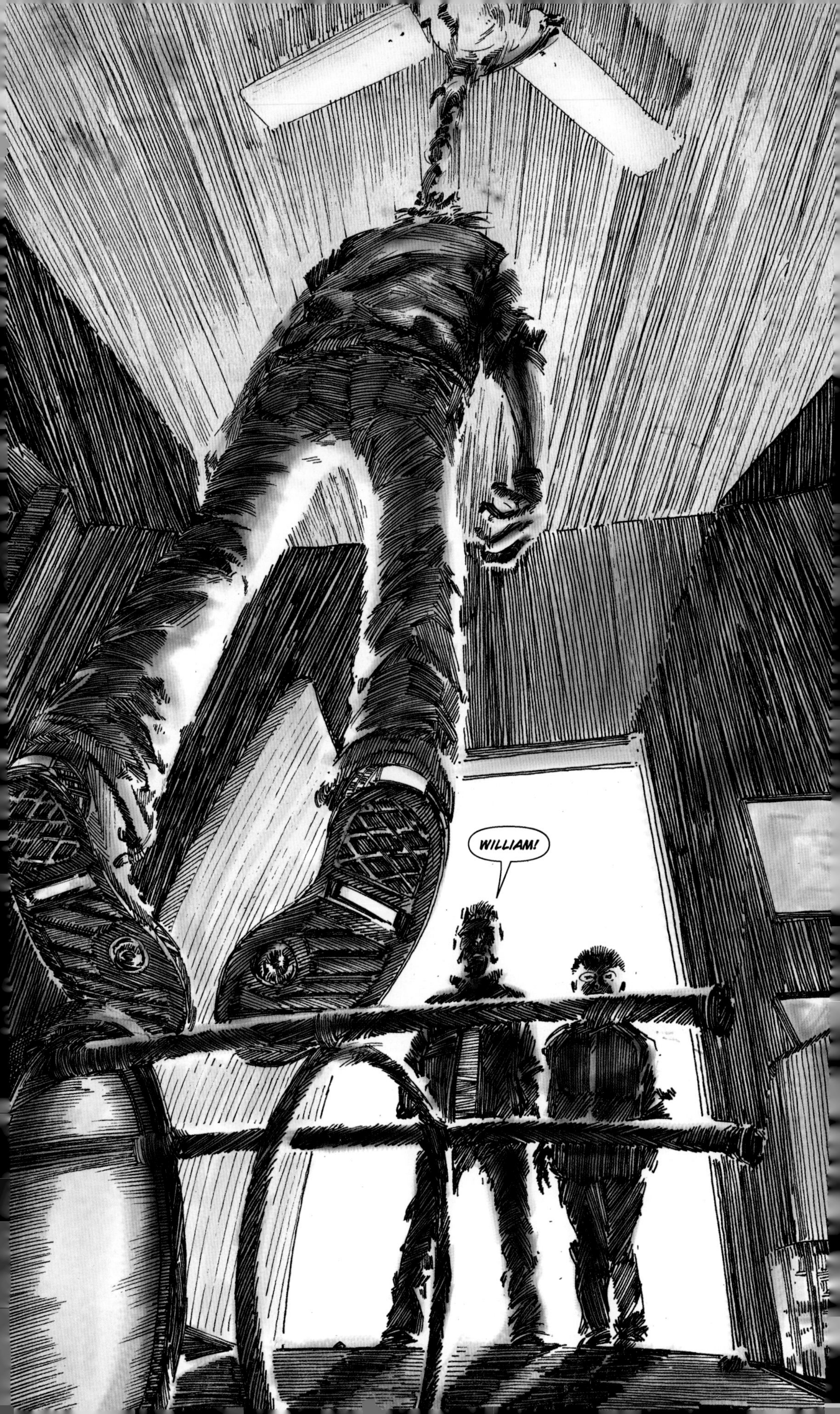
WILLIAM!

chapter two

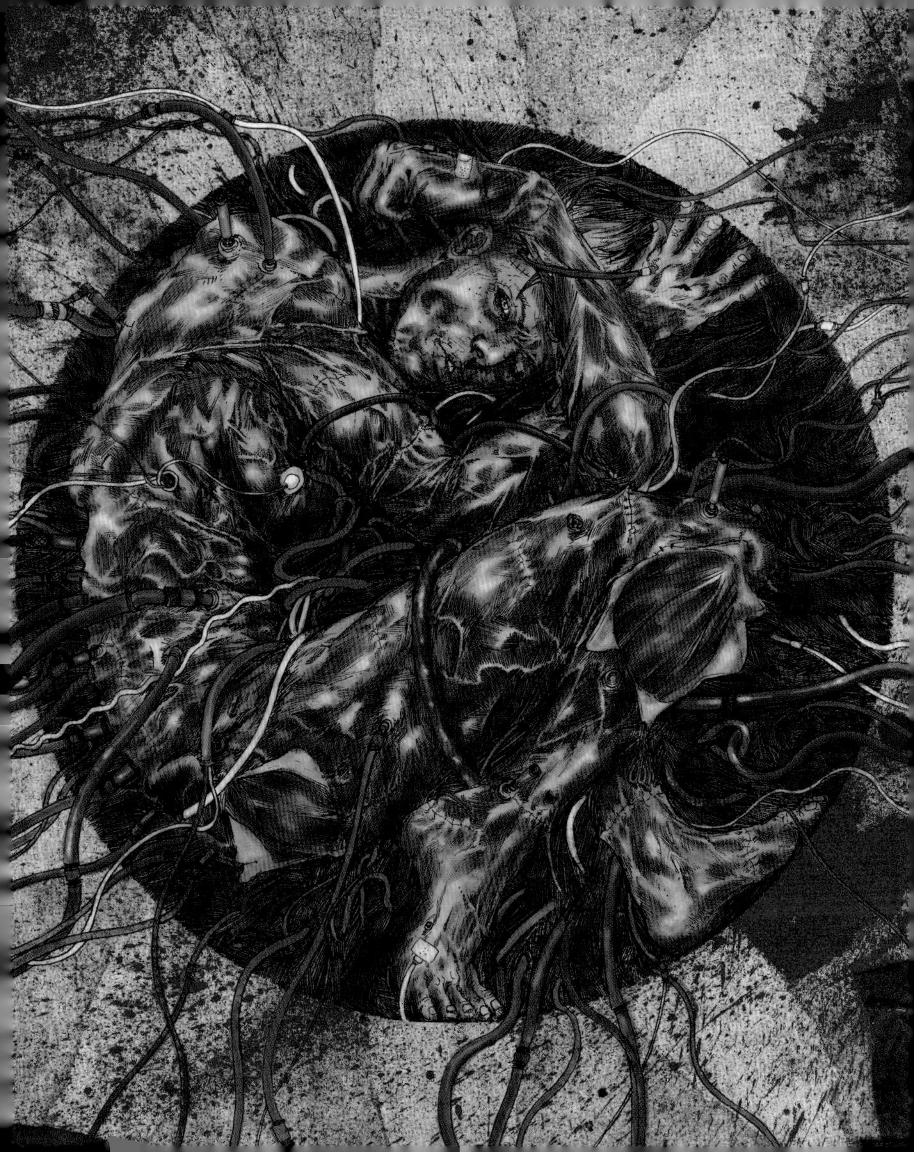

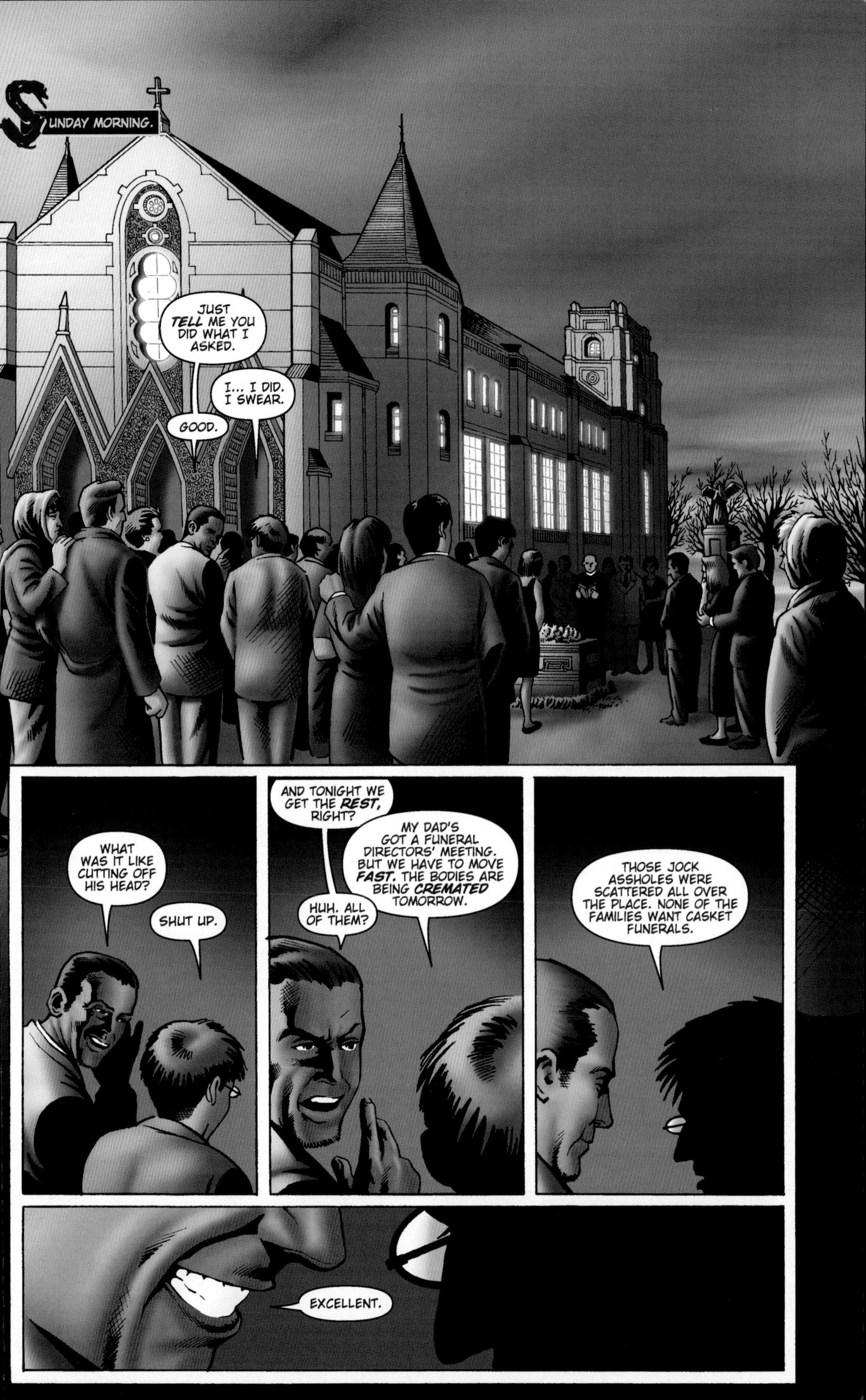
SUNDAY MORNING.
JUST TELL ME YOU DID WHAT I ASKED.
I... I DID. I SWEAR.
GOOD.
WHAT WAS IT LIKE CUTTING OFF HIS HEAD?
SHUT UP.
AND TONIGHT WE GET THE REST, RIGHT?
MY DAD'S GOT A FUNERAL DIRECTORS' MEETING. BUT WE HAVE TO MOVE FAST. THE BODIES ARE BEING CREMATED TOMORROW.
HUH. ALL OF THEM?
THOSE JOCK ASSHOLES WERE SCATTERED ALL OVER THE PLACE. NONE OF THE FAMILIES WANT CASKET FUNERALS.
EXCELLENT.

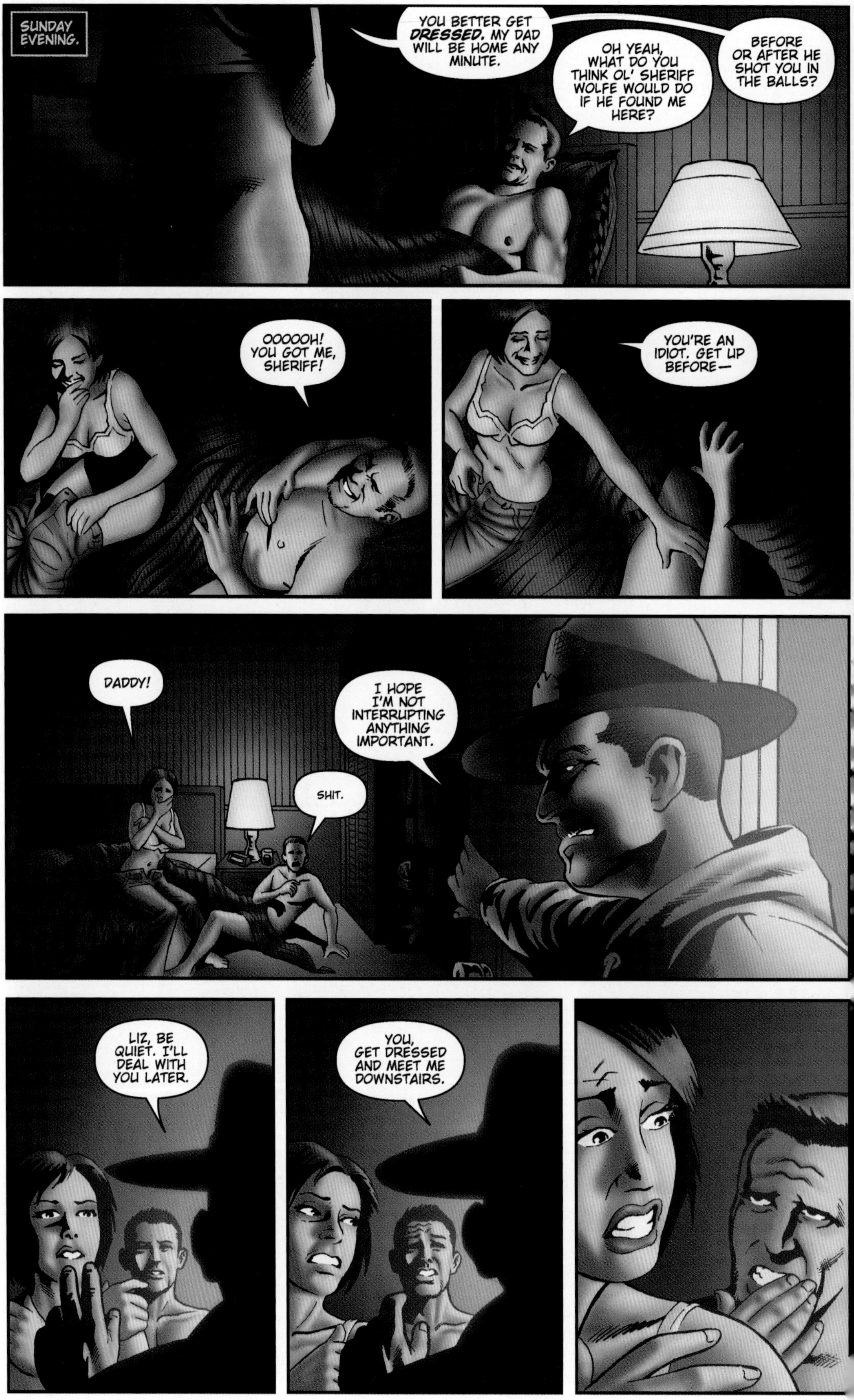
SUNDAY EVENING.
YOU BETTER GET DRESSED. MY DAD WILL BE HOME ANY MINUTE.
OH YEAH, WHAT DO YOU THINK OL' SHERIFF WOLFE WOULD DO IF HE FOUND ME HERE?
BEFORE OR AFTER HE SHOT YOU IN THE BALLS?
OOOOOH! YOU GOT ME, SHERIFF!
YOU'RE AN IDIOT. GET UP BEFORE—
DADDY!
I HOPE I'M NOT INTERRUPTING ANYTHING IMPORTANT.
SHIT.
LIZ, BE QUIET. I'LL DEAL WITH YOU LATER.
YOU, GET DRESSED AND MEET ME DOWNSTAIRS.

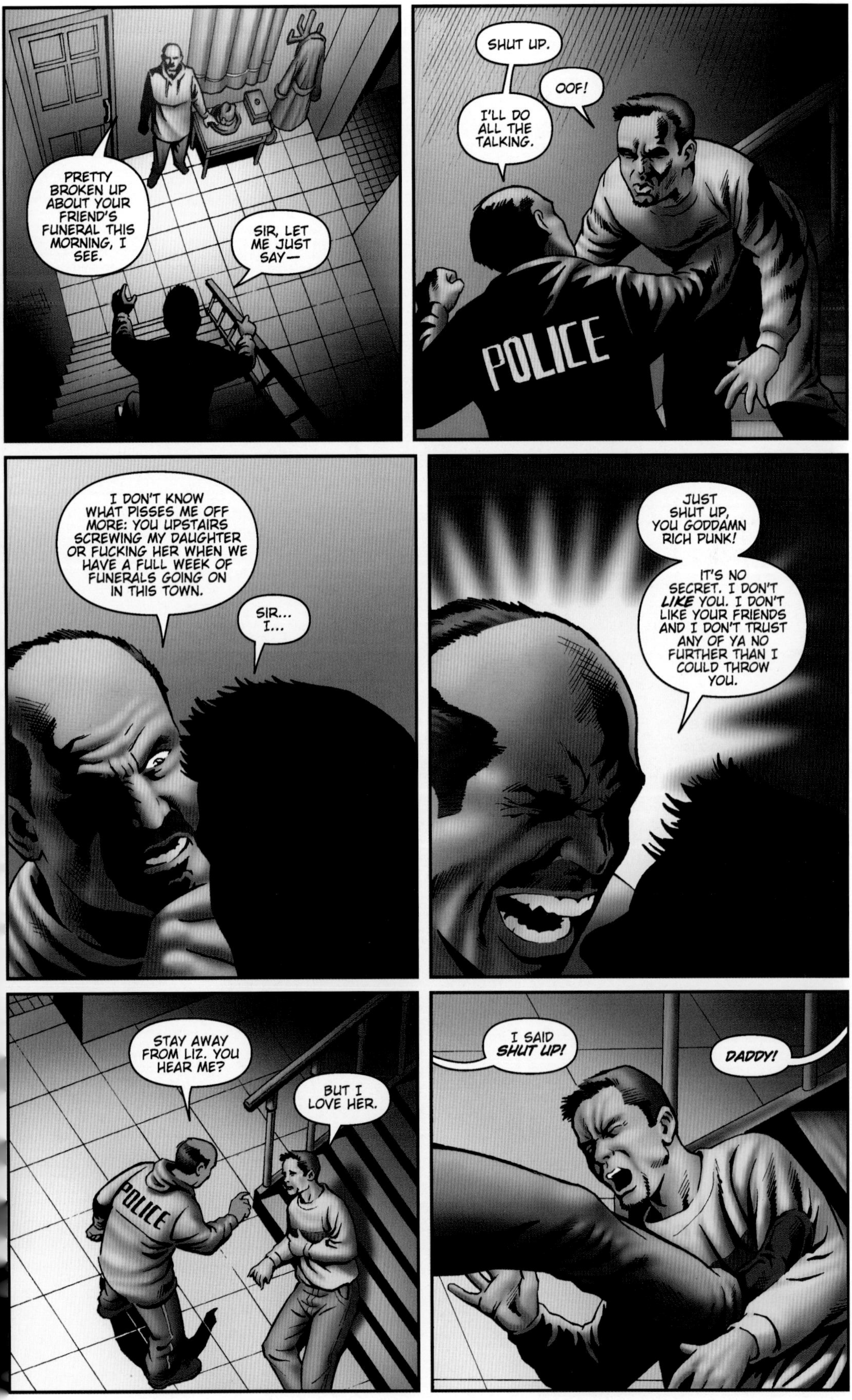
PRETTY BROKEN UP ABOUT YOUR FRIEND'S FUNERAL THIS MORNING, I SEE.
SIR, LET ME JUST SAY—
SHUT UP.
I'LL DO ALL THE TALKING.
OOF!
POLICE
I DON'T KNOW WHAT PISSES ME OFF MORE: YOU UPSTAIRS SCREWING MY DAUGHTER OR FUCKING HER WHEN WE HAVE A FULL WEEK OF FUNERALS GOING ON IN THIS TOWN.
SIR... I...
JUST SHUT UP, YOU GODDAMN RICH PUNK!
IT'S NO SECRET. I DON'T *LIKE* YOU. I DON'T LIKE YOUR FRIENDS AND I DON'T TRUST ANY OF YA NO FURTHER THAN I COULD THROW YOU.
STAY AWAY FROM LIZ. YOU HEAR ME?
BUT I LOVE HER.
POLICE
I SAID *SHUT UP!*
DADDY!

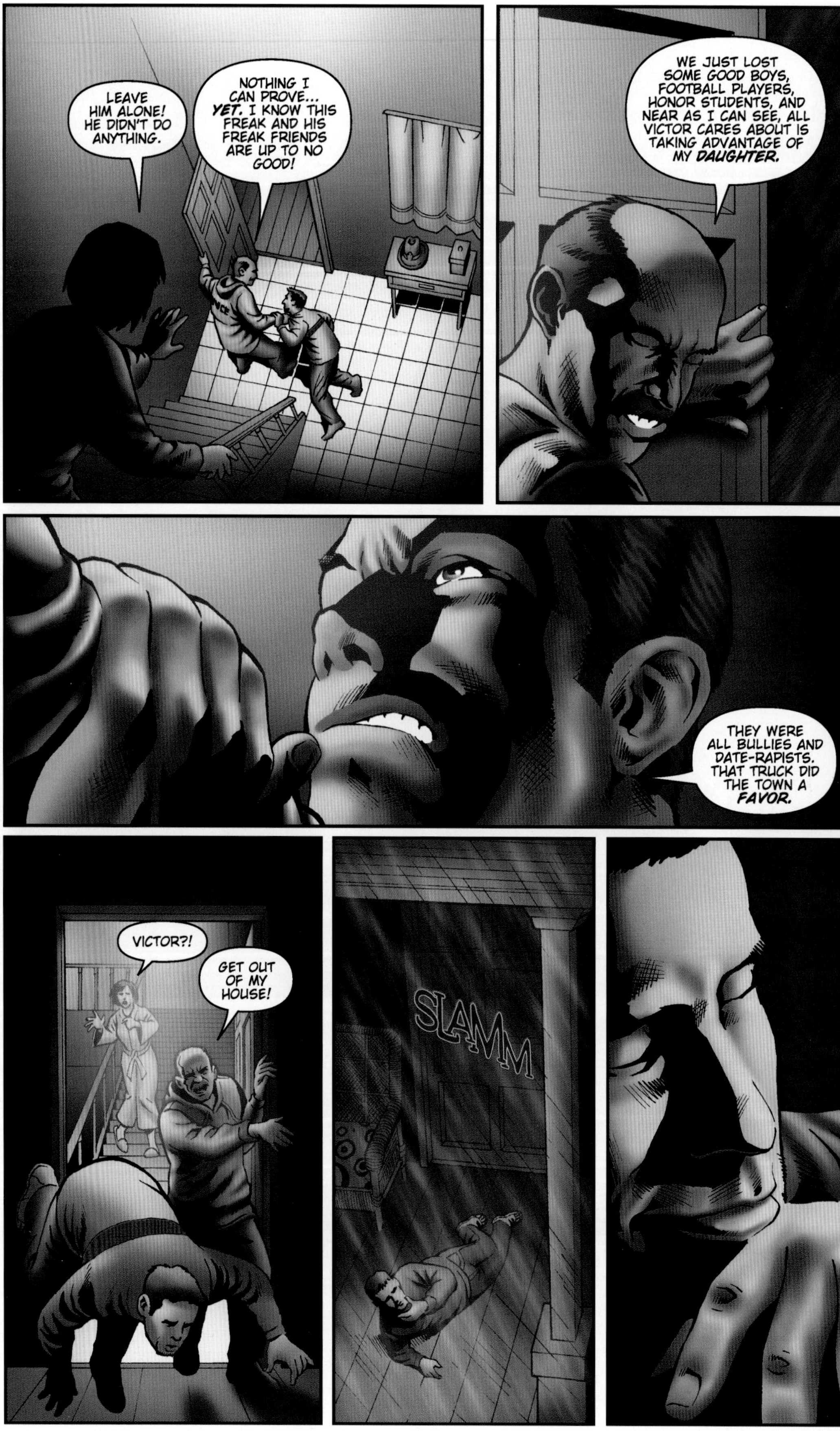
LEAVE HIM ALONE! HE DIDN'T DO ANYTHING.
NOTHING I CAN PROVE... YET. I KNOW THIS FREAK AND HIS FREAK FRIENDS ARE UP TO NO GOOD!
WE JUST LOST SOME GOOD BOYS, FOOTBALL PLAYERS, HONOR STUDENTS, AND NEAR AS I CAN SEE, ALL VICTOR CARES ABOUT IS TAKING ADVANTAGE OF MY DAUGHTER.
THEY WERE ALL BULLIES AND DATE-RAPISTS. THAT TRUCK DID THE TOWN A FAVOR.
VICTOR?!
GET OUT OF MY HOUSE!
SLAMM

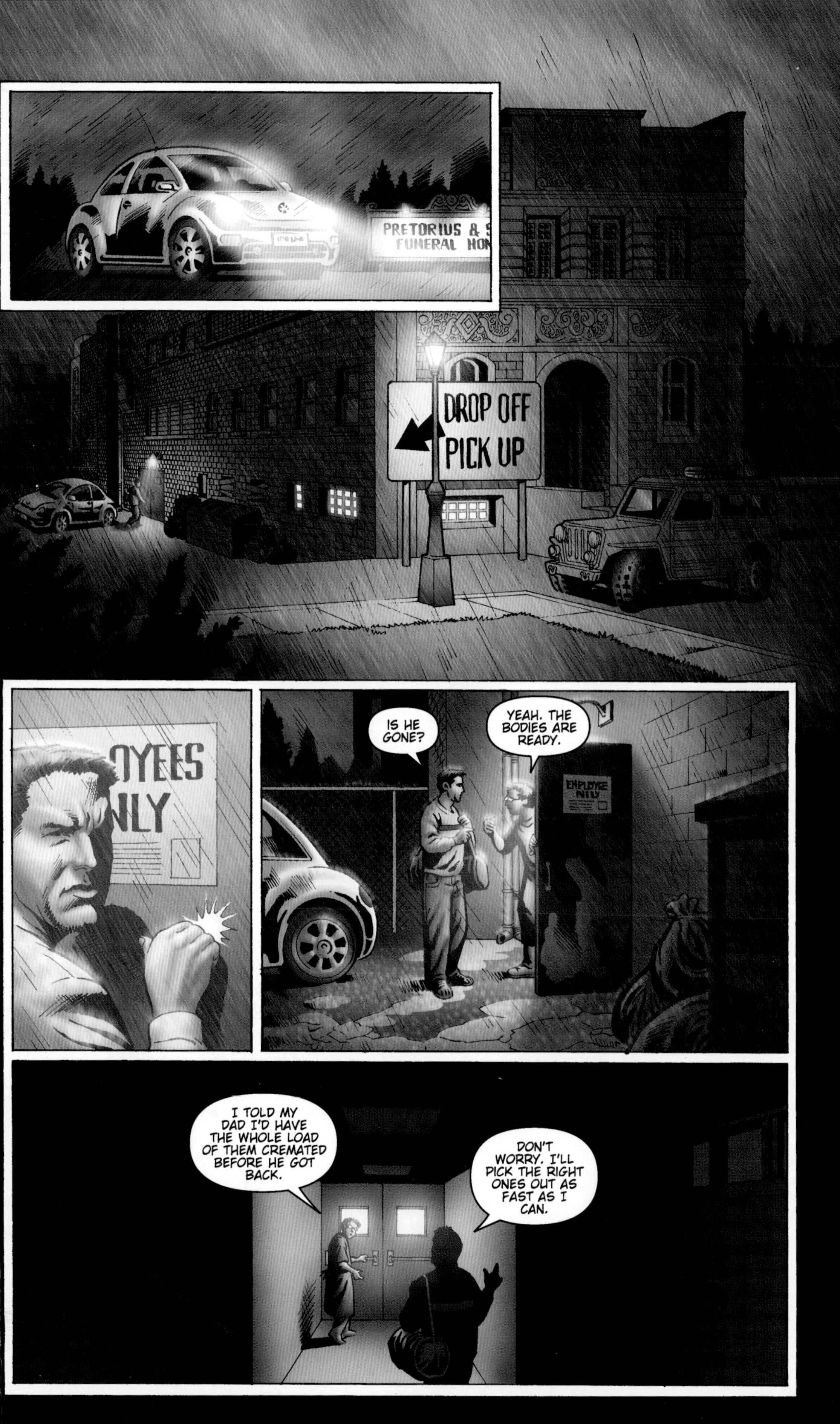
PRETORIUS & S
FUNERAL HON
DROP OFF
PICK UP
OYEES
NLY
IS HE GONE?
YEAH. THE BODIES ARE READY.
I TOLD MY DAD I'D HAVE THE WHOLE LOAD OF THEM CREMATED BEFORE HE GOT BACK.
DON'T WORRY. I'LL PICK THE RIGHT ONES OUT AS FAST AS I CAN.

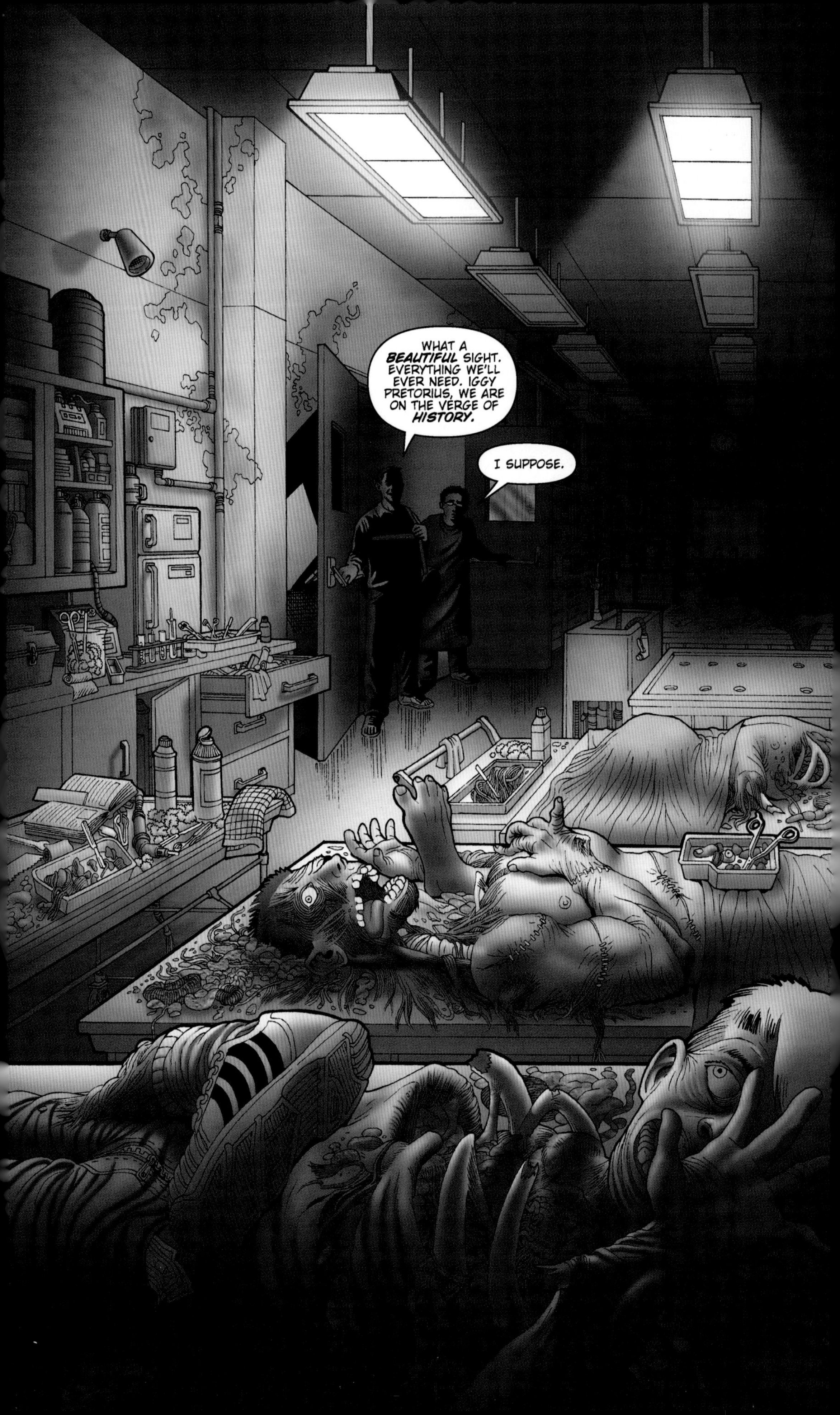
WHAT A BEAUTIFUL SIGHT. EVERYTHING WE'LL EVER NEED. IGGY PRETORIUS, WE ARE ON THE VERGE OF HISTORY.
I SUPPOSE.

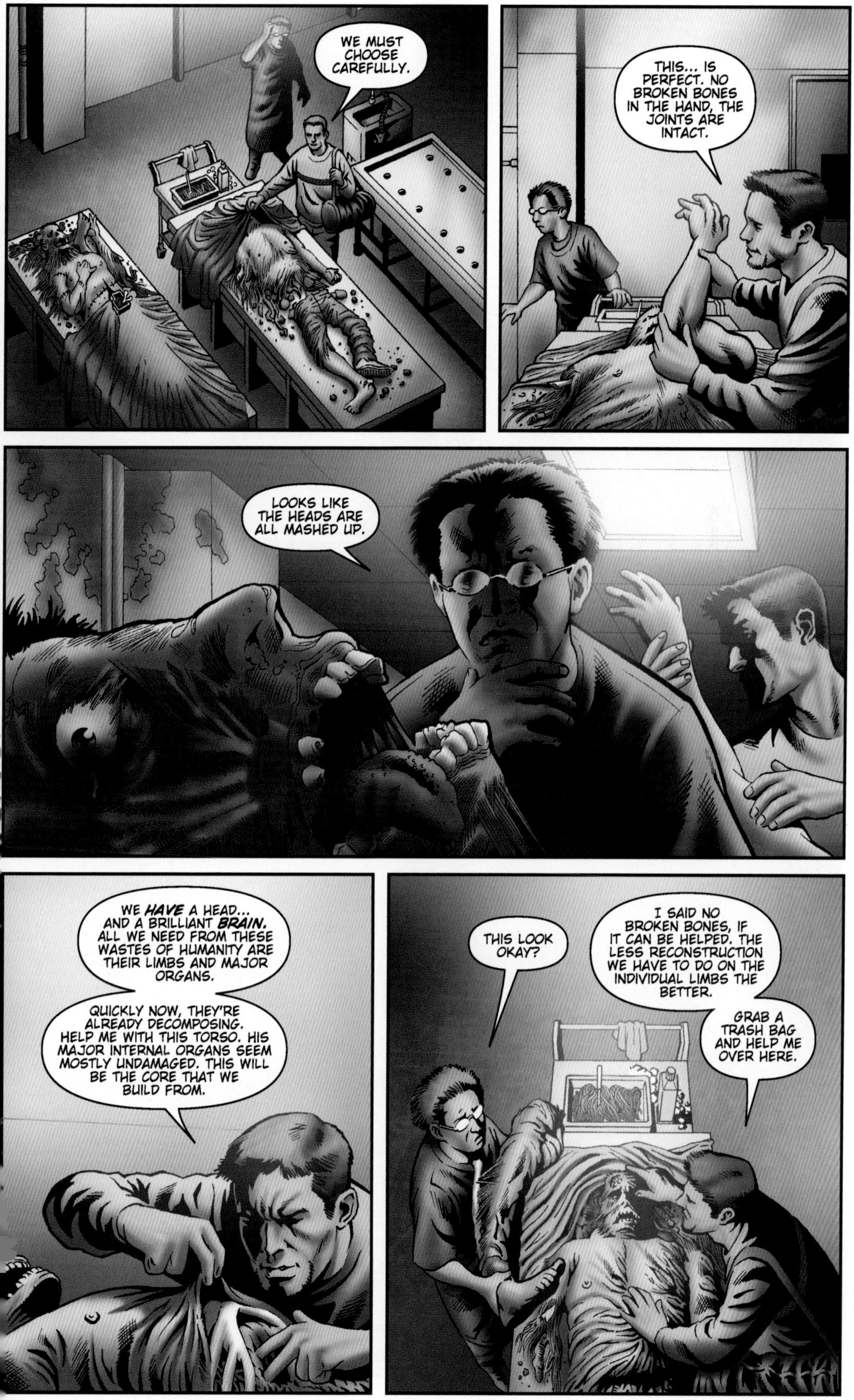
WE MUST CHOOSE CAREFULLY.
THIS... IS PERFECT. NO BROKEN BONES IN THE HAND, THE JOINTS ARE INTACT.
LOOKS LIKE THE HEADS ARE ALL MASHED UP.
WE HAVE A HEAD... AND A BRILLIANT BRAIN. ALL WE NEED FROM THESE WASTES OF HUMANITY ARE THEIR LIMBS AND MAJOR ORGANS.
QUICKLY NOW, THEY'RE ALREADY DECOMPOSING. HELP ME WITH THIS TORSO. HIS MAJOR INTERNAL ORGANS SEEM MOSTLY UNDAMAGED. THIS WILL BE THE CORE THAT WE BUILD FROM.
THIS LOOK OKAY?
I SAID NO BROKEN BONES, IF IT CAN BE HELPED. THE LESS RECONSTRUCTION WE HAVE TO DO ON THE INDIVIDUAL LIMBS THE BETTER.
GRAB A TRASH BAG AND HELP ME OVER HERE.

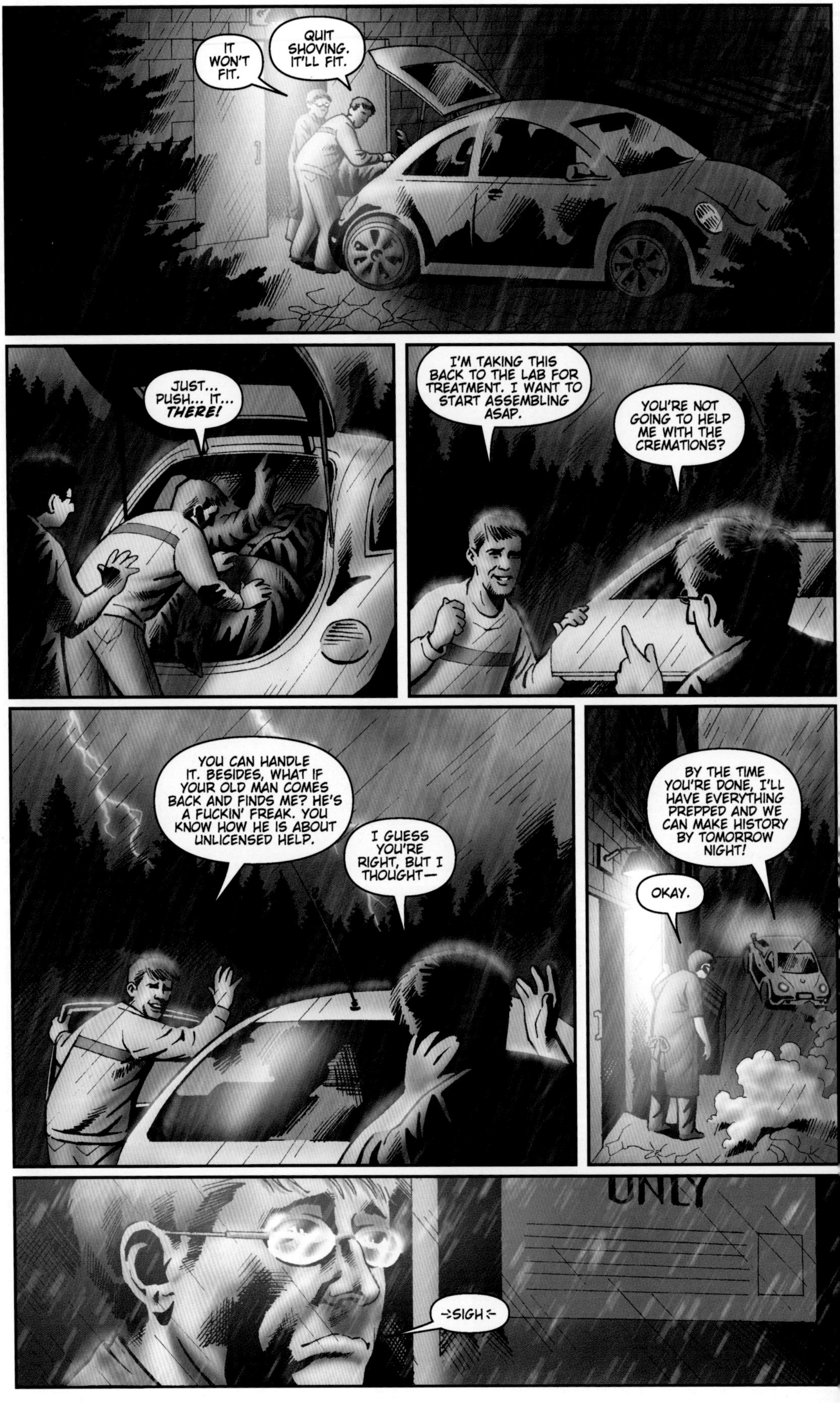
IT WON'T FIT.
QUIT SHOVING. IT'LL FIT.
JUST... PUSH... IT... THERE!
I'M TAKING THIS BACK TO THE LAB FOR TREATMENT. I WANT TO START ASSEMBLING ASAP.
YOU'RE NOT GOING TO HELP ME WITH THE CREMATIONS?
YOU CAN HANDLE IT. BESIDES, WHAT IF YOUR OLD MAN COMES BACK AND FINDS ME? HE'S A FUCKIN' FREAK. YOU KNOW HOW HE IS ABOUT UNLICENSED HELP.
I GUESS YOU'RE RIGHT, BUT I THOUGHT—
BY THE TIME YOU'RE DONE, I'LL HAVE EVERYTHING PREPPED AND WE CAN MAKE HISTORY BY TOMORROW NIGHT!
OKAY.
ONLY
⇉SIGH⇇

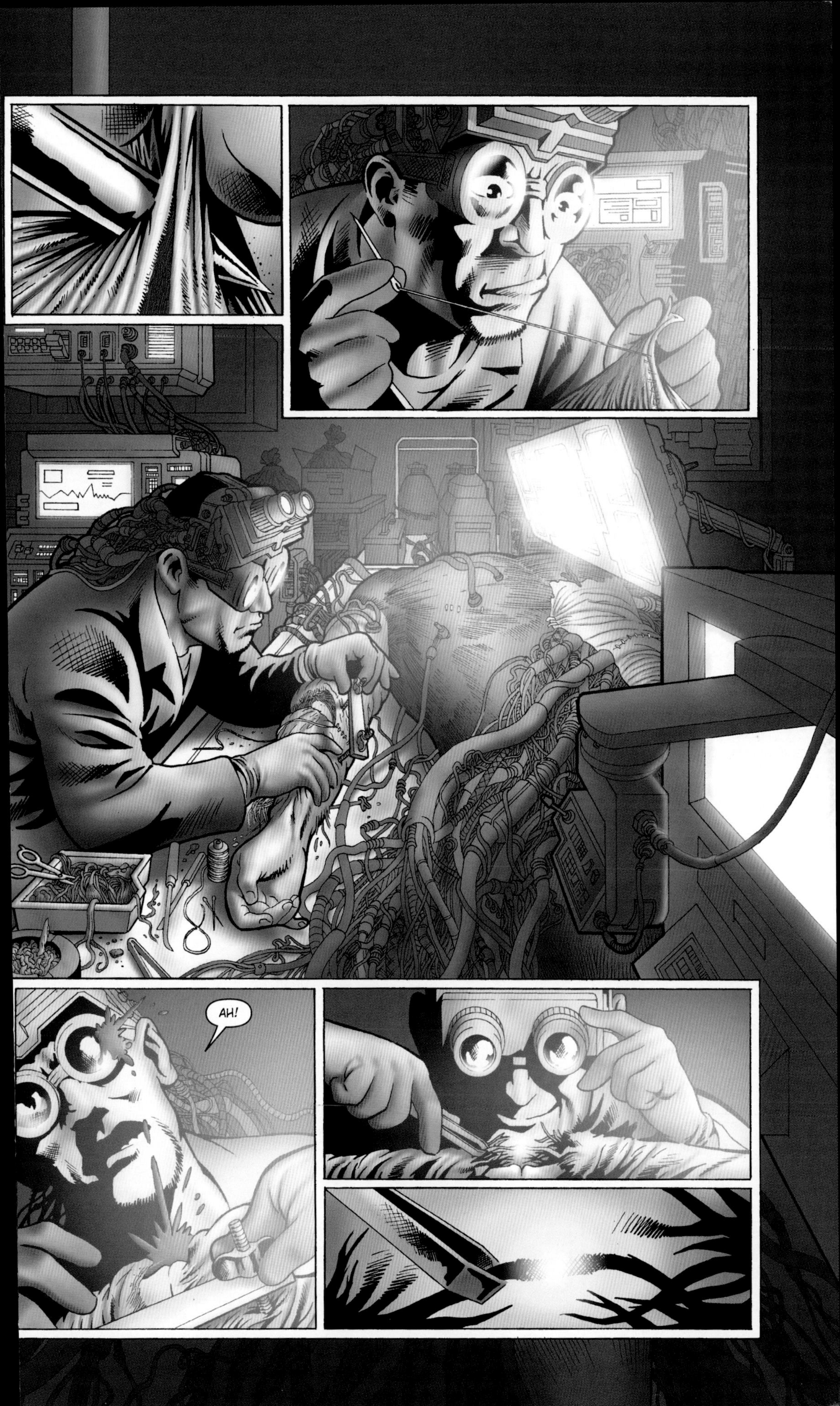
AH!

bing-bong
bing-bong

WHO THE FUCK?

YES?

IT'S MR. SHELLEY... WILLIAM'S FATHER... MAY I SPEAK WITH YOU?

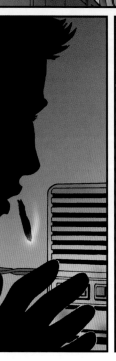

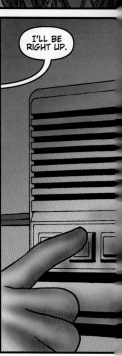

I'LL BE RIGHT UP.

MR. SHELLEY... IT'S THREE IN THE MORNING.

CAN I COME IN, VICTOR?

I SUPPOSE... OF COURSE. PLEASE COME IN. WE CAN TALK IN THE LIBRARY.

IS YOUR MOTHER HOME?

NO, SHE LEFT FOR PARIS.

ALL ALONE. I'M ALONE NOW... WITHOUT MY WILLIAM.

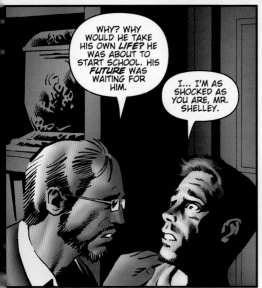

WHY? WHY WOULD HE TAKE HIS OWN LIFE? HE WAS ABOUT TO START SCHOOL. HIS FUTURE WAS WAITING FOR HIM.

I... I'M AS SHOCKED AS YOU ARE, MR. SHELLEY.

ARE YOU, VICTOR? ARE YOU SHOCKED?

WHAT DO YOU MEAN? I... I DON'T UNDERSTAND.

43

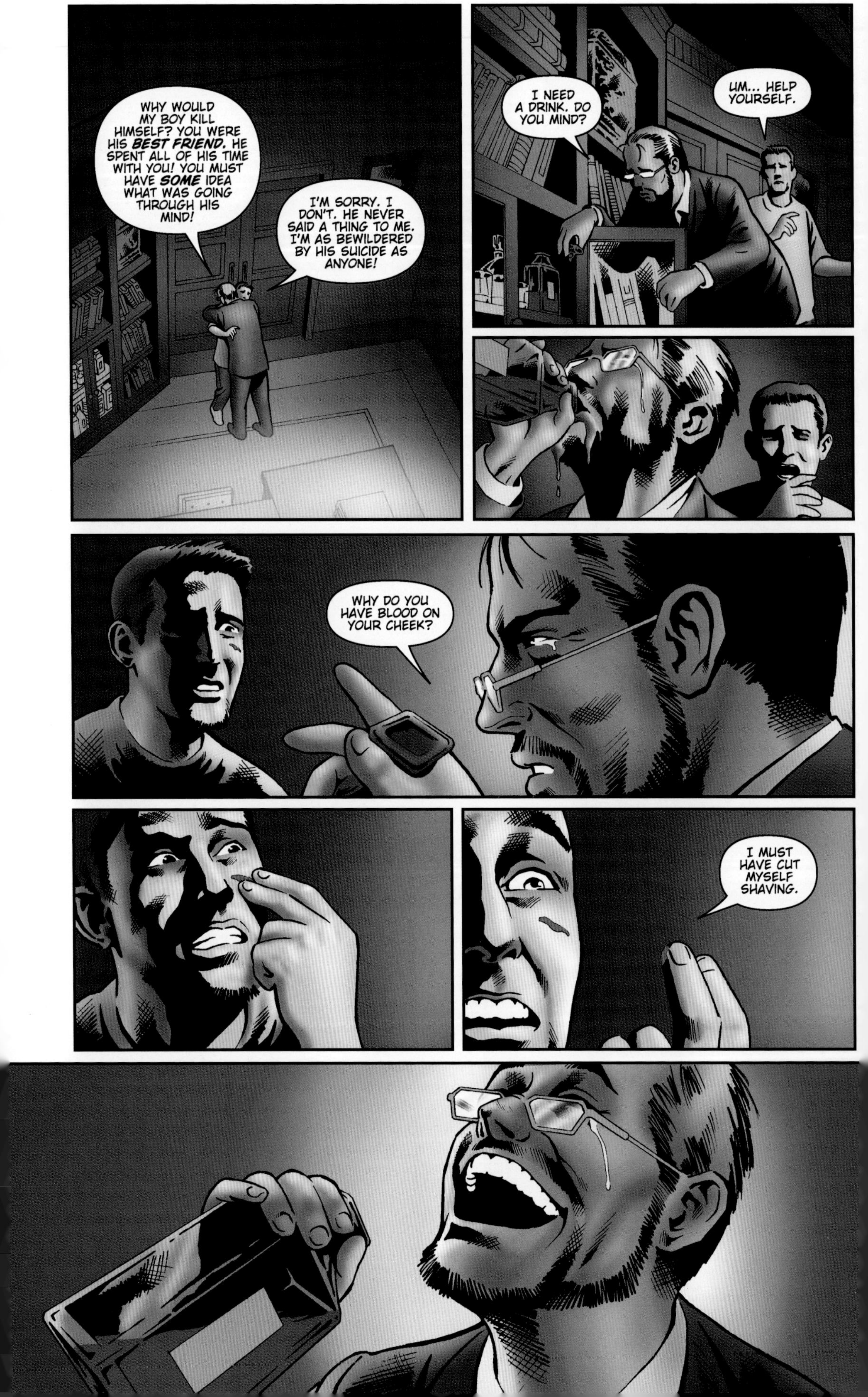
WHY WOULD MY BOY KILL HIMSELF? YOU WERE HIS BEST FRIEND. HE SPENT ALL OF HIS TIME WITH YOU! YOU MUST HAVE SOME IDEA WHAT WAS GOING THROUGH HIS MIND!
I'M SORRY. I DON'T. HE NEVER SAID A THING TO ME. I'M AS BEWILDERED BY HIS SUICIDE AS ANYONE!
I NEED A DRINK. DO YOU MIND?
UM... HELP YOURSELF.
WHY DO YOU HAVE BLOOD ON YOUR CHEEK?
I MUST HAVE CUT MYSELF SHAVING.

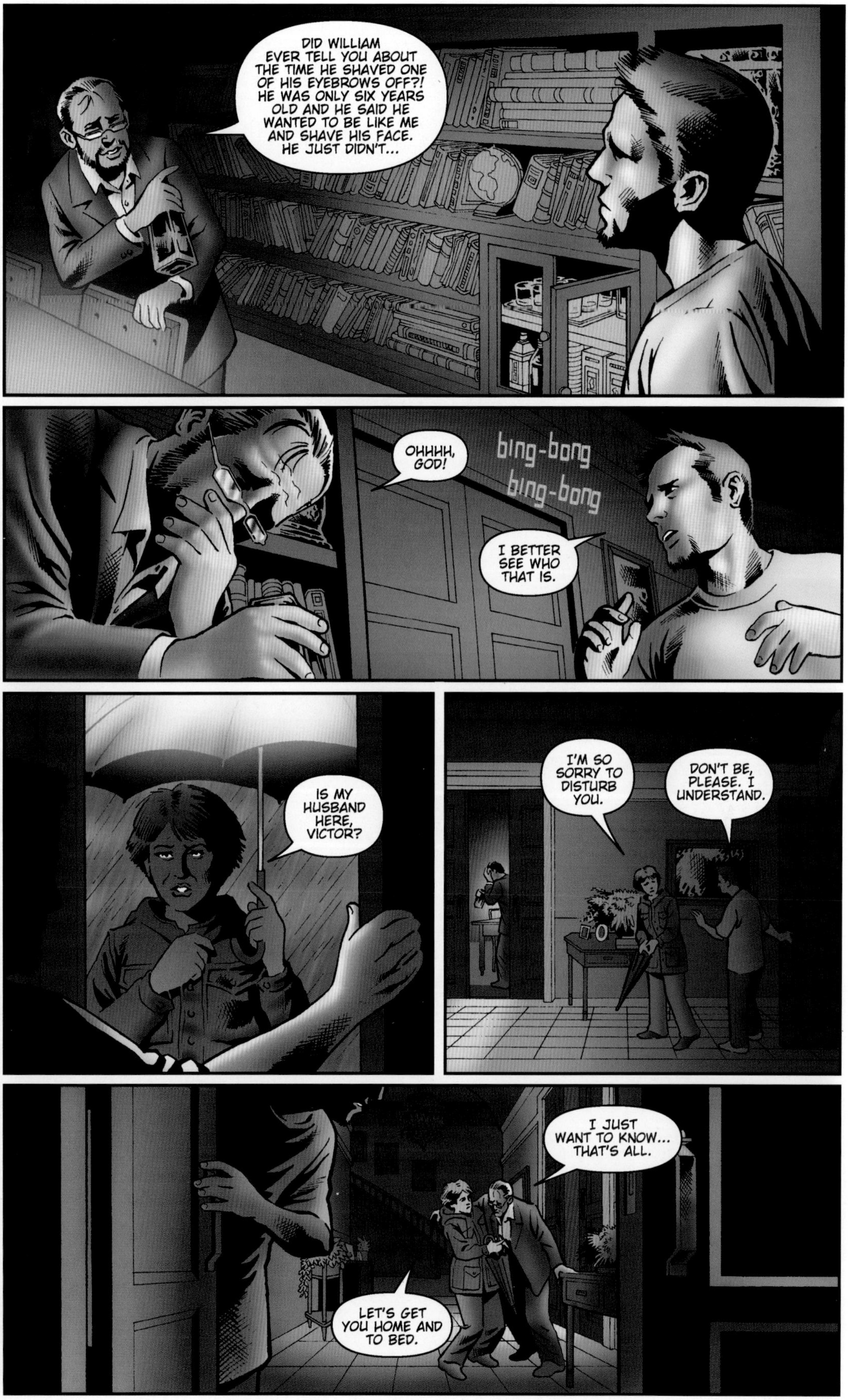
DID WILLIAM EVER TELL YOU ABOUT THE TIME HE SHAVED ONE OF HIS EYEBROWS OFF?! HE WAS ONLY SIX YEARS OLD AND HE SAID HE WANTED TO BE LIKE ME AND SHAVE HIS FACE. HE JUST DIDN'T...
OHHHH, GOD!
bing-bong
bing-bong
I BETTER SEE WHO THAT IS.
IS MY HUSBAND HERE, VICTOR?
I'M SO SORRY TO DISTURB YOU.
DON'T BE, PLEASE. I UNDERSTAND.
I JUST WANT TO KNOW... THAT'S ALL.
LET'S GET YOU HOME AND TO BED.

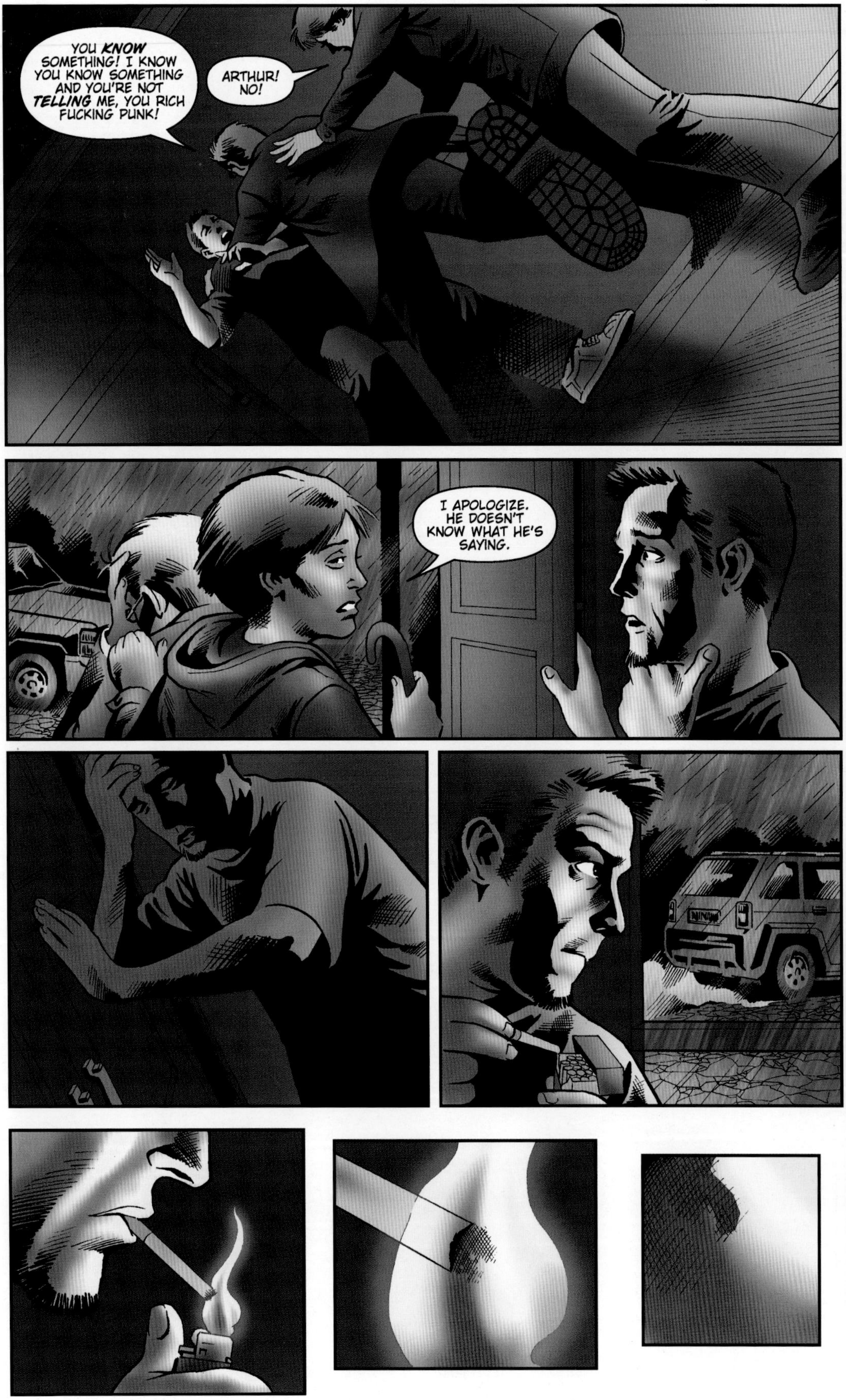
YOU KNOW SOMETHING! I KNOW YOU KNOW SOMETHING AND YOU'RE NOT TELLING ME, YOU RICH FUCKING PUNK!
ARTHUR! NO!
I APOLOGIZE. HE DOESN'T KNOW WHAT HE'S SAYING.

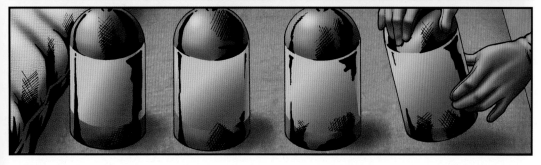

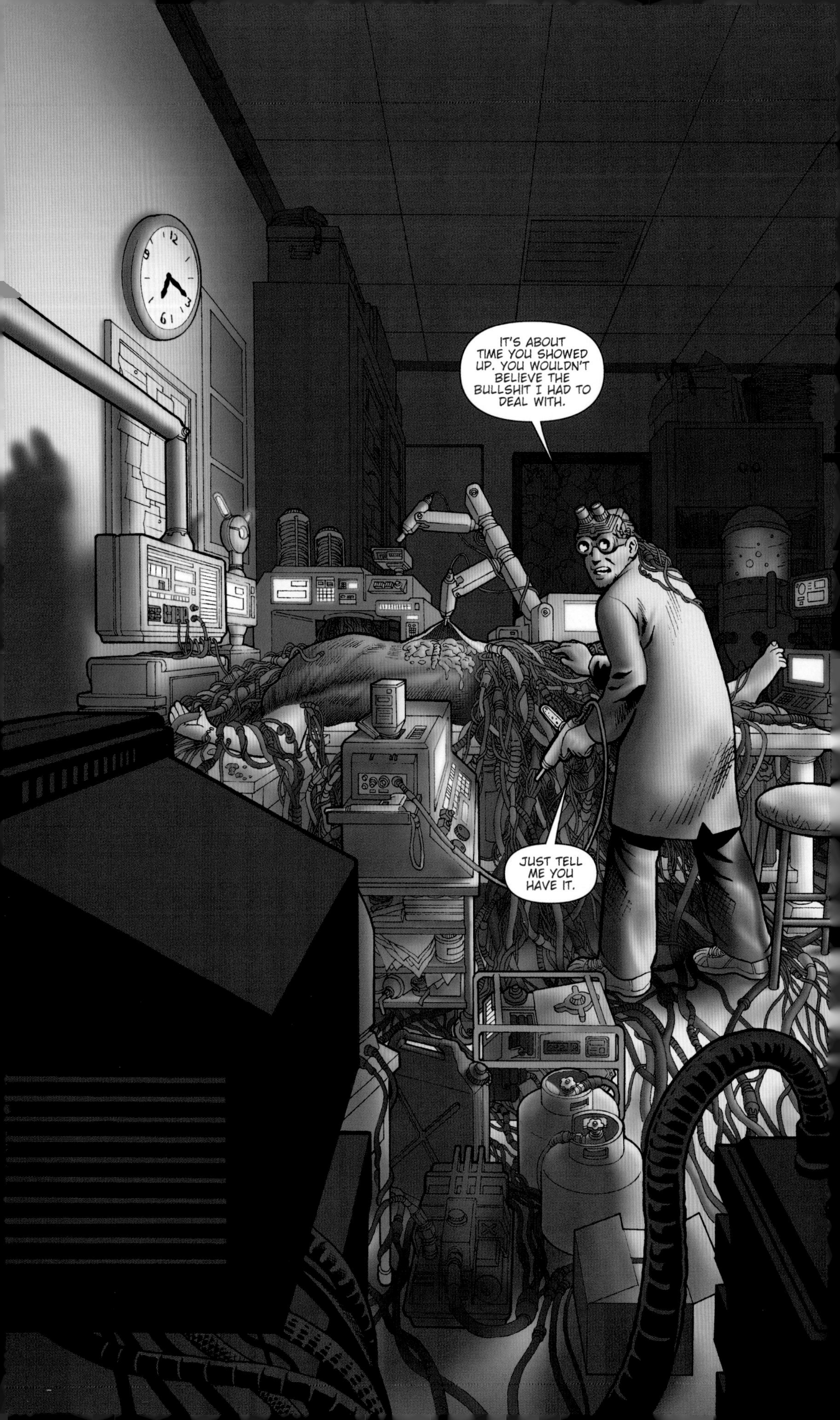
IT'S ABOUT TIME YOU SHOWED UP. YOU WOULDN'T BELIEVE THE BULLSHIT I HAD TO DEAL WITH.
JUST TELL ME YOU HAVE IT.

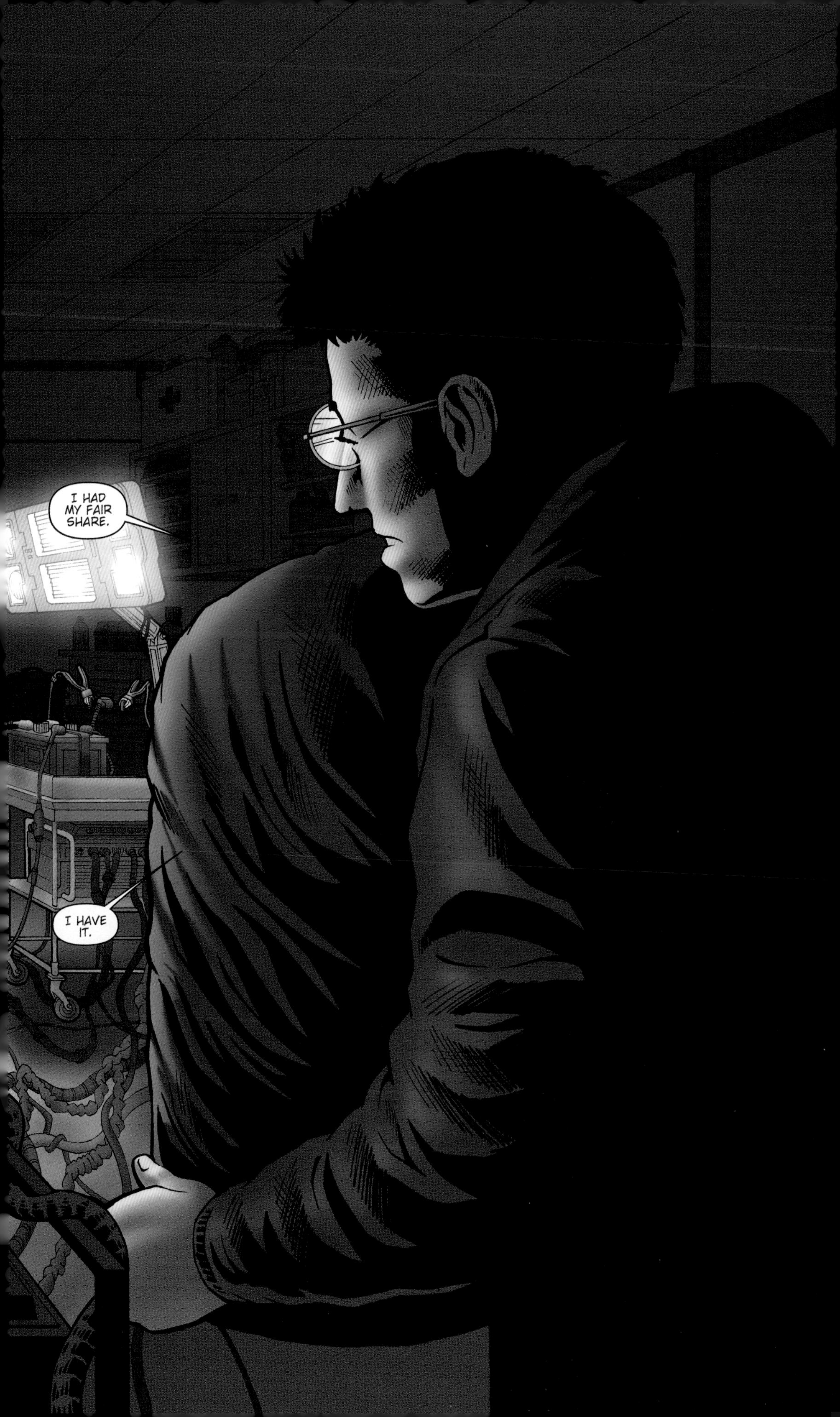
I HAD MY FAIR SHARE.
I HAVE IT.

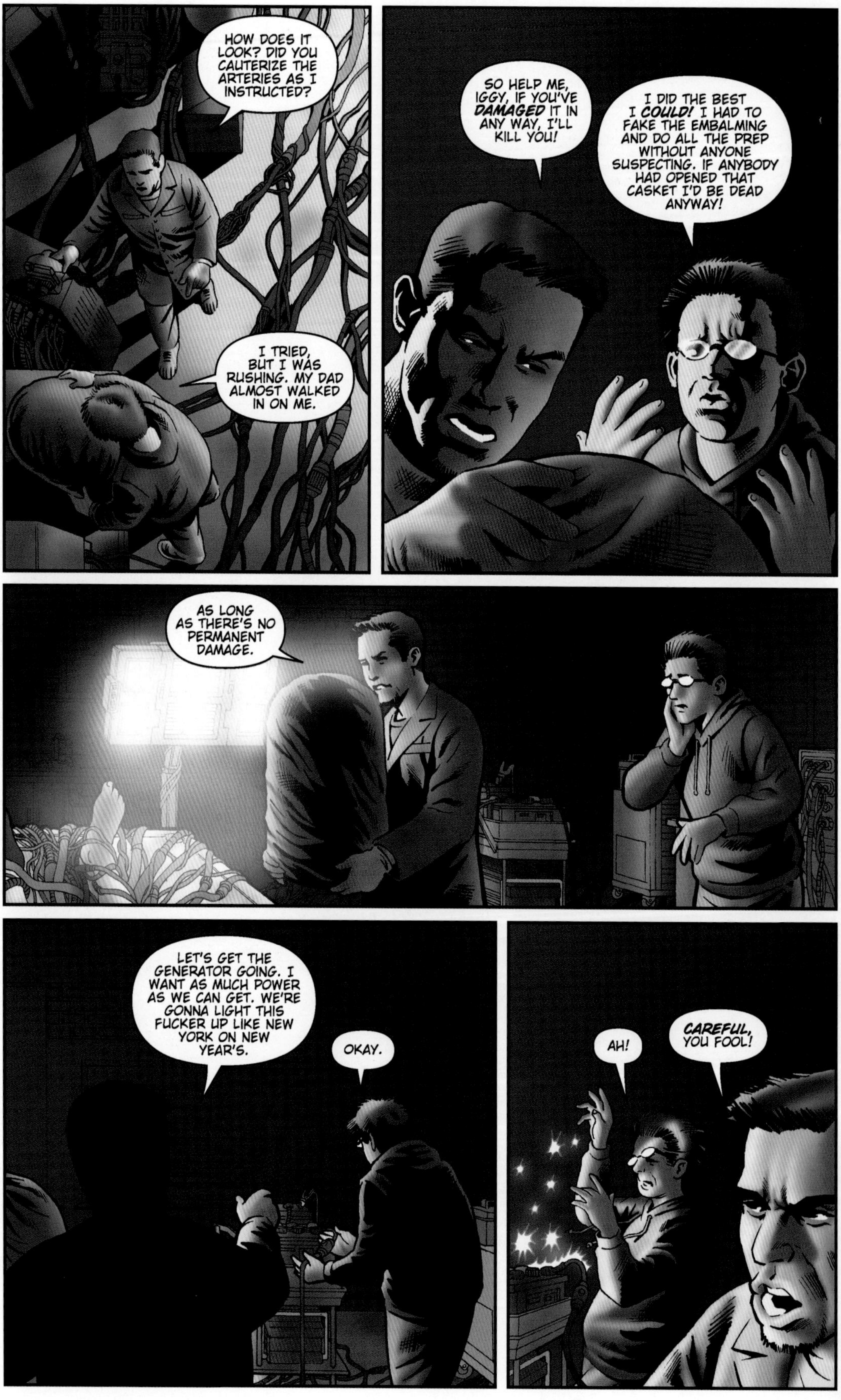
HOW DOES IT LOOK? DID YOU CAUTERIZE THE ARTERIES AS I INSTRUCTED?
I TRIED, BUT I WAS RUSHING. MY DAD ALMOST WALKED IN ON ME.
SO HELP ME, IGGY, IF YOU'VE DAMAGED IT IN ANY WAY, I'LL KILL YOU!
I DID THE BEST I COULD! I HAD TO FAKE THE EMBALMING AND DO ALL THE PREP WITHOUT ANYONE SUSPECTING. IF ANYBODY HAD OPENED THAT CASKET I'D BE DEAD ANYWAY!
AS LONG AS THERE'S NO PERMANENT DAMAGE.
LET'S GET THE GENERATOR GOING. I WANT AS MUCH POWER AS WE CAN GET. WE'RE GONNA LIGHT THIS FUCKER UP LIKE NEW YORK ON NEW YEAR'S.
OKAY.
AH!
CAREFUL, YOU FOOL!

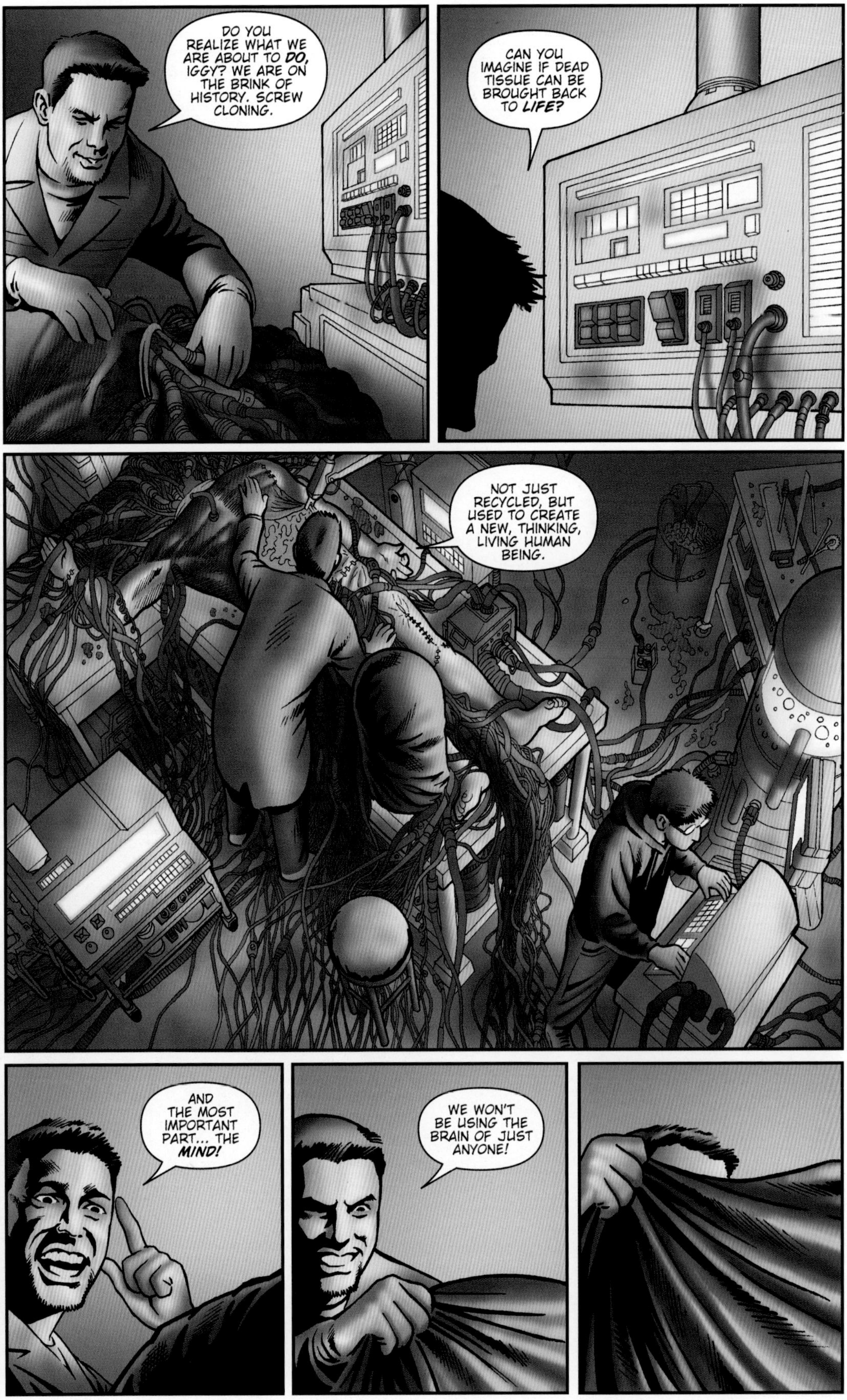
DO YOU REALIZE WHAT WE ARE ABOUT TO DO, IGGY? WE ARE ON THE BRINK OF HISTORY. SCREW CLONING.
CAN YOU IMAGINE IF DEAD TISSUE CAN BE BROUGHT BACK TO LIFE?
NOT JUST RECYCLED, BUT USED TO CREATE A NEW, THINKING, LIVING HUMAN BEING.
AND THE MOST IMPORTANT PART... THE MIND!
WE WON'T BE USING THE BRAIN OF JUST ANYONE!

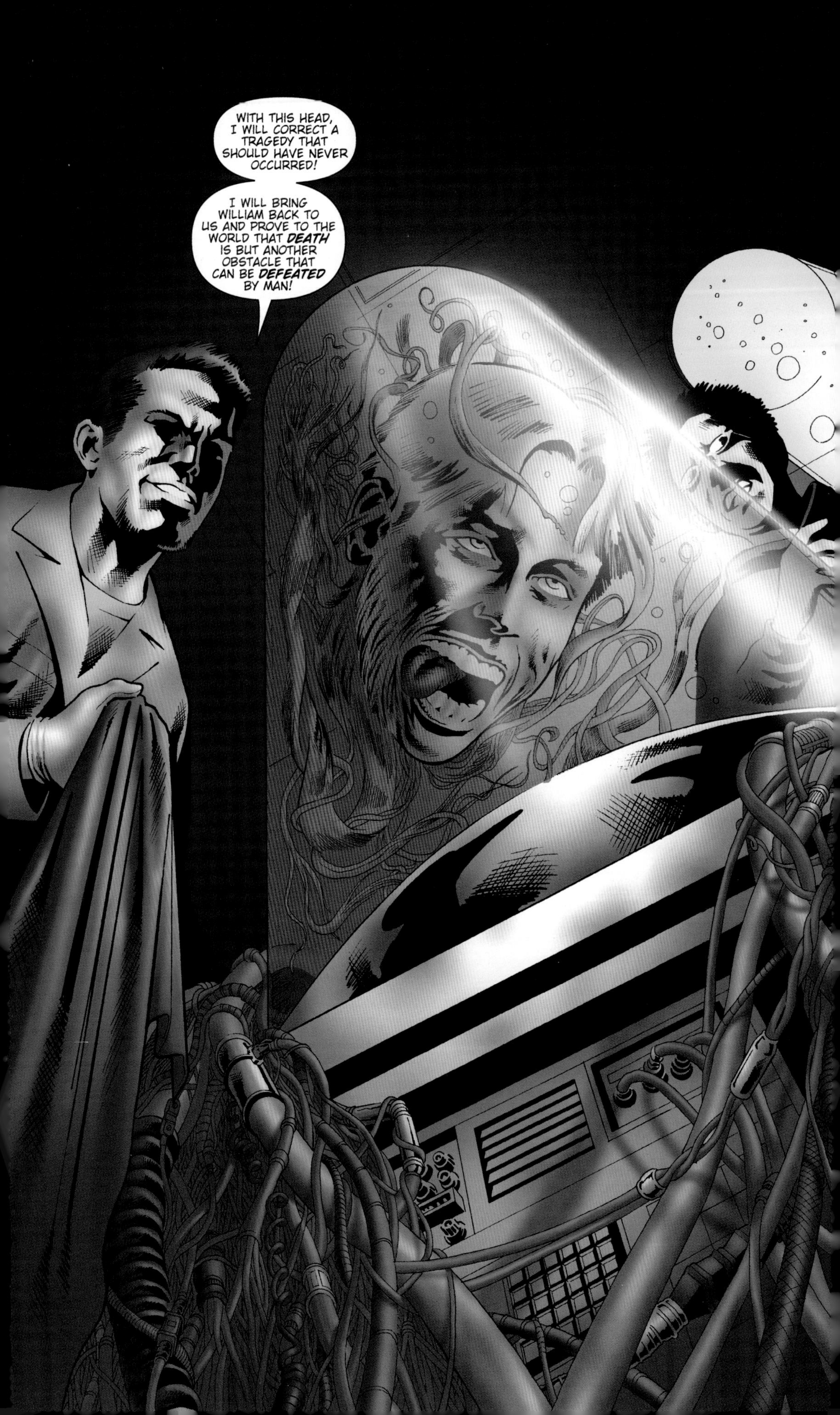
WITH THIS HEAD, I WILL CORRECT A TRAGEDY THAT SHOULD HAVE NEVER OCCURRED!
I WILL BRING WILLIAM BACK TO US AND PROVE TO THE WORLD THAT *DEATH* IS BUT ANOTHER OBSTACLE THAT CAN BE *DEFEATED* BY MAN!

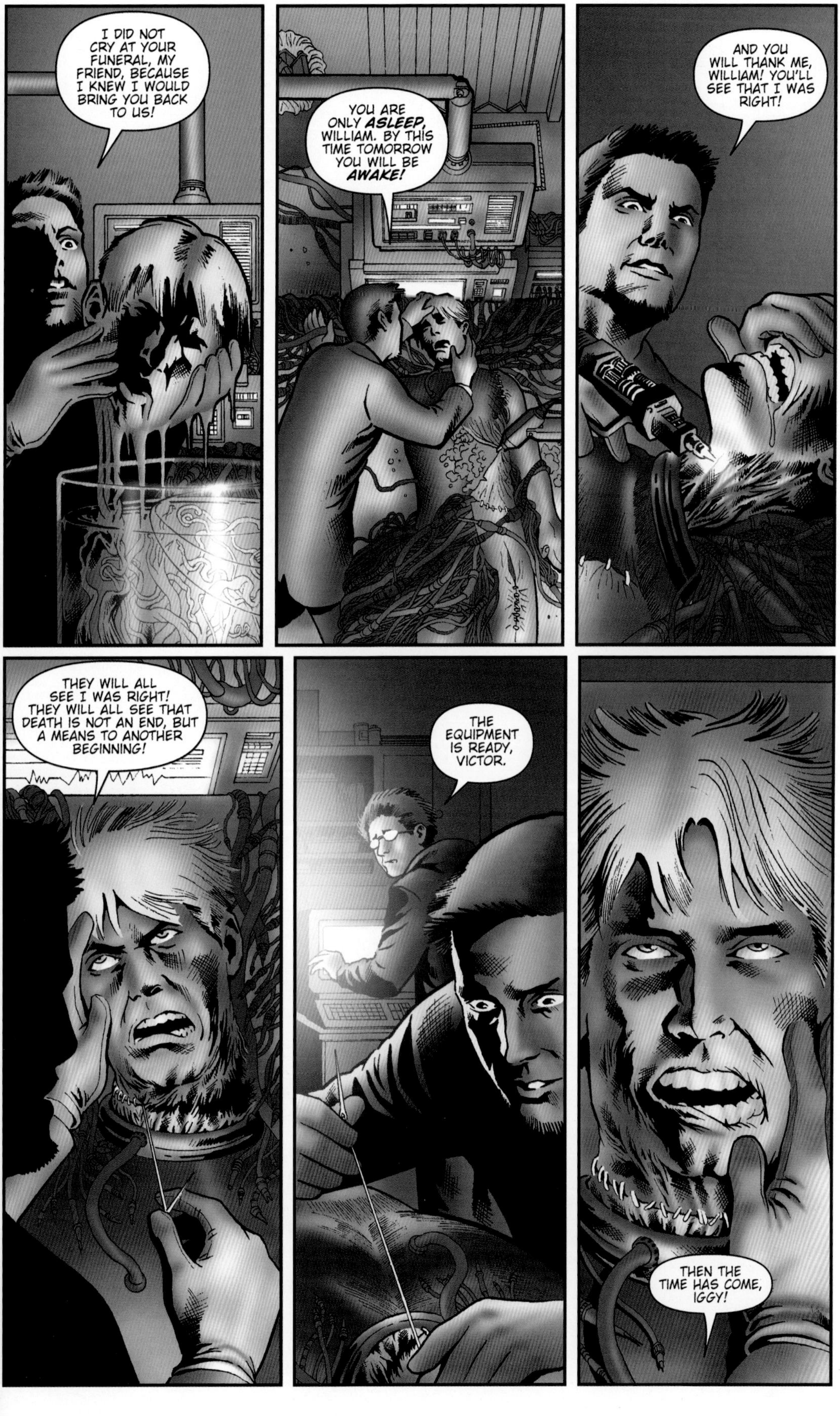
I DID NOT CRY AT YOUR FUNERAL, MY FRIEND, BECAUSE I KNEW I WOULD BRING YOU BACK TO US!
YOU ARE ONLY ASLEEP, WILLIAM. BY THIS TIME TOMORROW YOU WILL BE AWAKE!
AND YOU WILL THANK ME, WILLIAM! YOU'LL SEE THAT I WAS RIGHT!
THEY WILL ALL SEE I WAS RIGHT! THEY WILL ALL SEE THAT DEATH IS NOT AN END, BUT A MEANS TO ANOTHER BEGINNING!
THE EQUIPMENT IS READY, VICTOR.
THEN THE TIME HAS COME, IGGY!

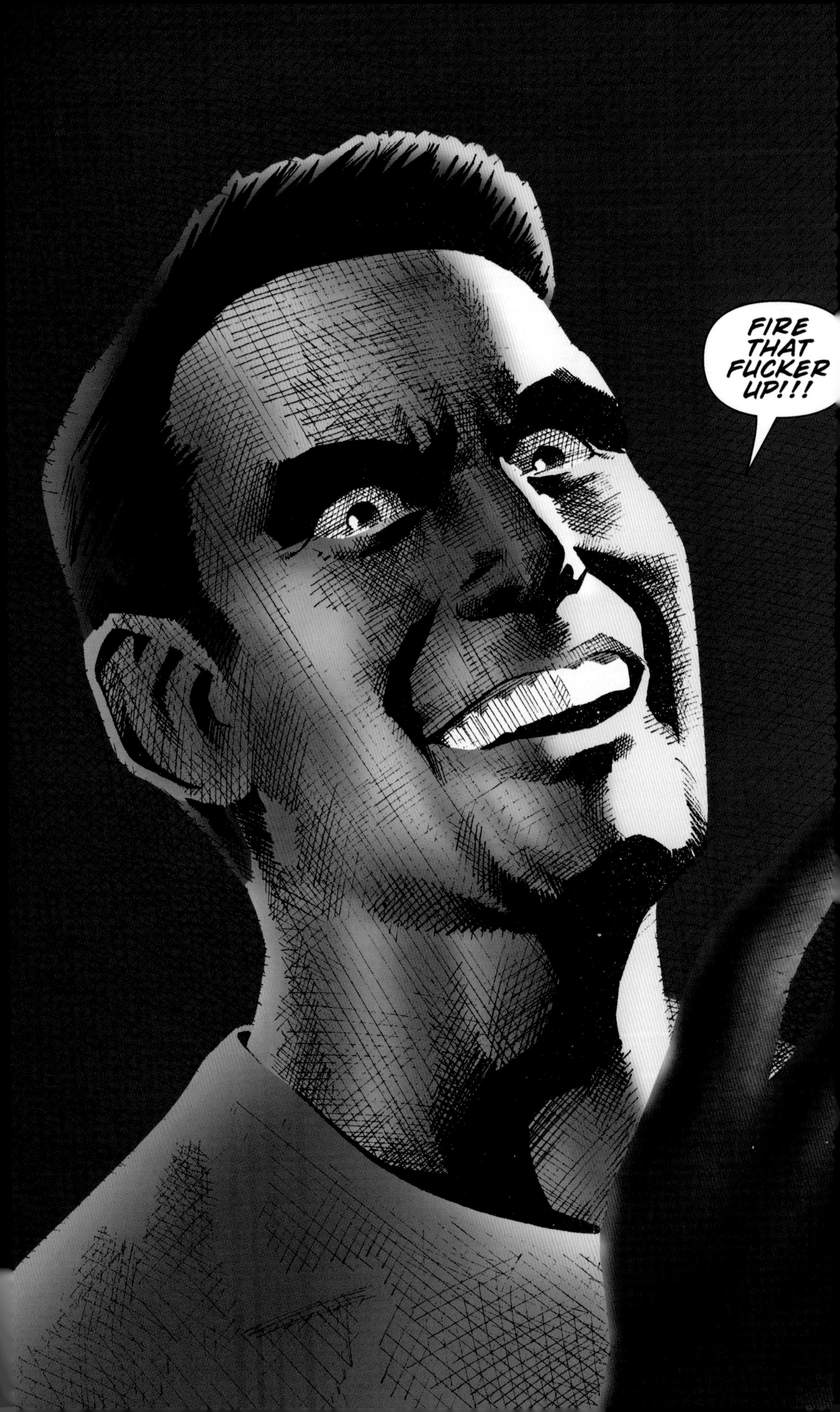
FIRE THAT FUCKER UP!!!

chapter three

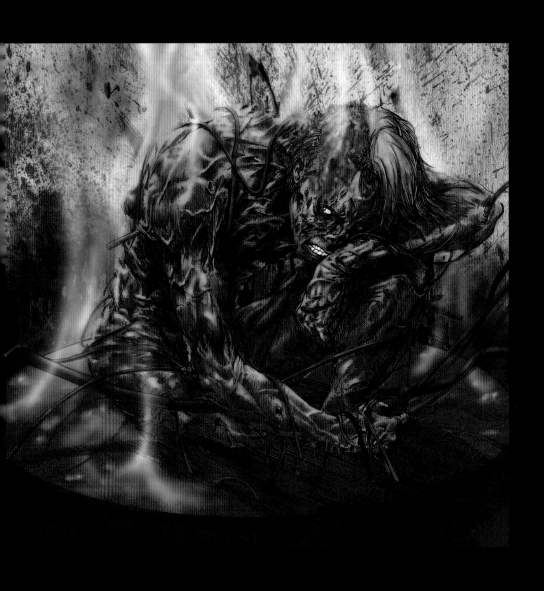

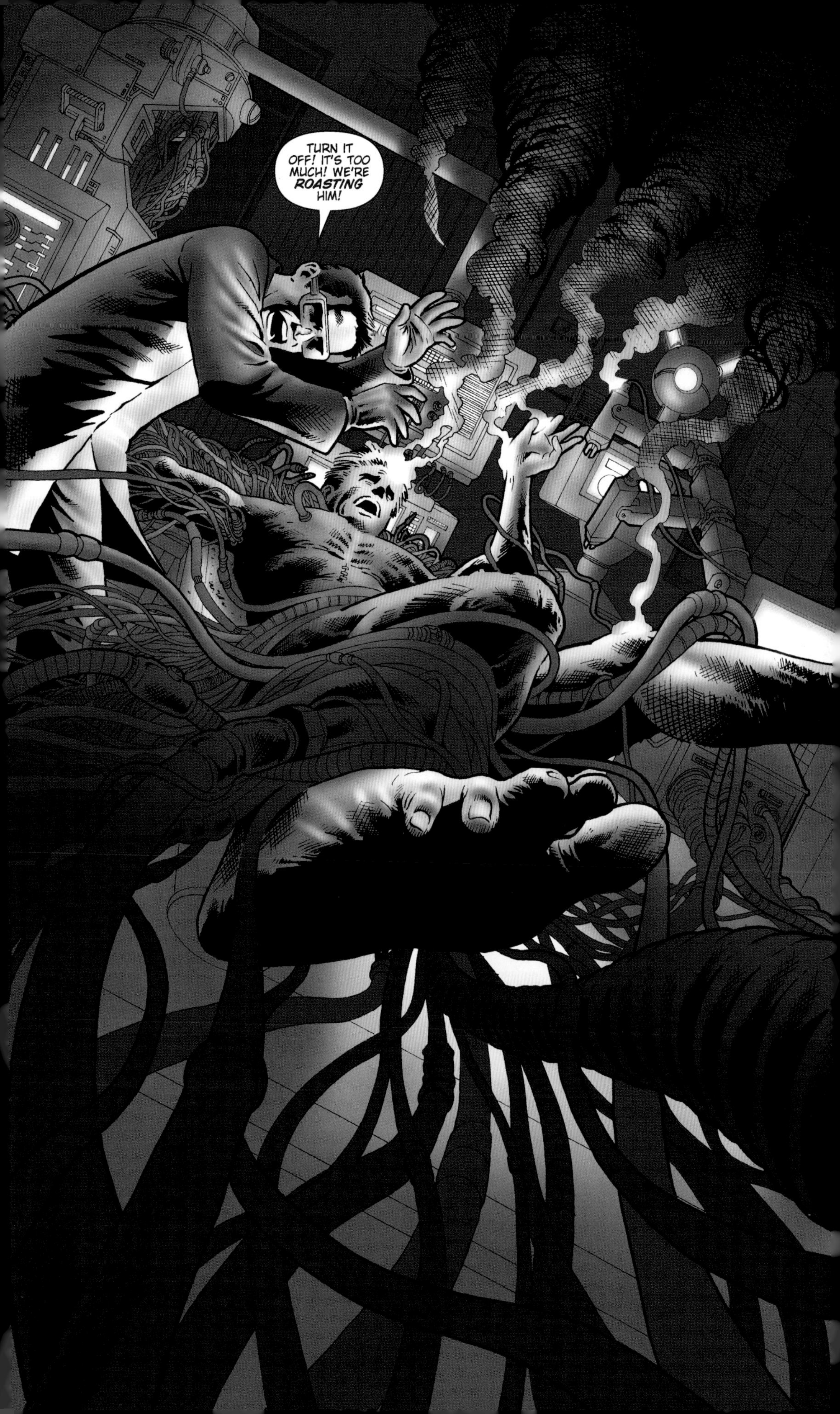
TURN IT OFF! IT'S TOO MUCH! WE'RE *ROASTING* HIM!

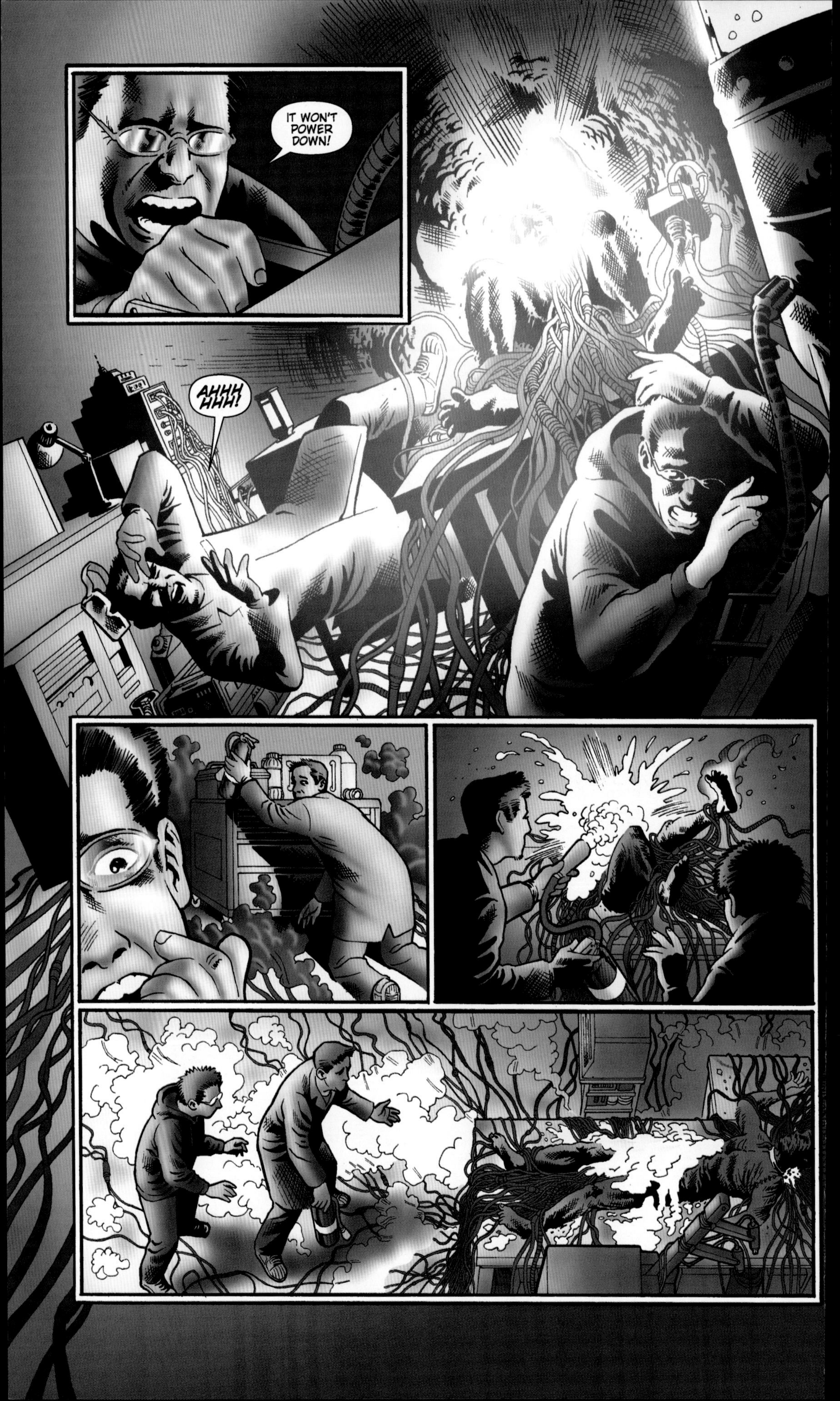
IT WON'T POWER DOWN!
AHHH HHH!

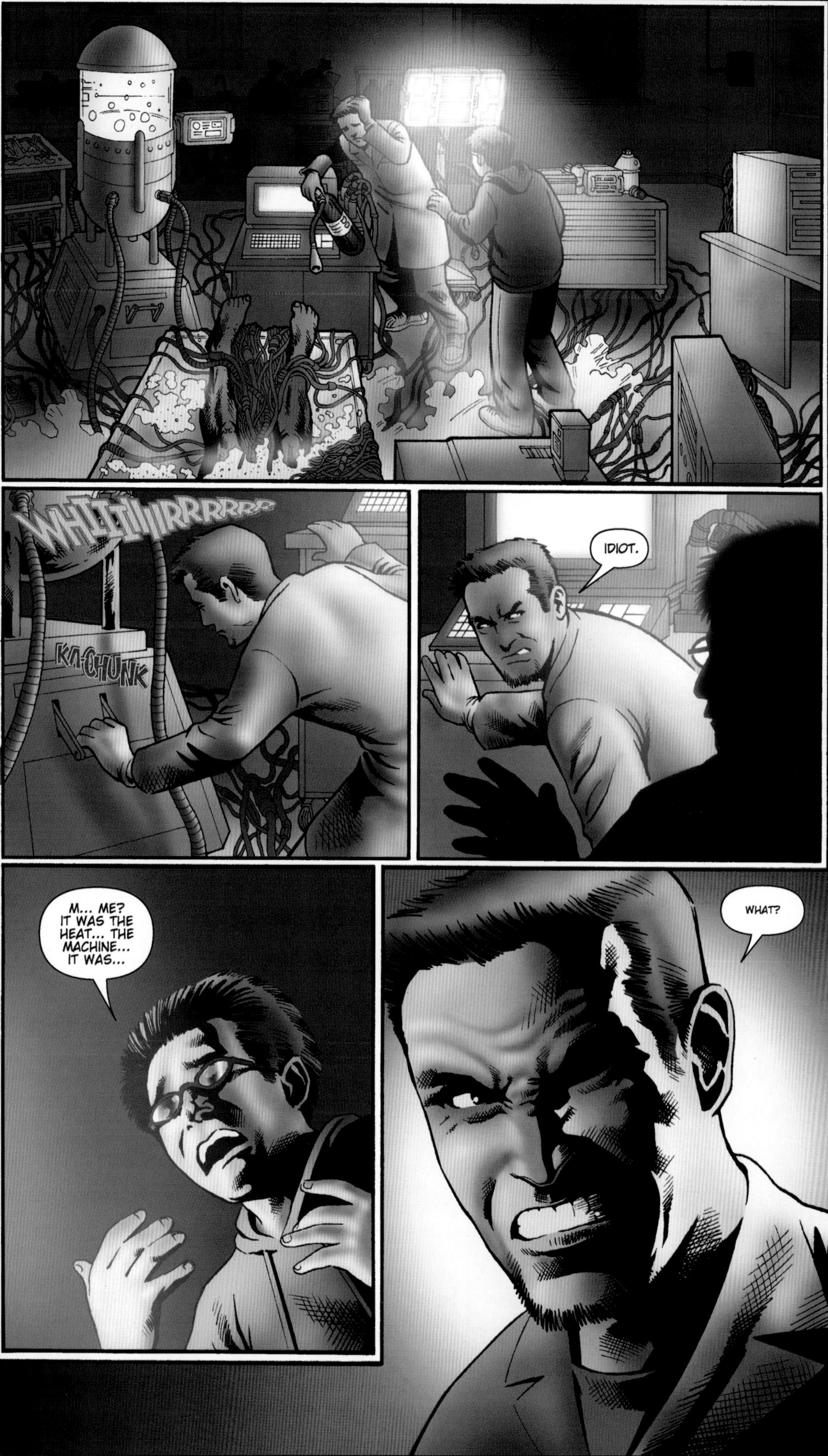
WHIIIIIIRRRRRRR
KA-CHUNK
IDIOT.
M... ME? IT WAS THE HEAT... THE MACHINE... IT WAS...
WHAT?

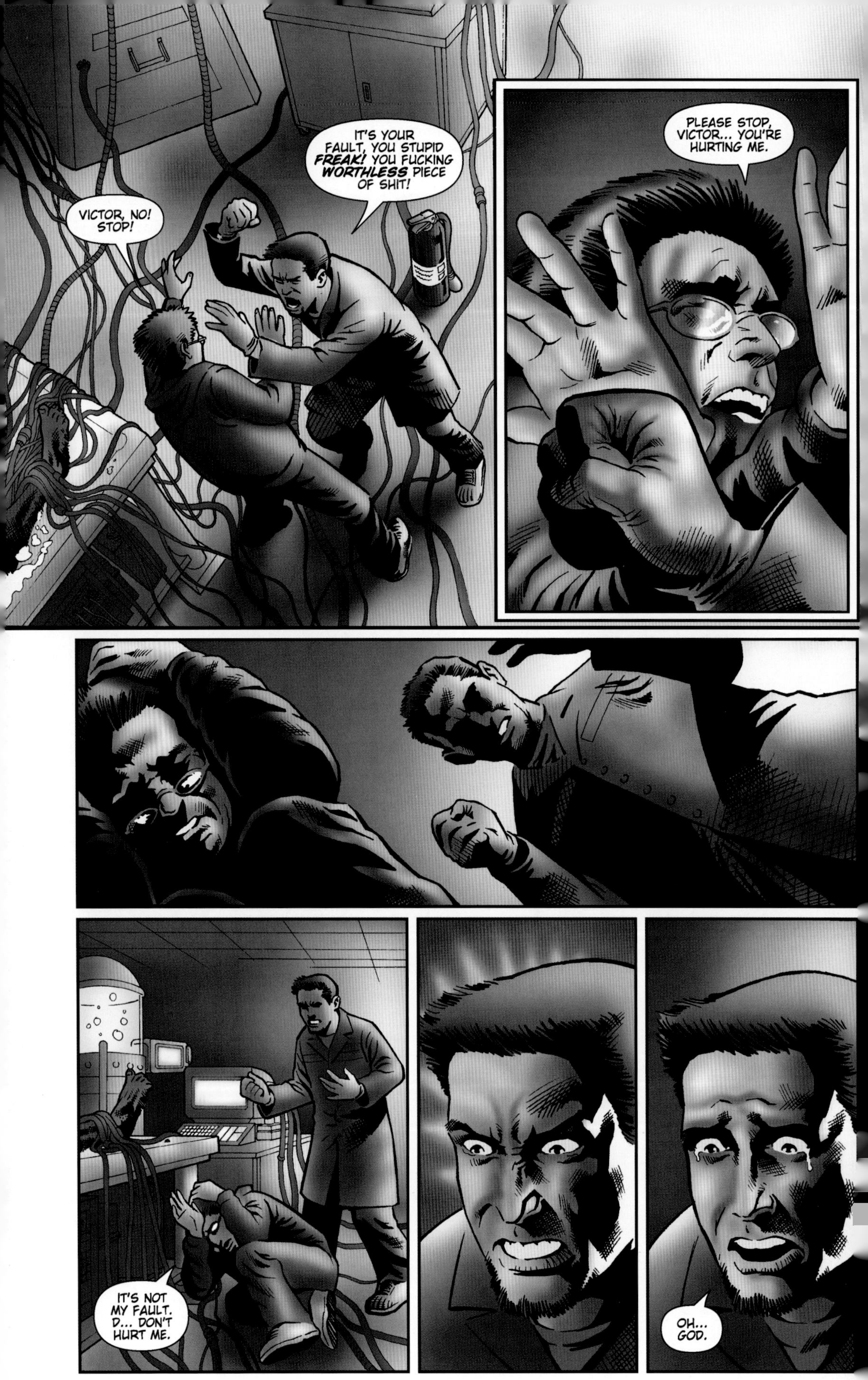
VICTOR, NO! STOP!
IT'S YOUR FAULT, YOU STUPID FREAK! YOU FUCKING WORTHLESS PIECE OF SHIT!
PLEASE STOP, VICTOR... YOU'RE HURTING ME.
IT'S NOT MY FAULT. D... DON'T HURT ME.
OH... GOD.

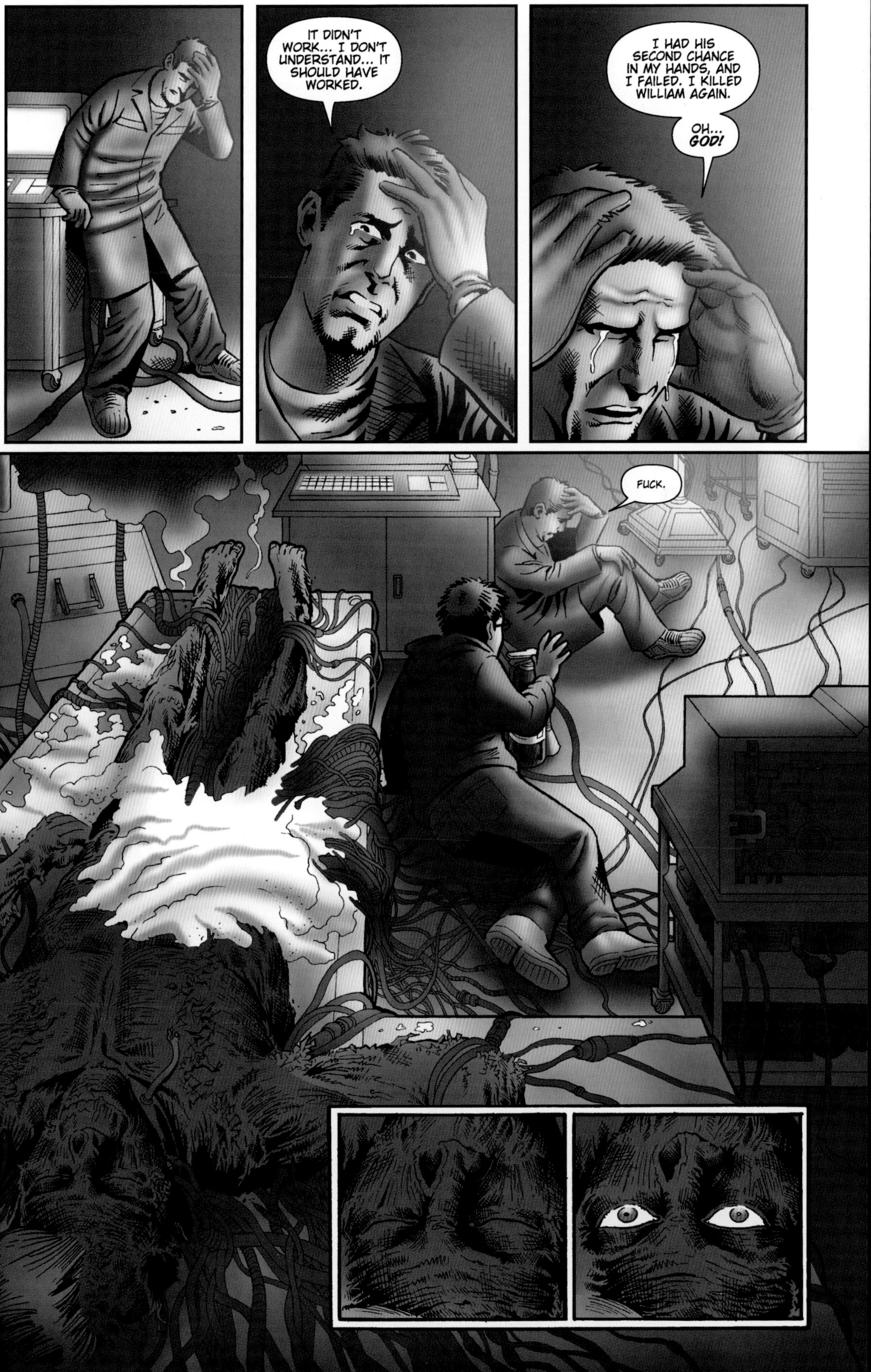
IT DIDN'T WORK... I DON'T UNDERSTAND... IT SHOULD HAVE WORKED.
I HAD HIS SECOND CHANCE IN MY HANDS, AND I FAILED. I KILLED WILLIAM AGAIN.
OH... GOD!
FUCK.

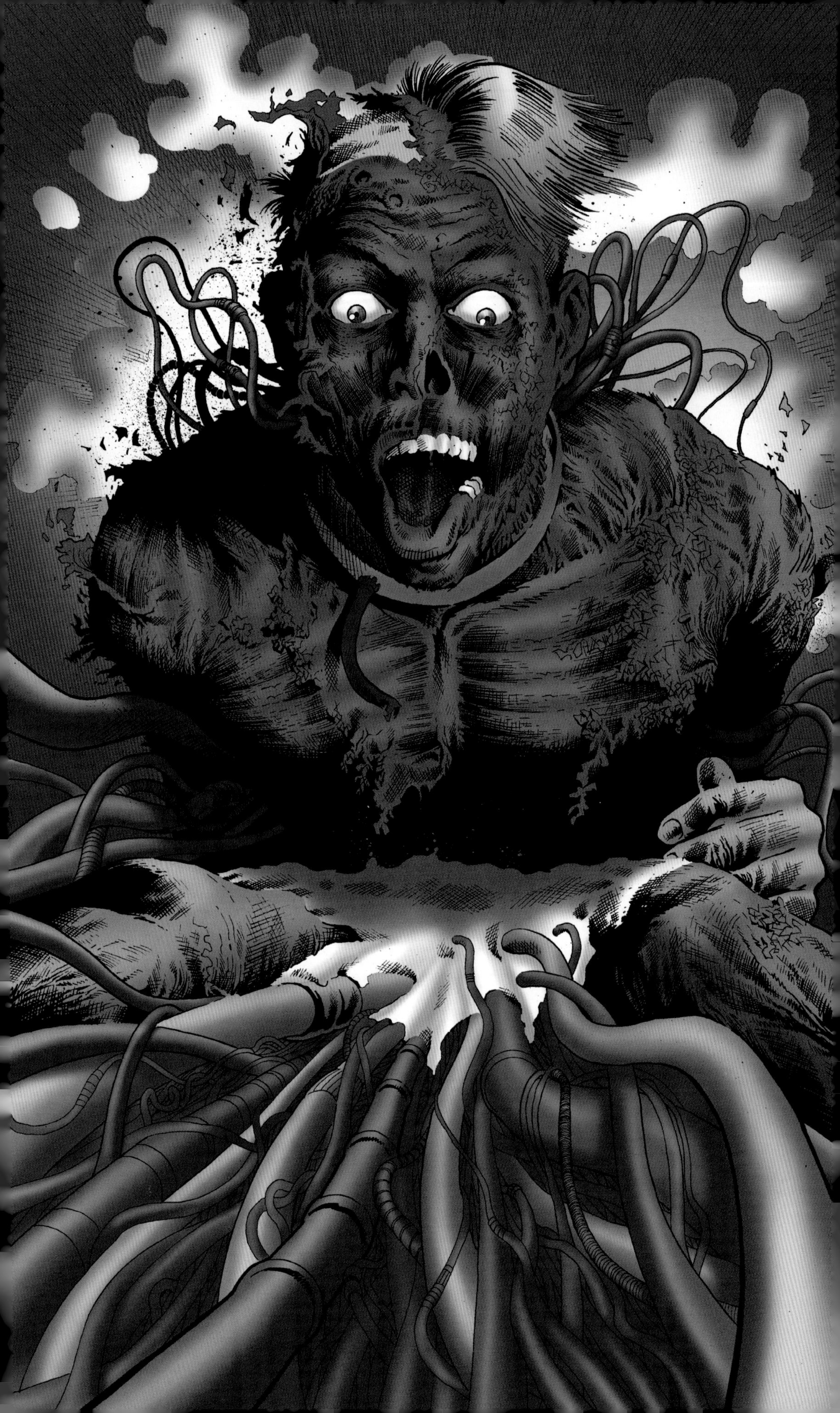

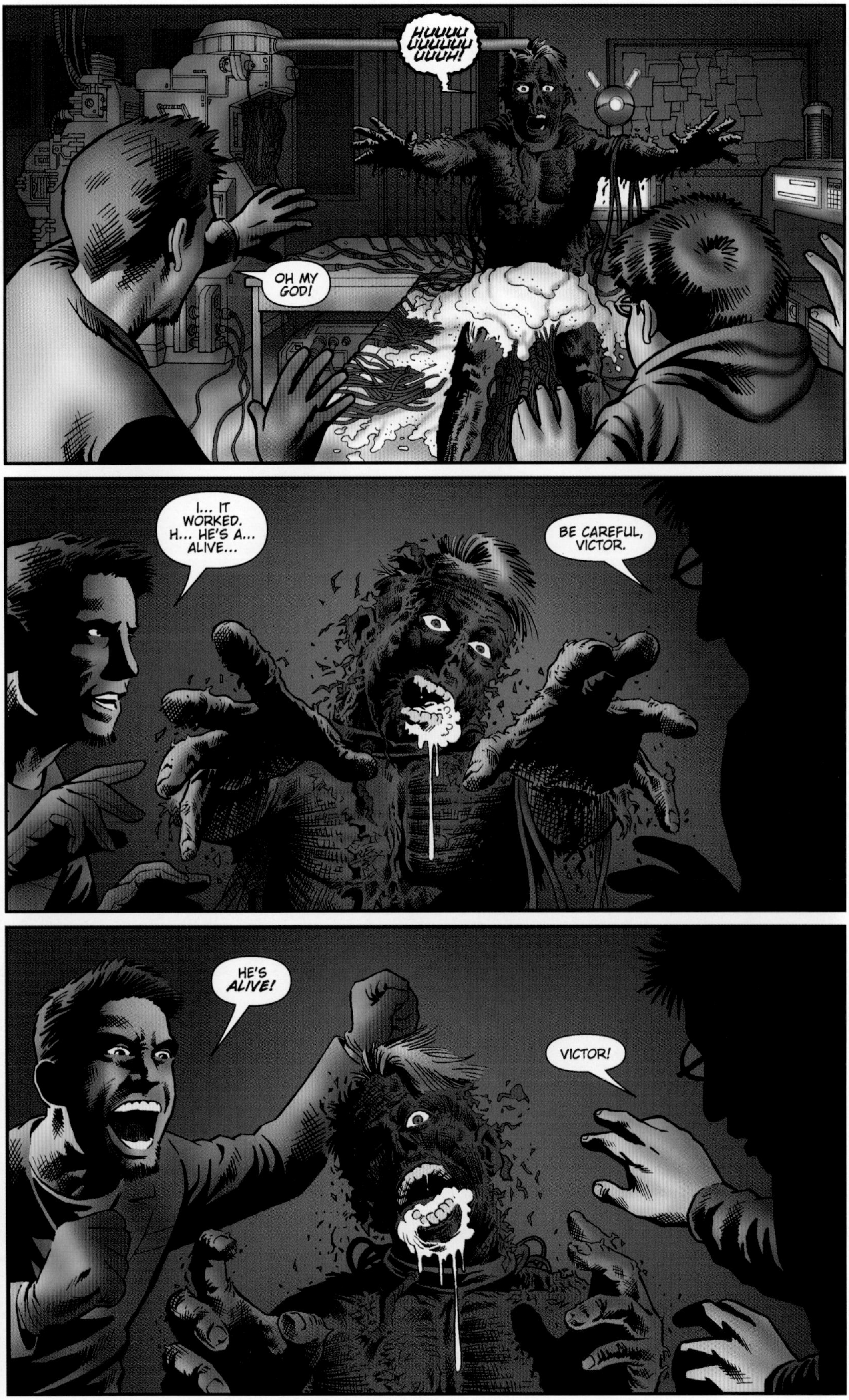
HUUUU UUUUUU UUUH!
OH MY GOD!
I... IT WORKED. H... HE'S A... ALIVE...
BE CAREFUL, VICTOR.
HE'S ALIVE!
VICTOR!

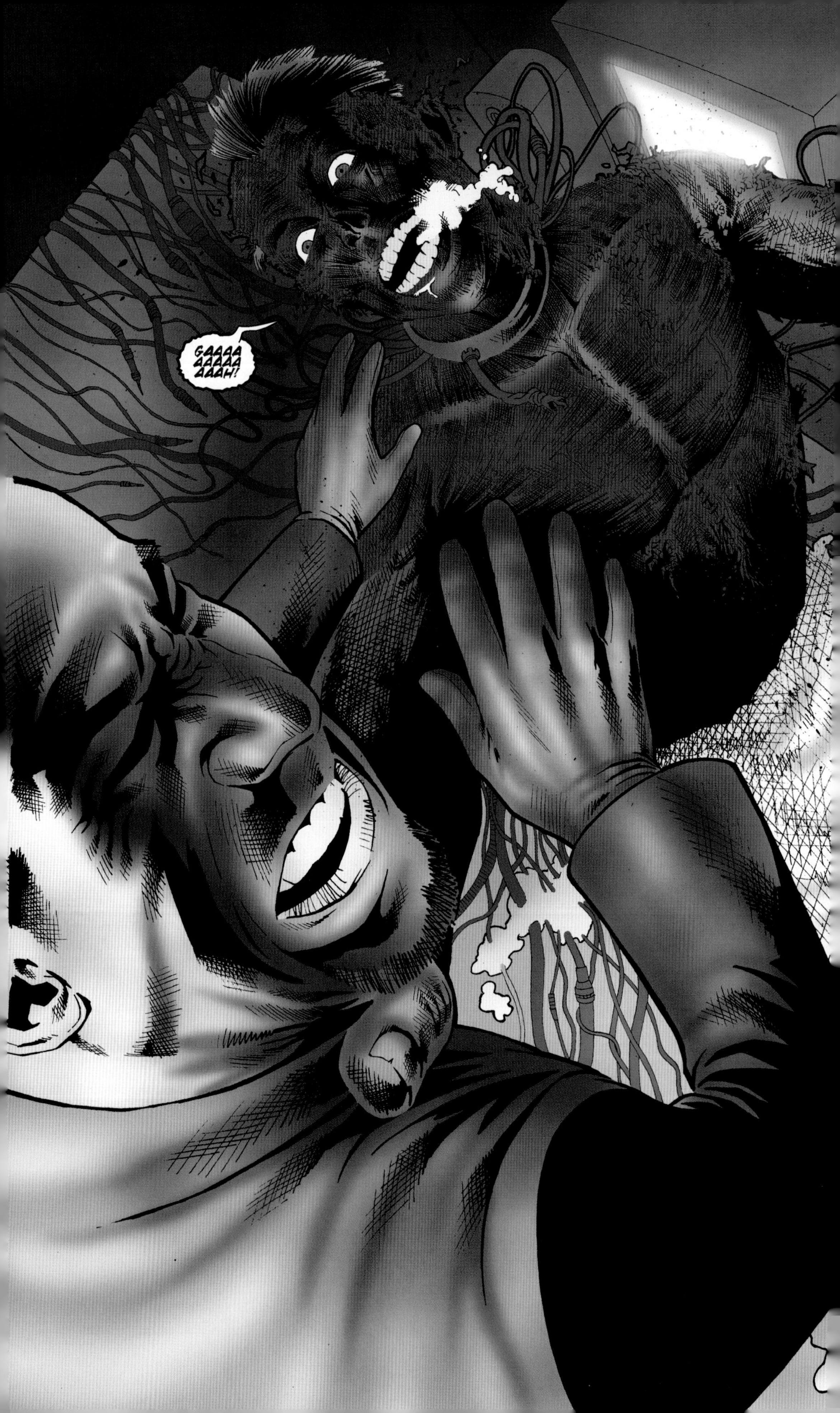
GAAAA AAAAA AAAH!

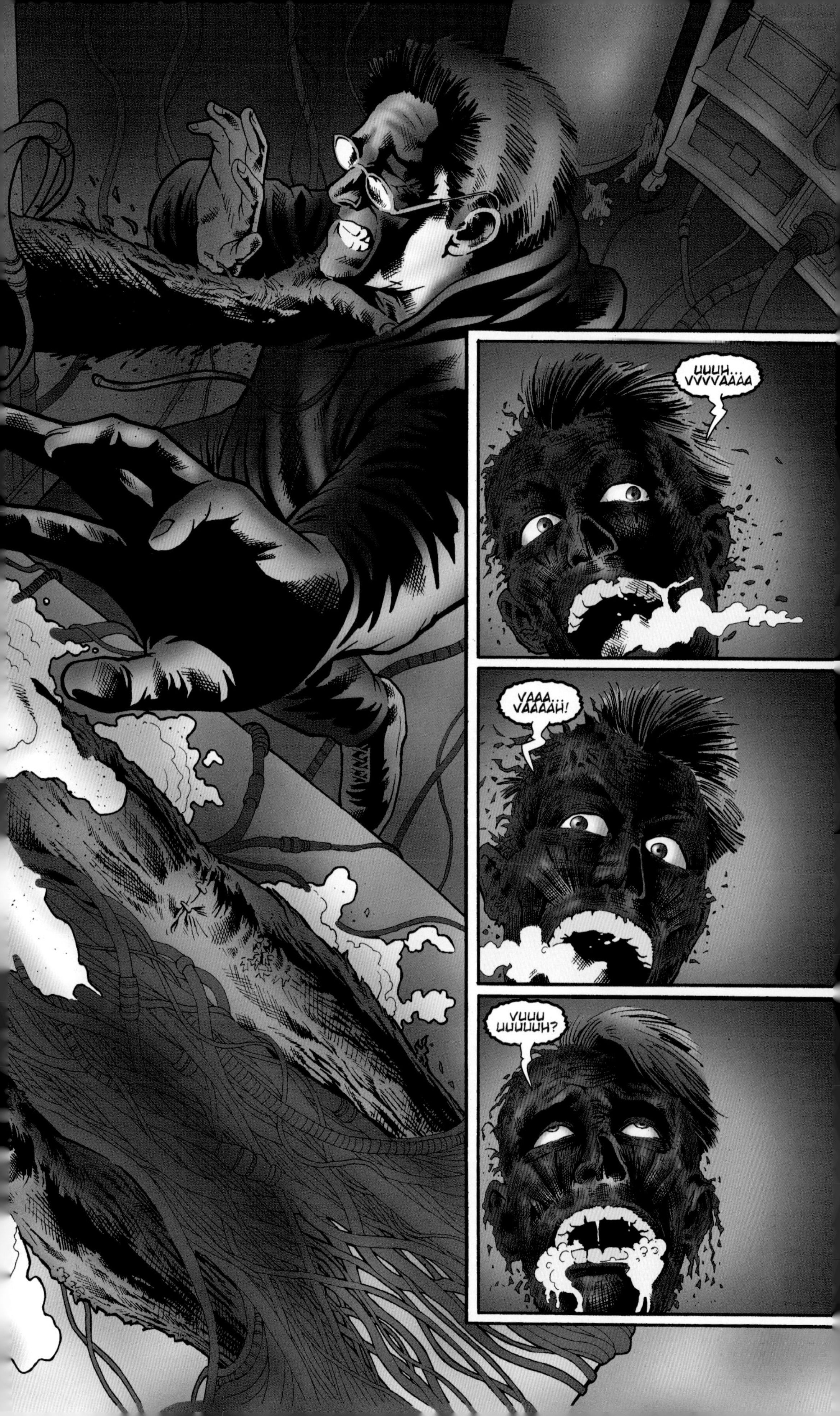
UUUH... VVVVAAAA
VAAA... VAAAAH!
VUUU UUUUUH?

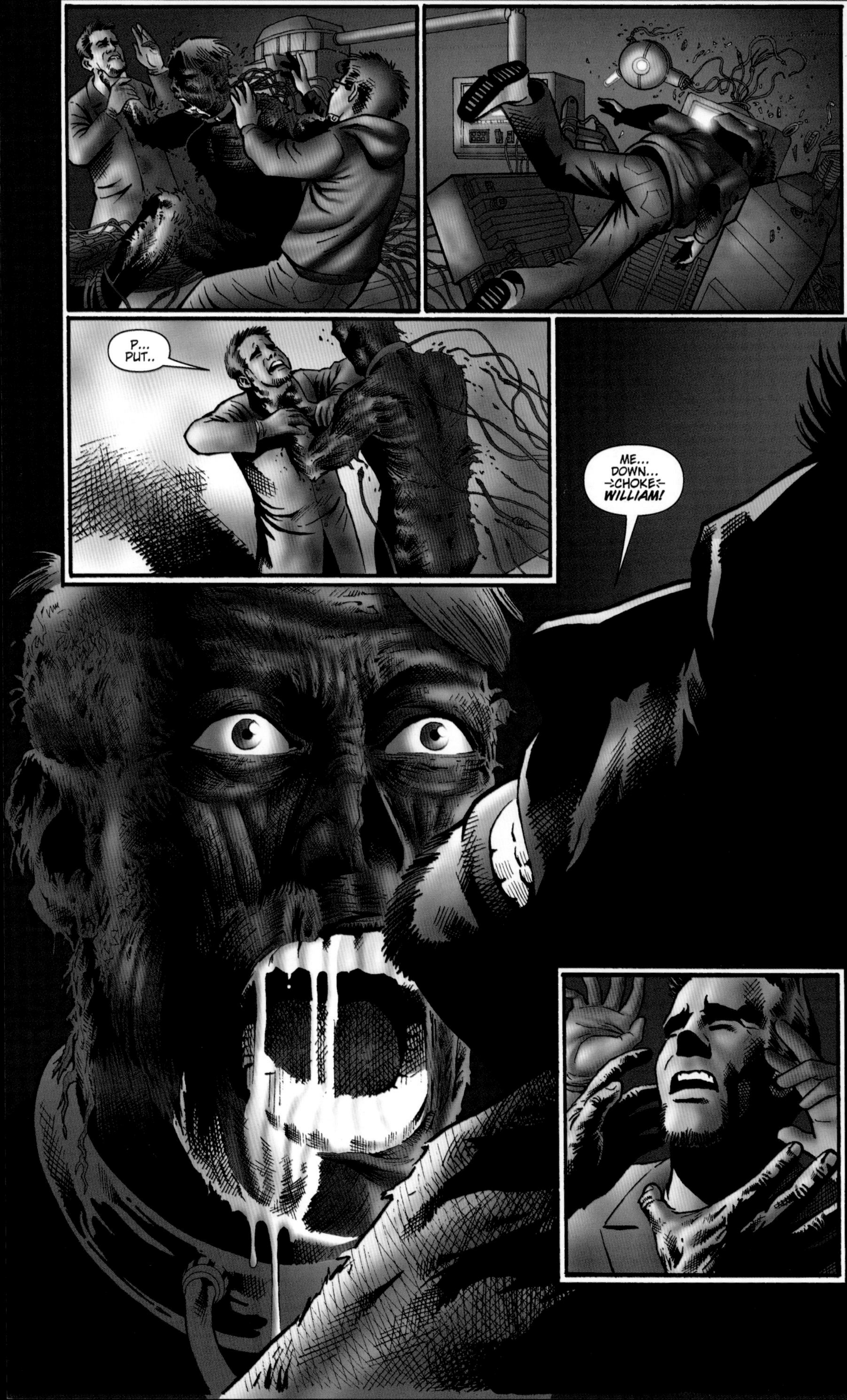
P... PUT..
ME... DOWN... -CHOKE- WILLIAM!

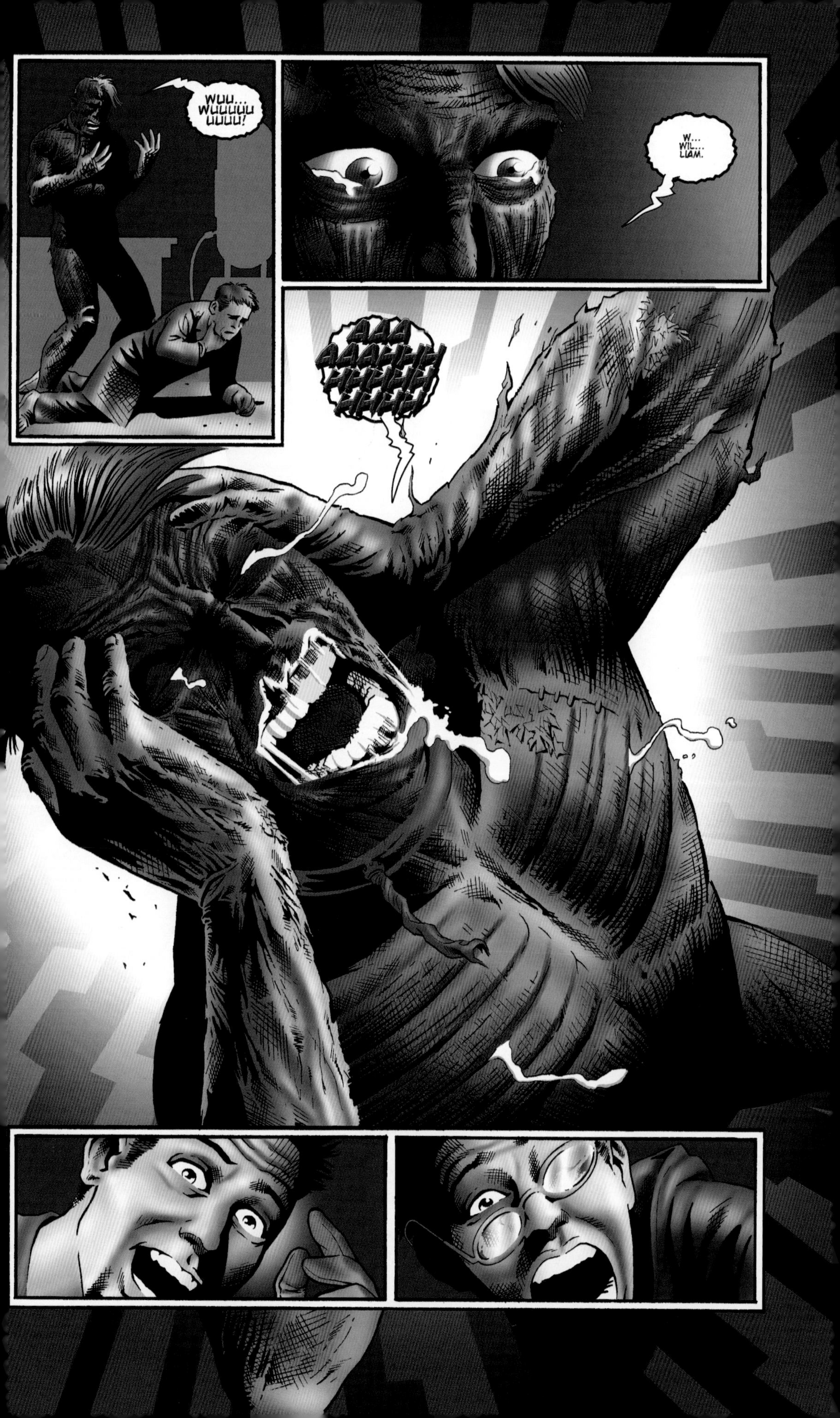
WUU... WUUUUU UUUU!
W... WIL... LIAM.
AAA AAAHHHH HHHHHH HHHHH

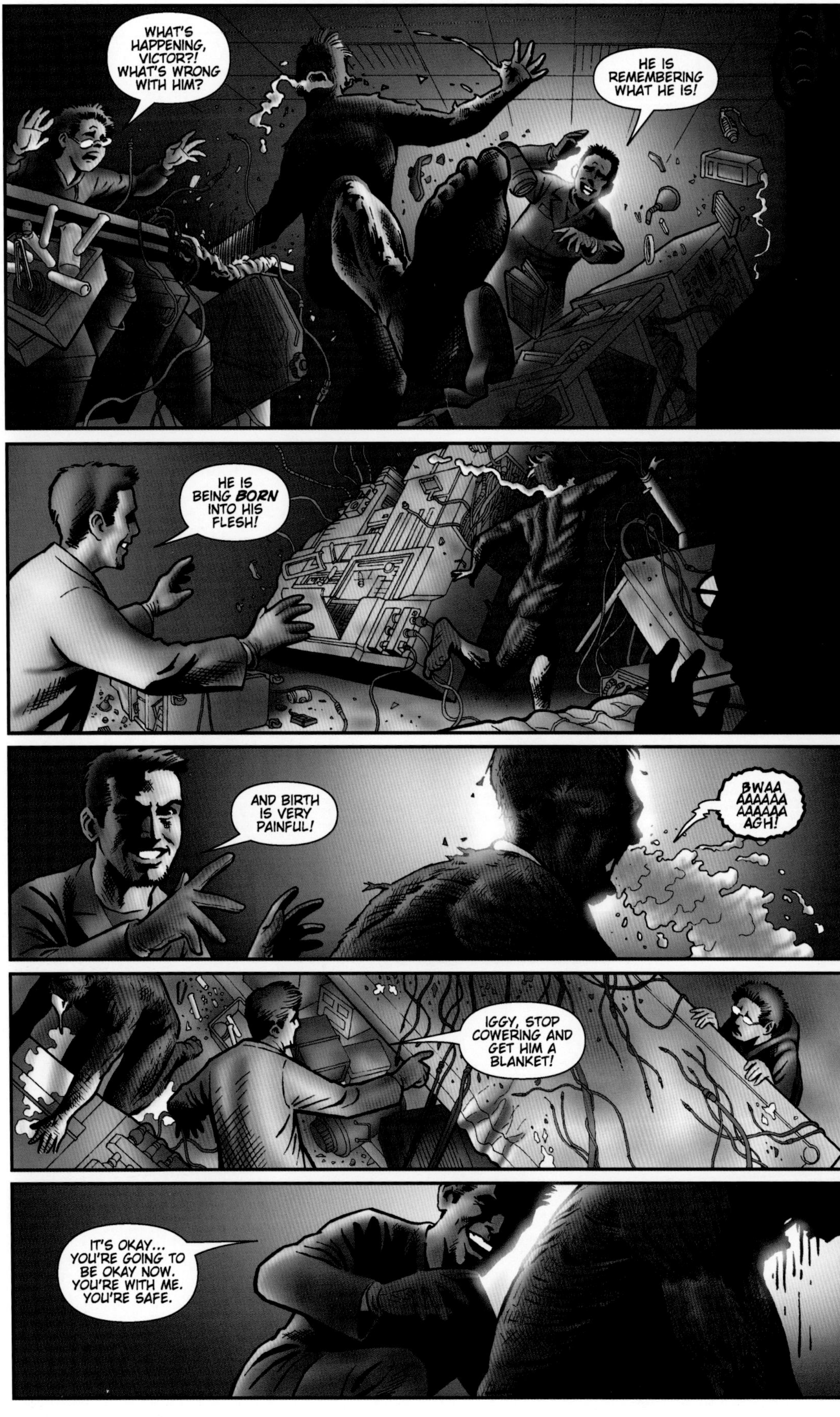
WHAT'S HAPPENING, VICTOR?! WHAT'S WRONG WITH HIM?
HE IS REMEMBERING WHAT HE IS!
HE IS BEING *BORN* INTO HIS FLESH!
AND BIRTH IS VERY PAINFUL!
BWAA AAAAAA AAAAAA AGH!
IGGY, STOP COWERING AND GET HIM A BLANKET!
IT'S OKAY... YOU'RE GOING TO BE OKAY NOW. YOU'RE WITH ME. YOU'RE SAFE.

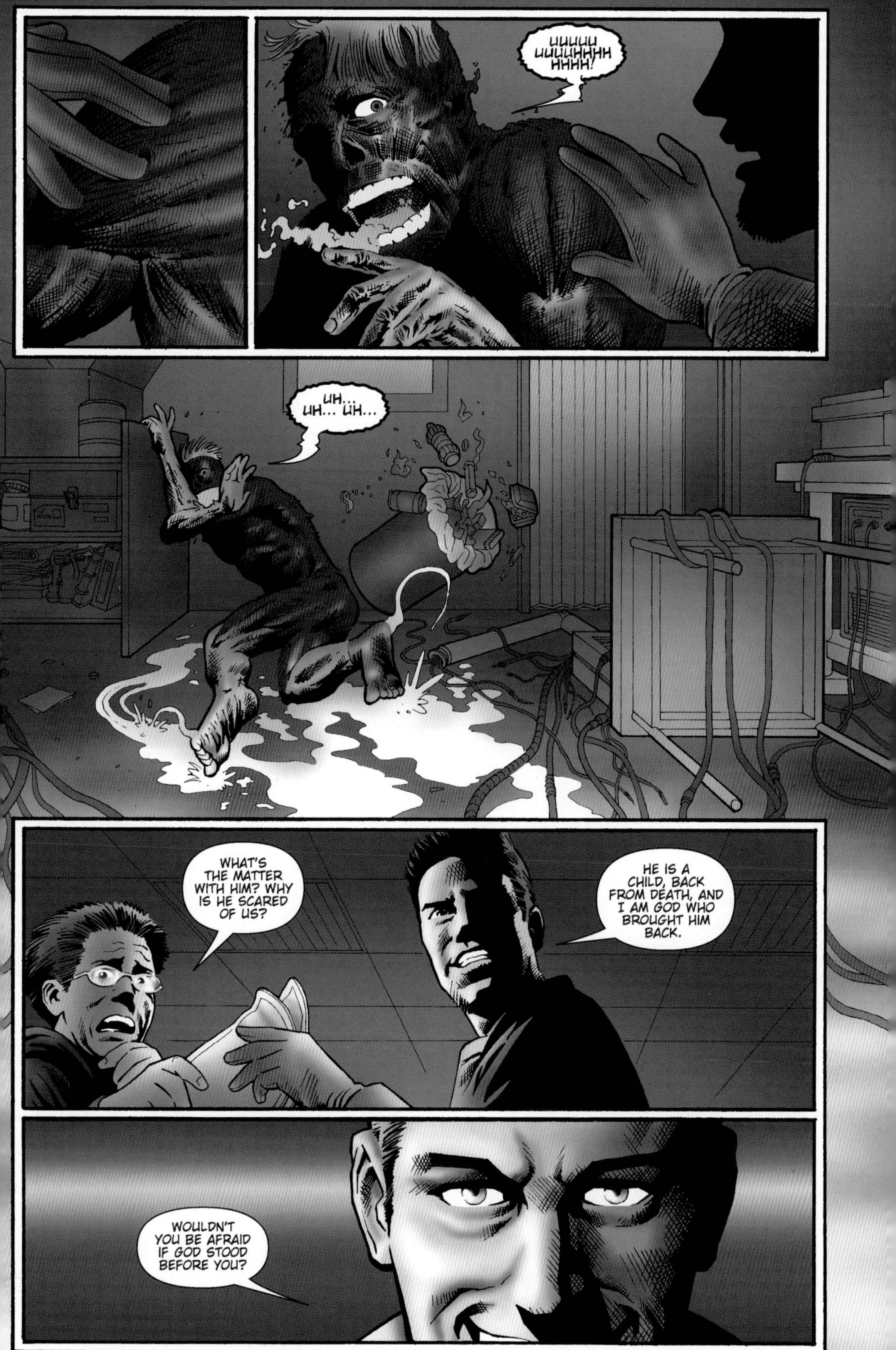
UUUUU UUUUHHHH HHHH!
UH... UH... UH...
WHAT'S THE MATTER WITH HIM? WHY IS HE SCARED OF US?
HE IS A CHILD, BACK FROM DEATH, AND I AM GOD WHO BROUGHT HIM BACK.
WOULDN'T YOU BE AFRAID IF GOD STOOD BEFORE YOU?

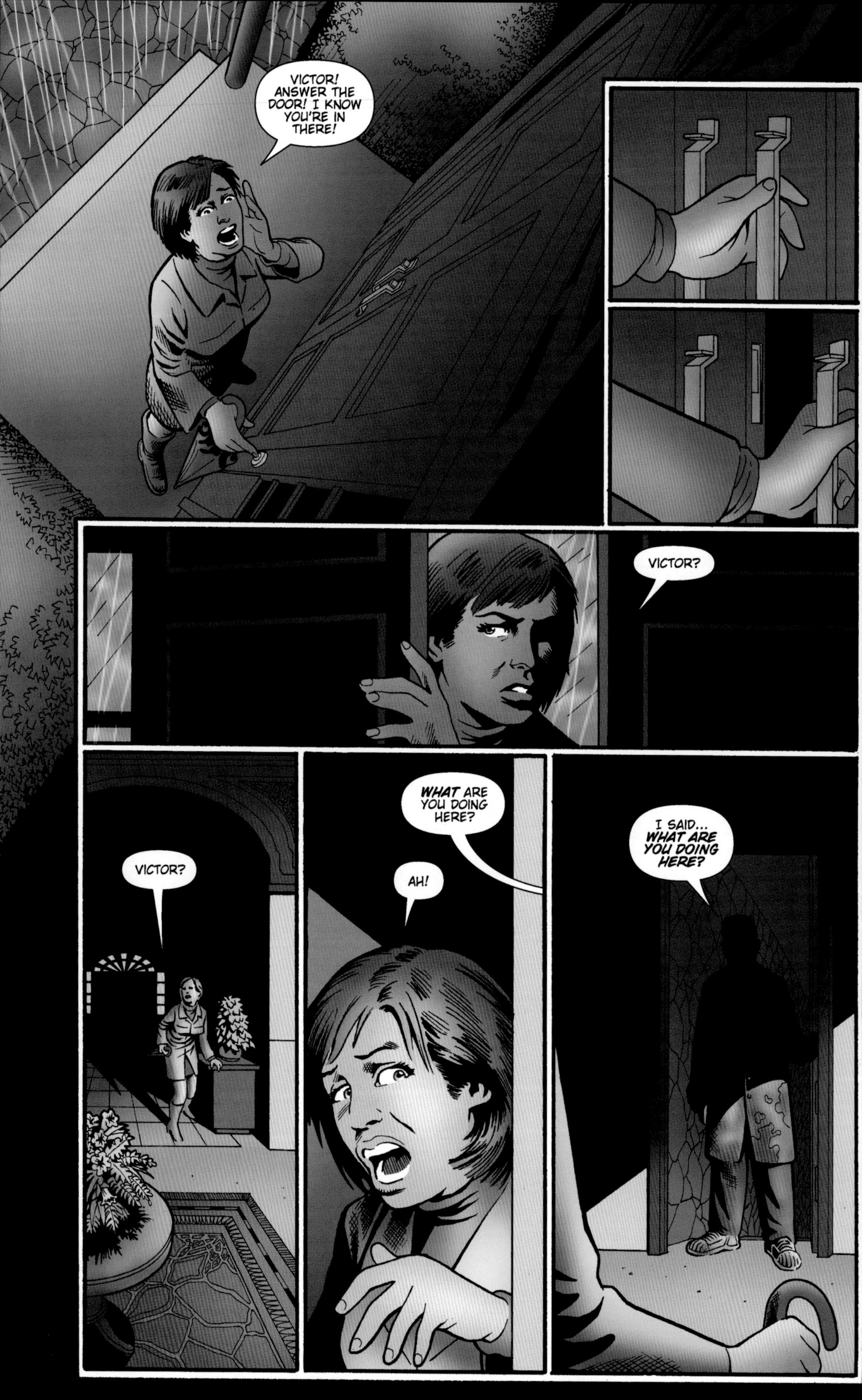
VICTOR! ANSWER THE DOOR! I KNOW YOU'RE IN THERE!
VICTOR?
VICTOR?
WHAT ARE YOU DOING HERE?
AH!
I SAID... WHAT ARE YOU DOING HERE?

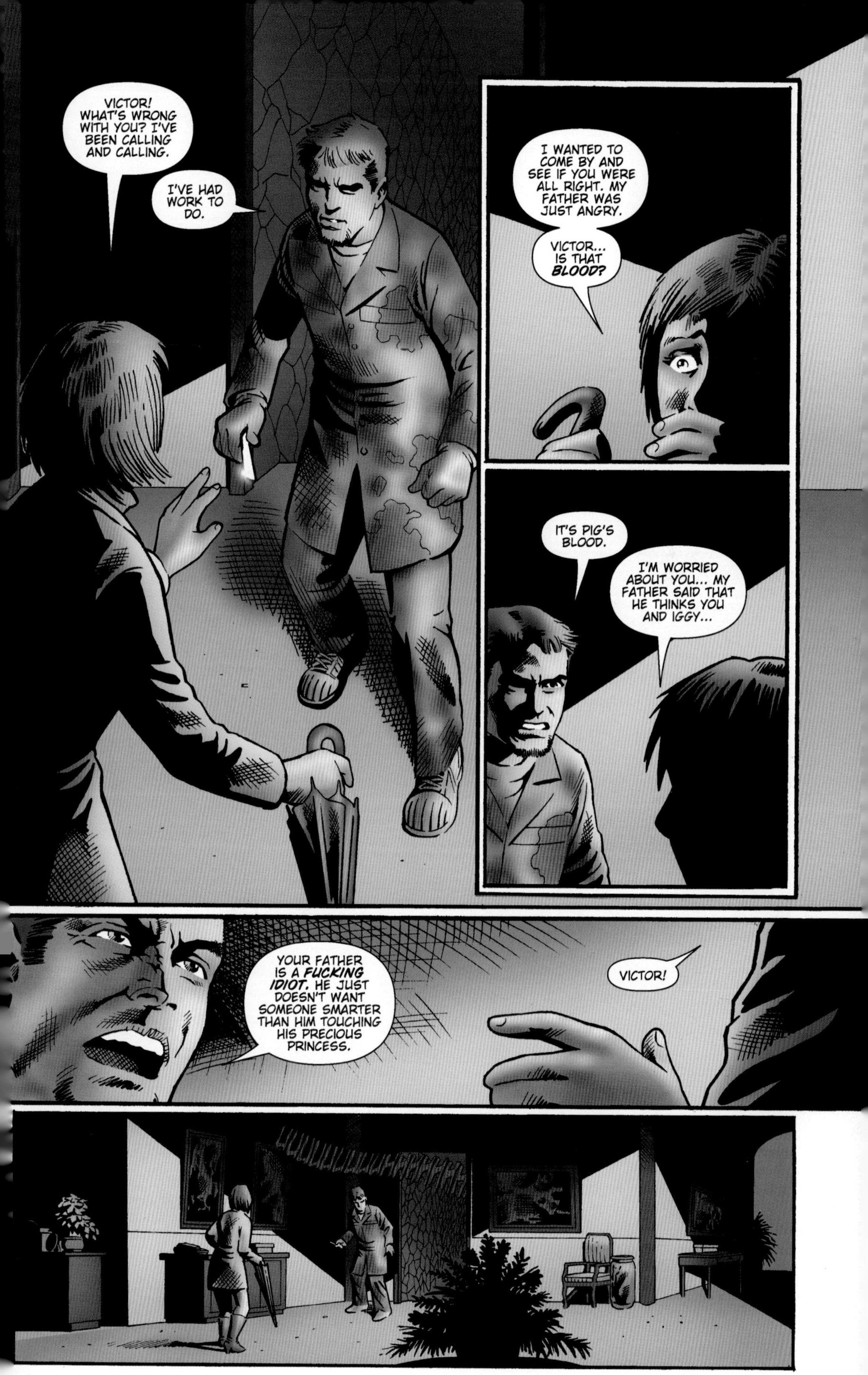
VICTOR! WHAT'S WRONG WITH YOU? I'VE BEEN CALLING AND CALLING.
I'VE HAD WORK TO DO.
I WANTED TO COME BY AND SEE IF YOU WERE ALL RIGHT. MY FATHER WAS JUST ANGRY.
VICTOR... IS THAT BLOOD?
IT'S PIG'S BLOOD.
I'M WORRIED ABOUT YOU... MY FATHER SAID THAT HE THINKS YOU AND IGGY...
YOUR FATHER IS A FUCKING IDIOT. HE JUST DOESN'T WANT SOMEONE SMARTER THAN HIM TOUCHING HIS PRECIOUS PRINCESS.
VICTOR!

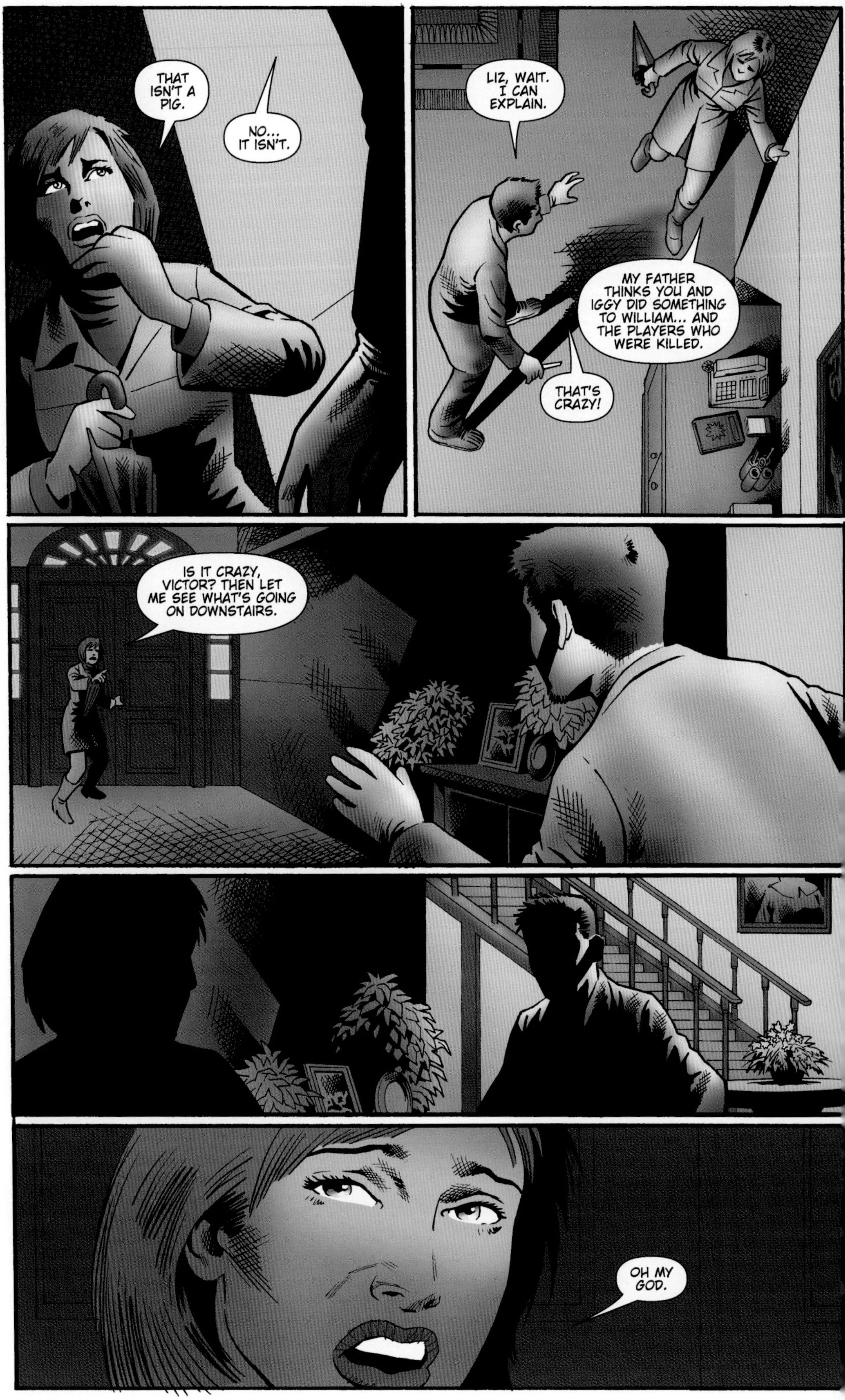
THAT ISN'T A PIG.
NO... IT ISN'T.
LIZ, WAIT. I CAN EXPLAIN.
MY FATHER THINKS YOU AND IGGY DID SOMETHING TO WILLIAM... AND THE PLAYERS WHO WERE KILLED.
THAT'S CRAZY!
IS IT CRAZY, VICTOR? THEN LET ME SEE WHAT'S GOING ON DOWNSTAIRS.
OH MY GOD.

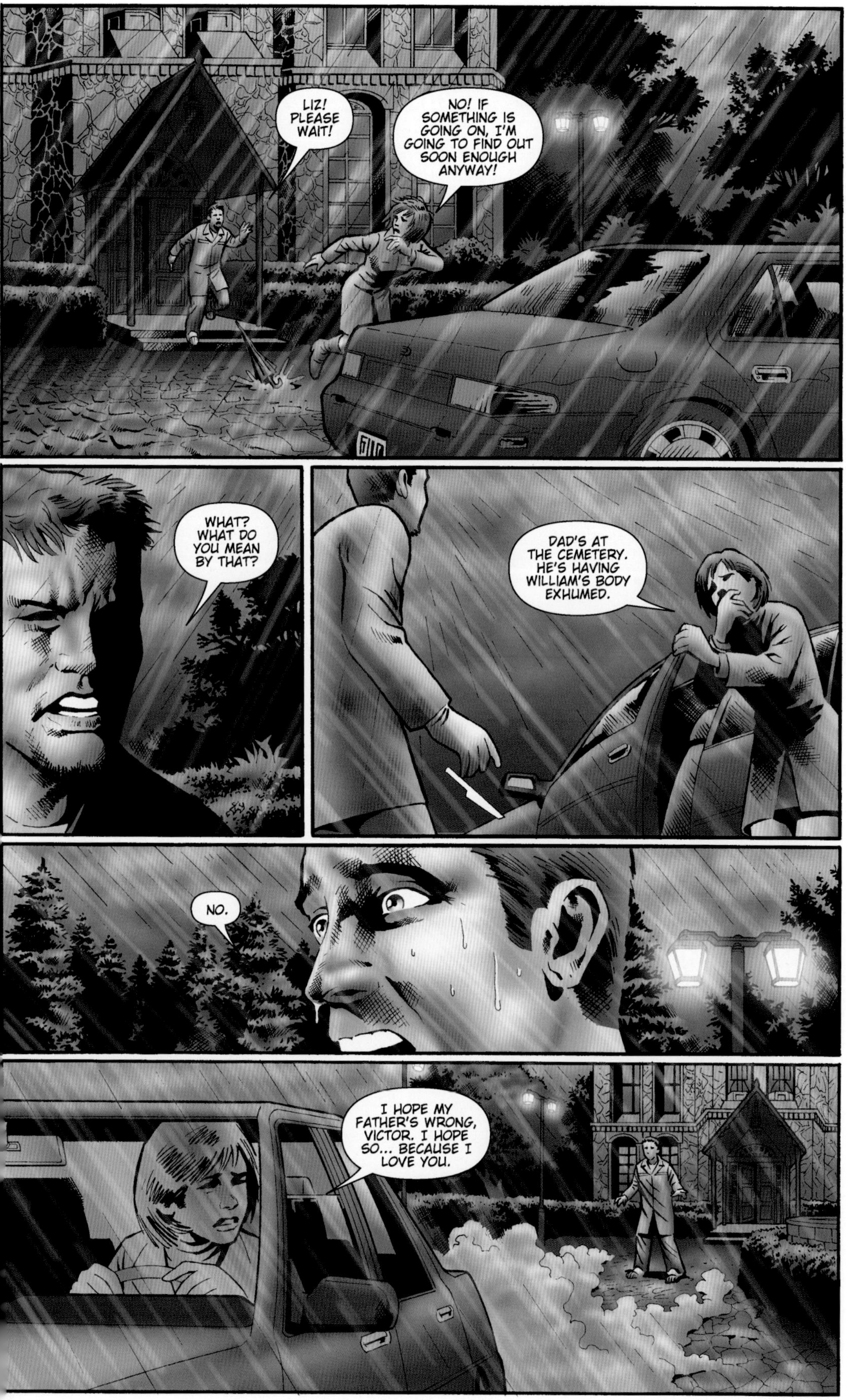
LIZ! PLEASE WAIT!
NO! IF SOMETHING IS GOING ON, I'M GOING TO FIND OUT SOON ENOUGH ANYWAY!
WHAT? WHAT DO YOU MEAN BY THAT?
DAD'S AT THE CEMETERY. HE'S HAVING WILLIAM'S BODY EXHUMED.
NO.
I HOPE MY FATHER'S WRONG, VICTOR. I HOPE SO... BECAUSE I LOVE YOU.

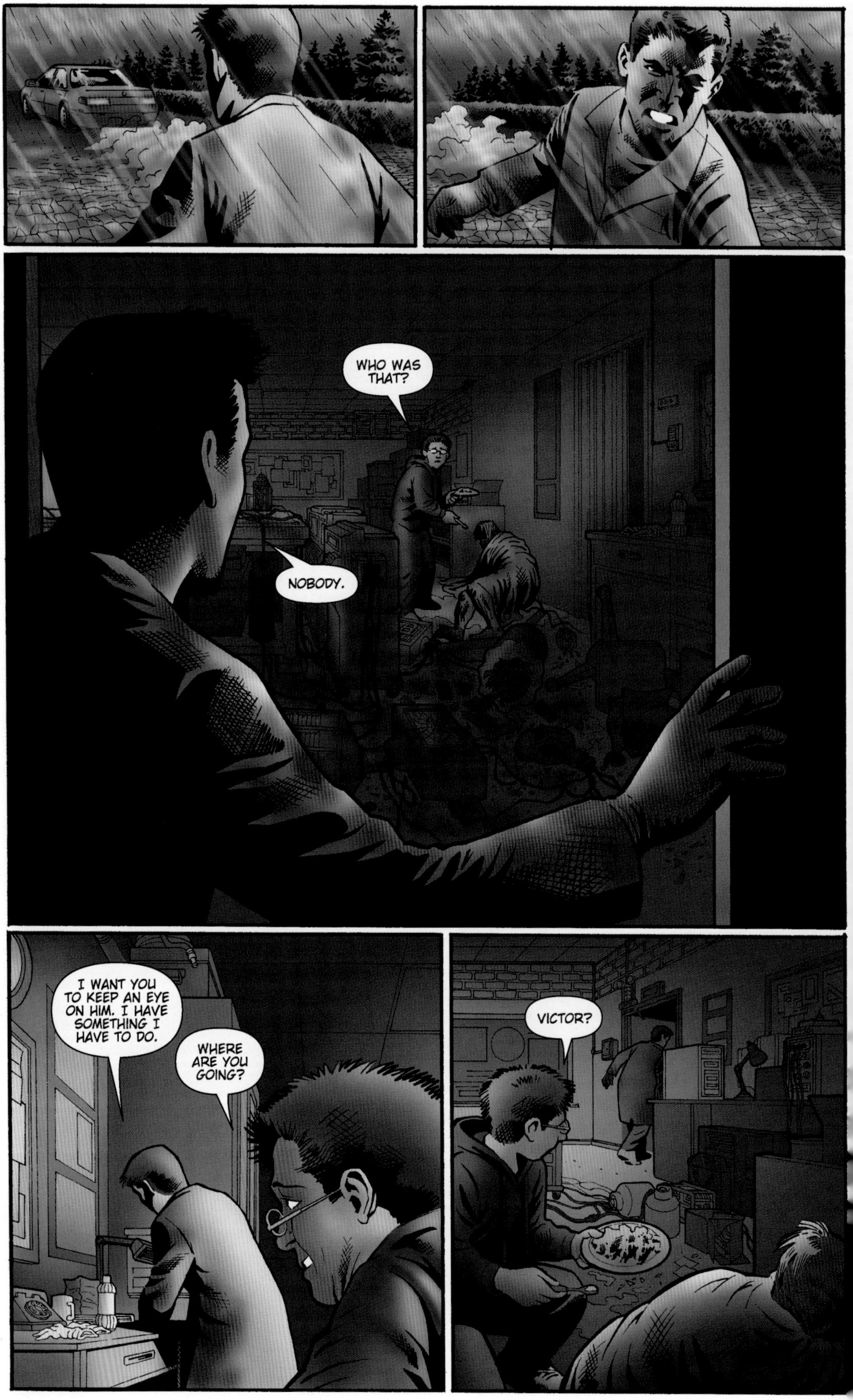
WHO WAS THAT?
NOBODY.
I WANT YOU TO KEEP AN EYE ON HIM. I HAVE SOMETHING I HAVE TO DO.
WHERE ARE YOU GOING?
VICTOR?

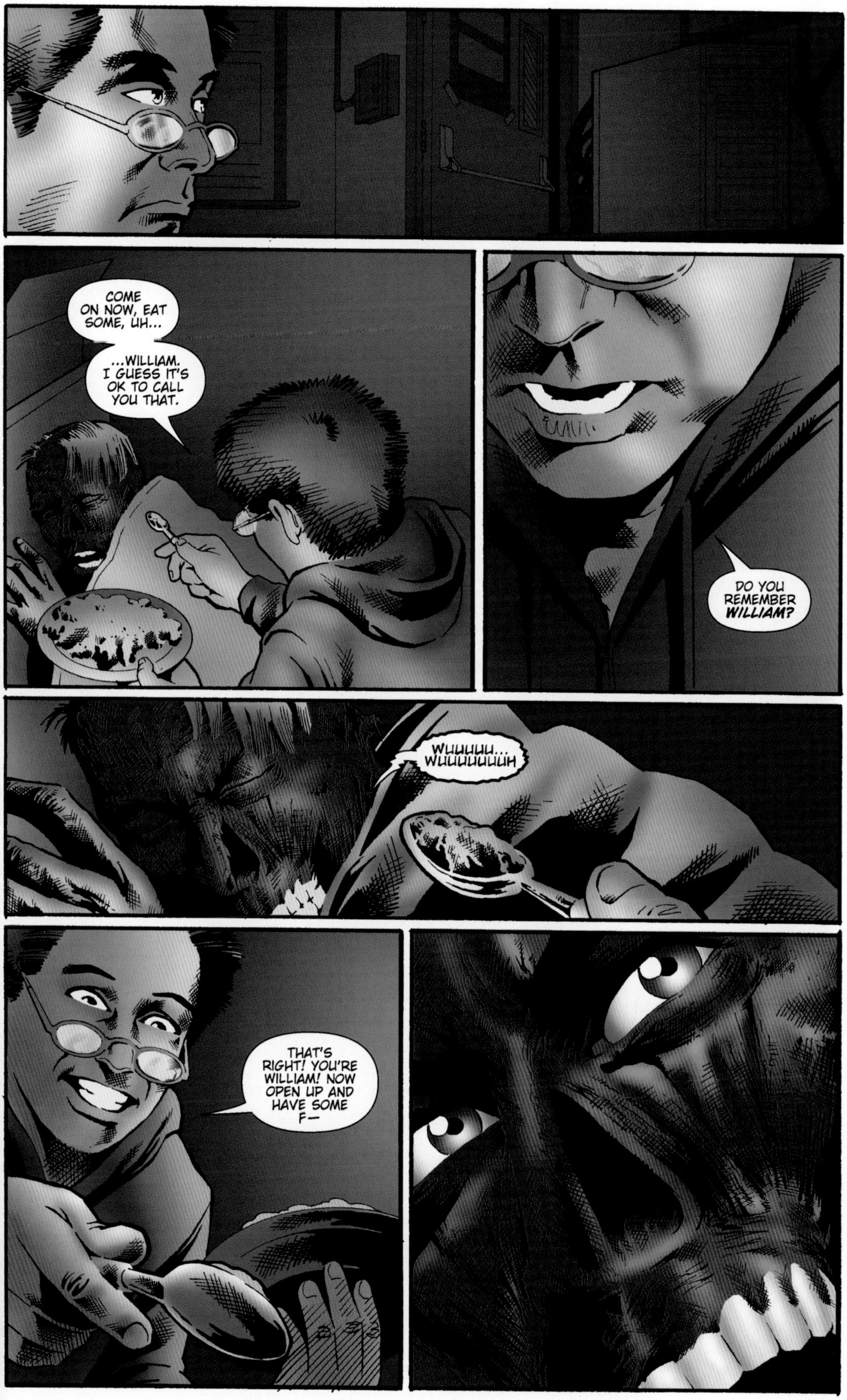
COME ON NOW, EAT SOME, UH...
...WILLIAM. I GUESS IT'S OK TO CALL YOU THAT.
DO YOU REMEMBER *WILLIAM?*
WUUUUU... WUUUUUUUH
THAT'S RIGHT! YOU'RE WILLIAM! NOW OPEN UP AND HAVE SOME F—

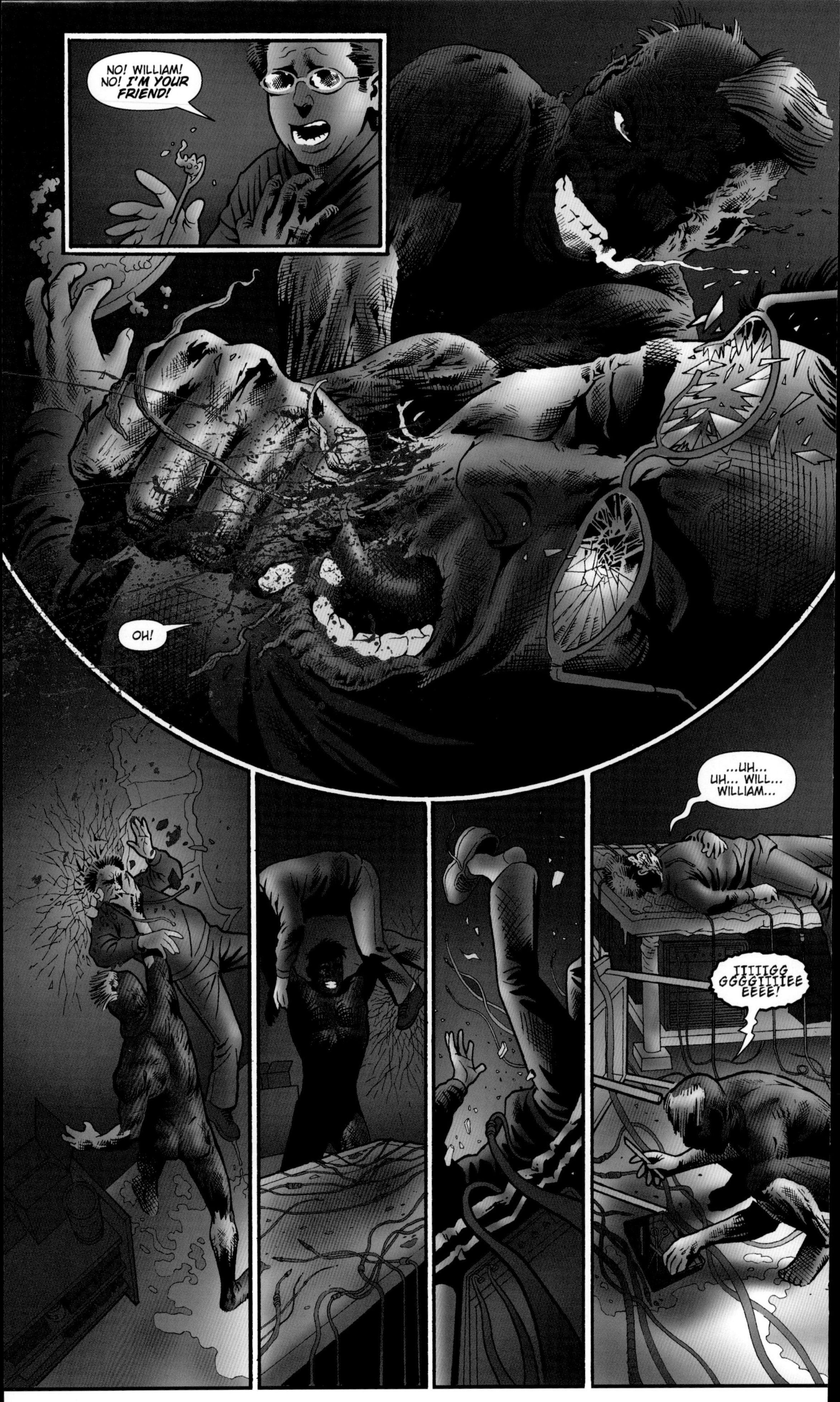

NO! WILLIAM! NO! I'M YOUR FRIEND!
OH!
...UH... UH... WILL... WILLIAM...
IIIIIGG GGGGIIIIEE EEEE!

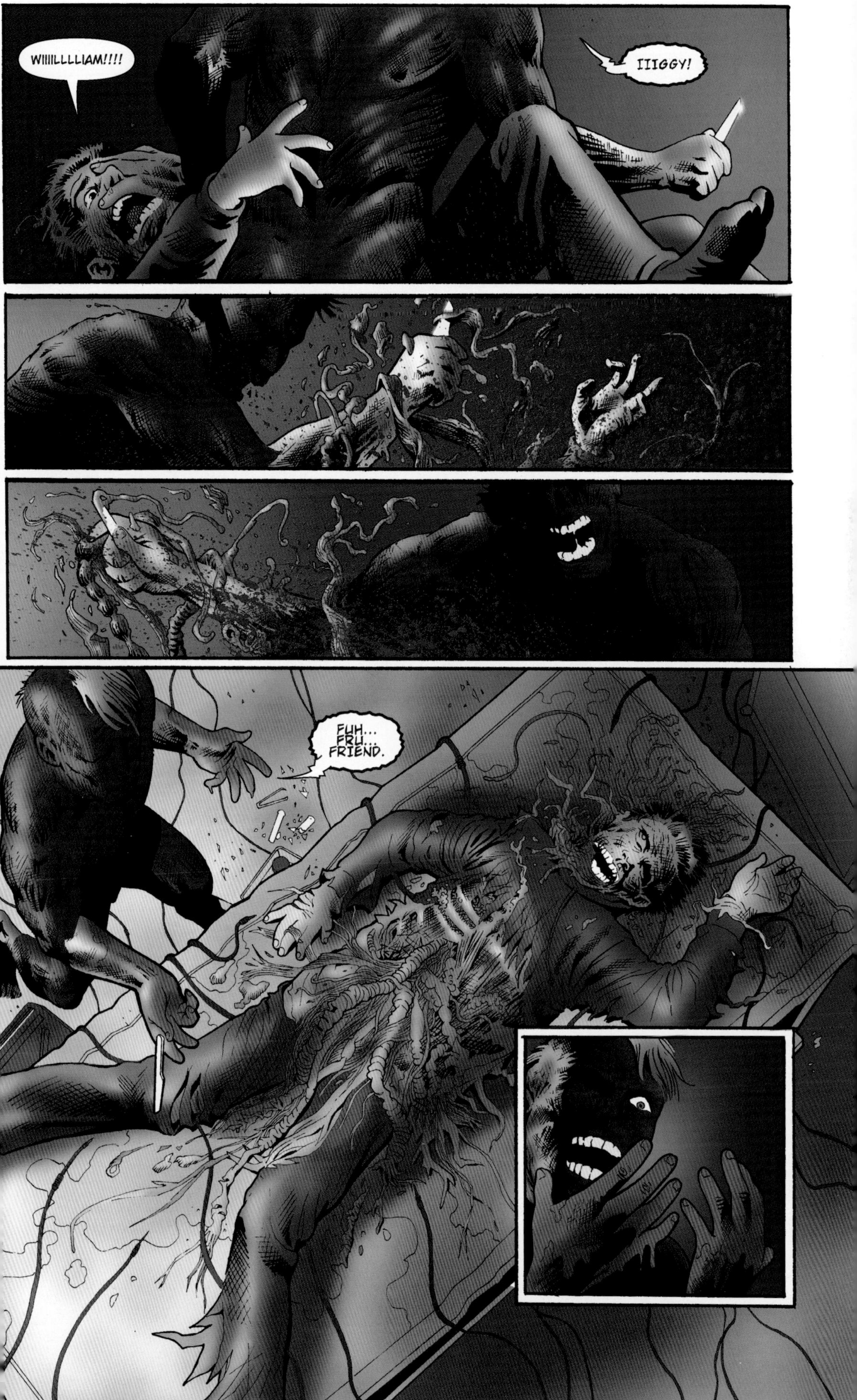
WIIIILLLLLIAM!!!!
IIIGGY!
FUH... FRU... FRIEND.

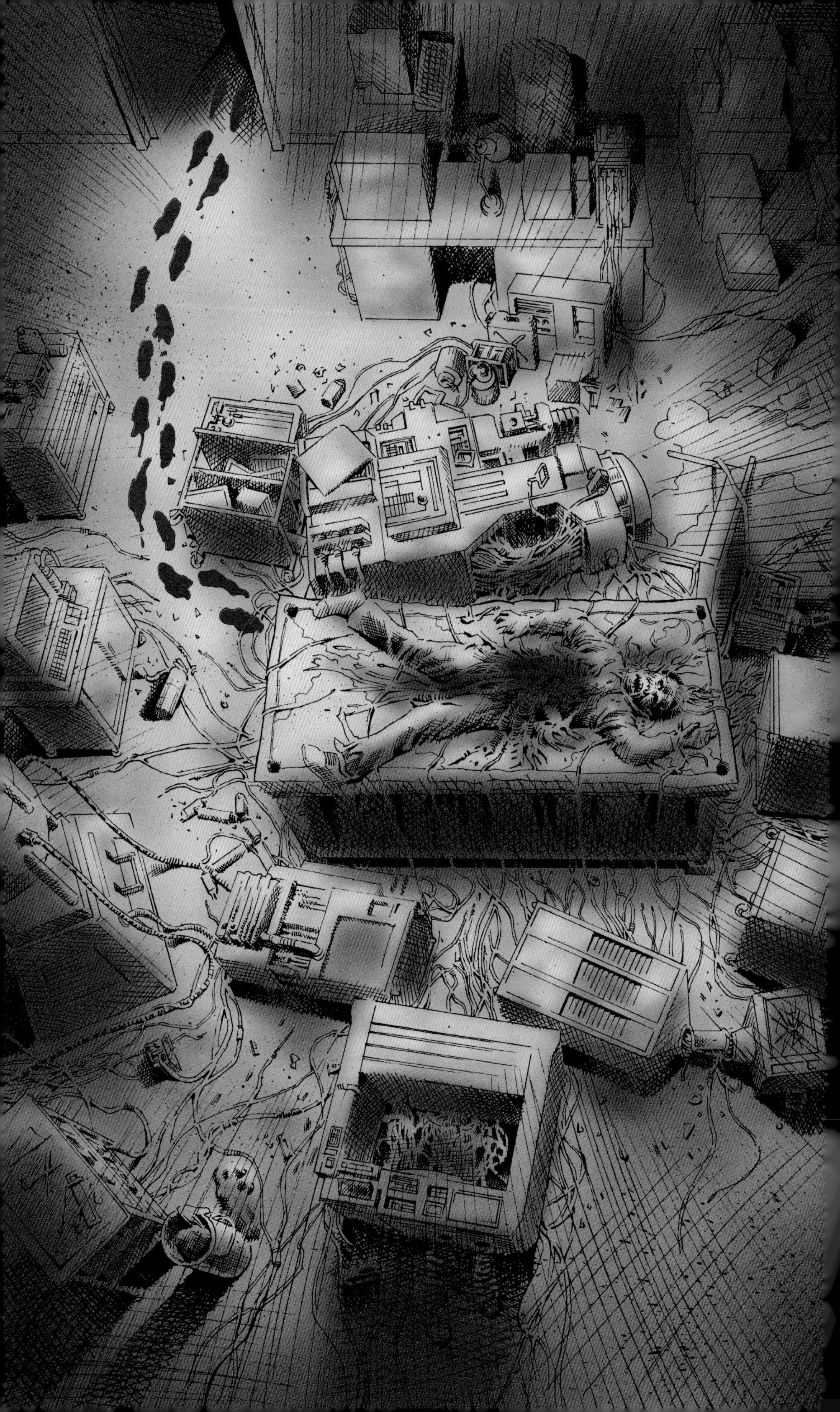

chapter four

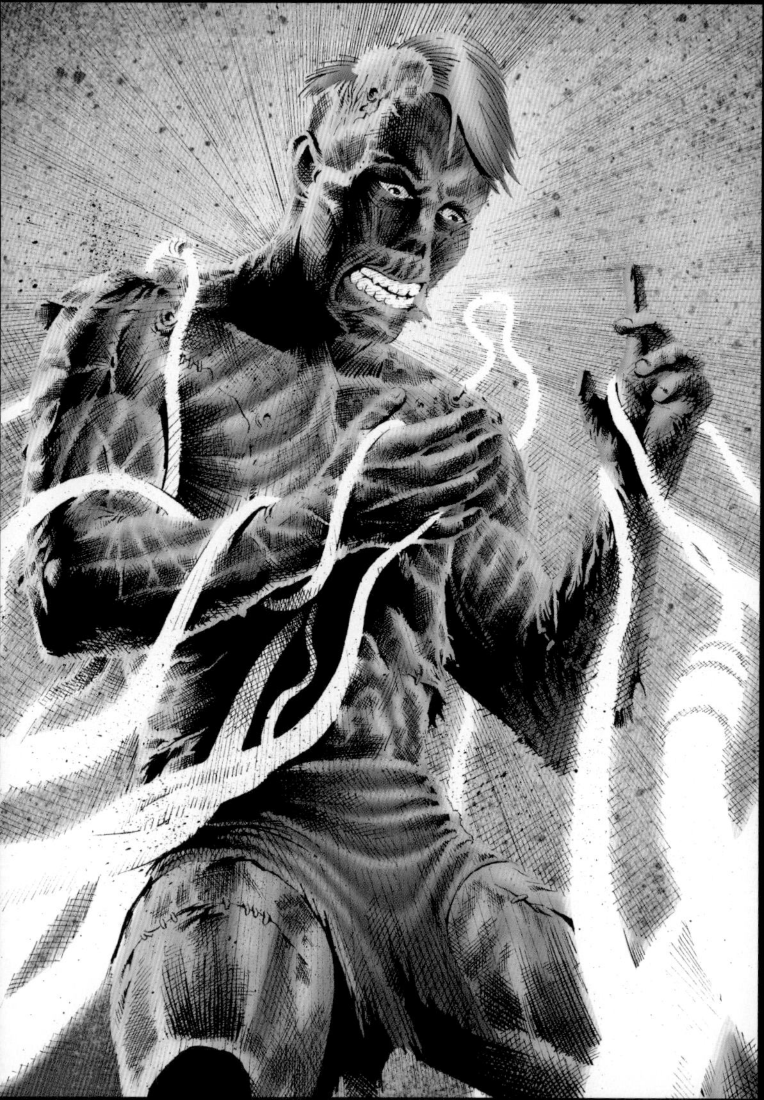

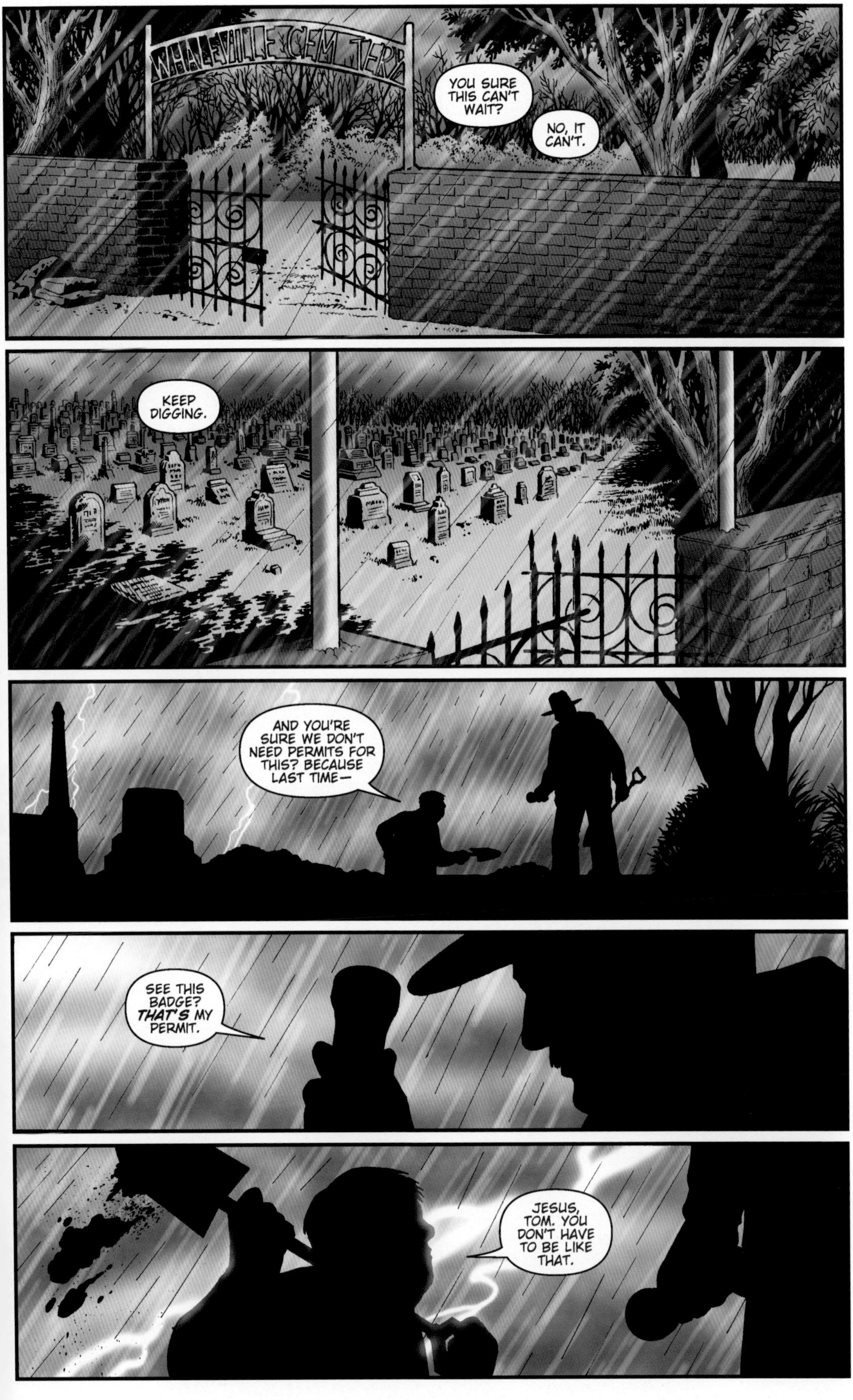
WHALEVILLE CEMETERY
YOU SURE THIS CAN'T WAIT?
NO, IT CAN'T.
KEEP DIGGING.
AND YOU'RE SURE WE DON'T NEED PERMITS FOR THIS? BECAUSE LAST TIME—
SEE THIS BADGE? *THAT'S* MY PERMIT.
JESUS, TOM. YOU DON'T HAVE TO BE LIKE THAT.

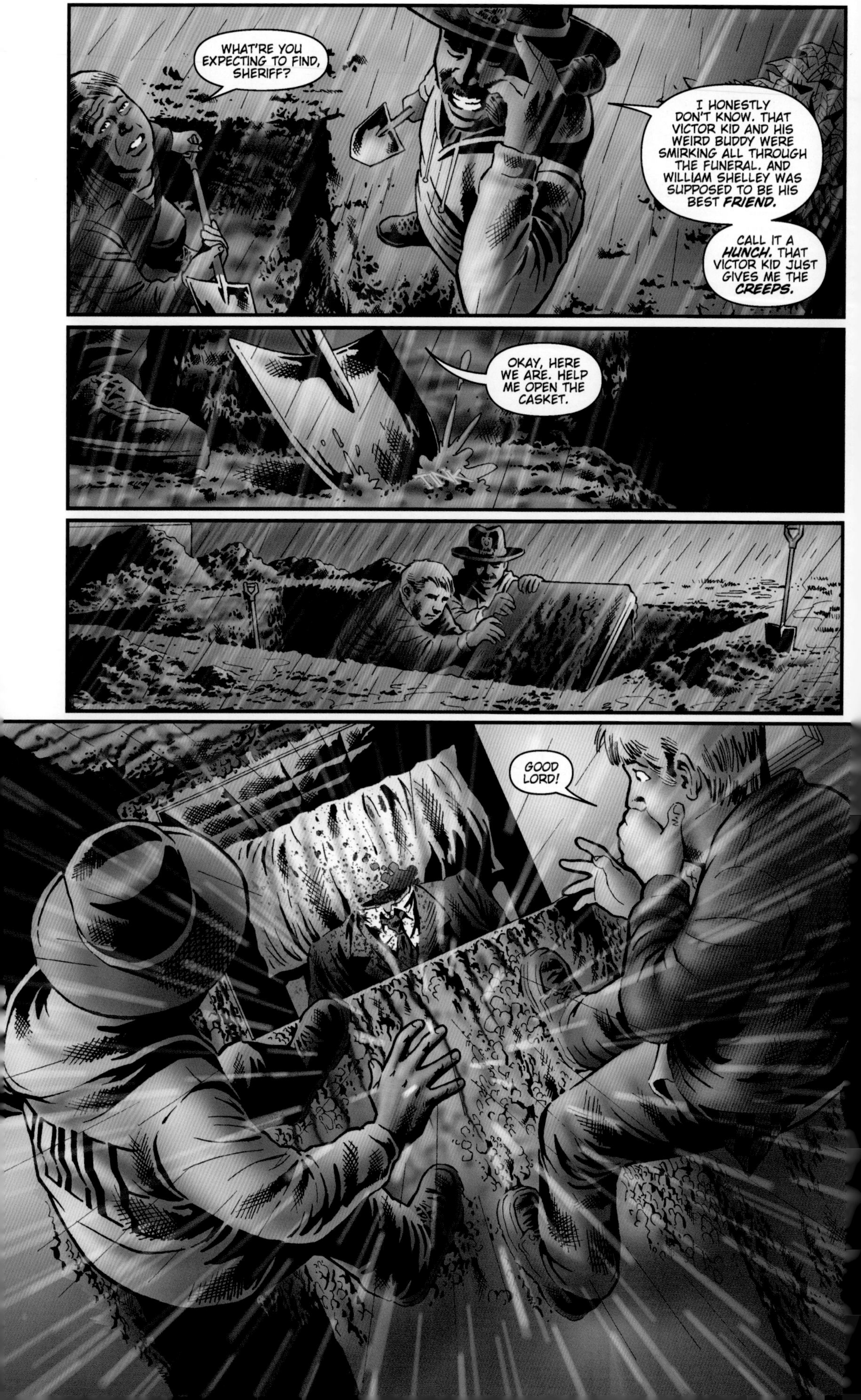

WHAT'RE YOU EXPECTING TO FIND, SHERIFF?
I HONESTLY DON'T KNOW. THAT VICTOR KID AND HIS WEIRD BUDDY WERE SMIRKING ALL THROUGH THE FUNERAL. AND WILLIAM SHELLEY WAS SUPPOSED TO BE HIS BEST FRIEND.
CALL IT A HUNCH. THAT VICTOR KID JUST GIVES ME THE CREEPS.
OKAY, HERE WE ARE. HELP ME OPEN THE CASKET.
TINK
GOOD LORD!

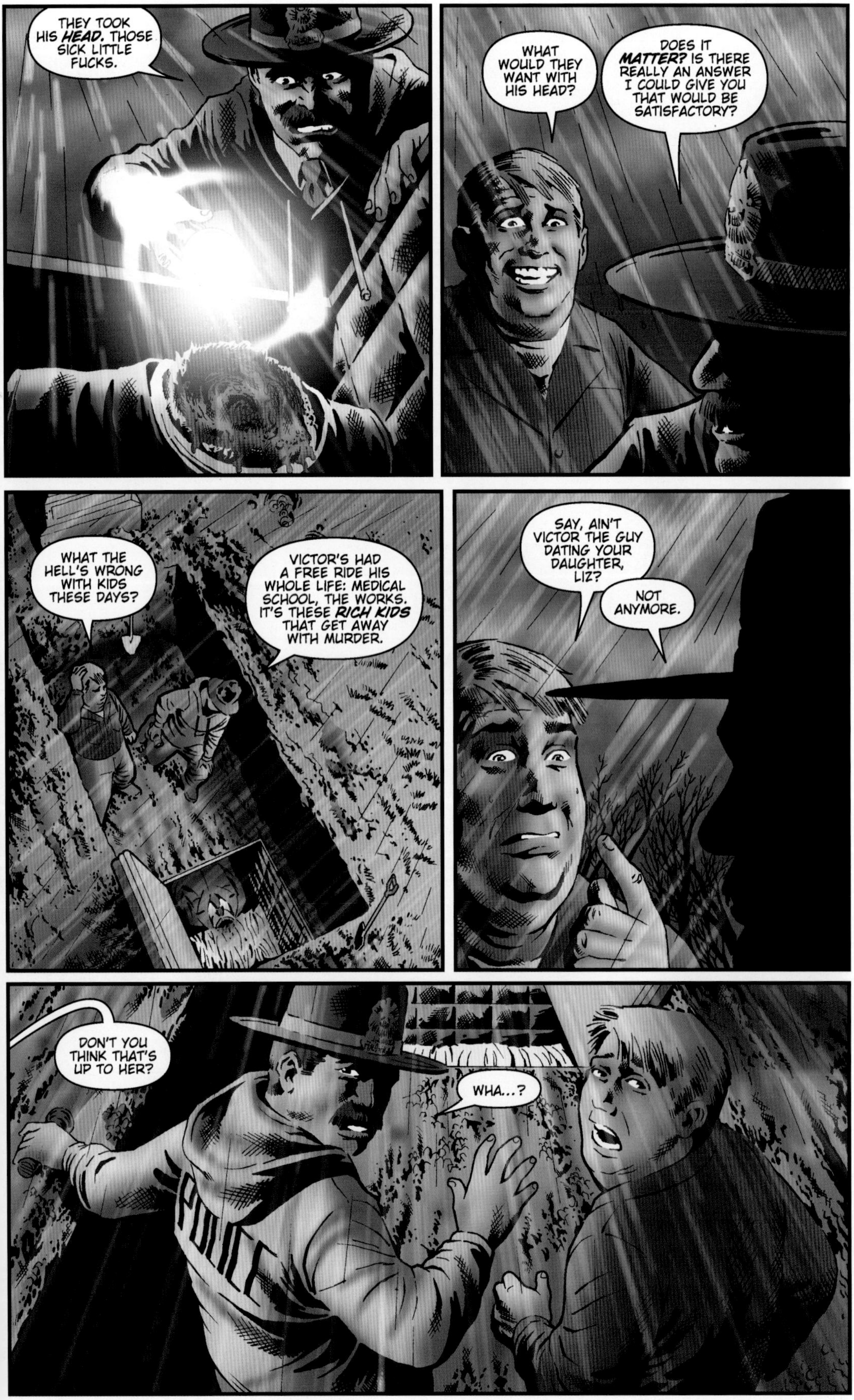
THEY TOOK HIS HEAD. THOSE SICK LITTLE FUCKS.
WHAT WOULD THEY WANT WITH HIS HEAD?
DOES IT MATTER? IS THERE REALLY AN ANSWER I COULD GIVE YOU THAT WOULD BE SATISFACTORY?
WHAT THE HELL'S WRONG WITH KIDS THESE DAYS?
VICTOR'S HAD A FREE RIDE HIS WHOLE LIFE: MEDICAL SCHOOL, THE WORKS. IT'S THESE RICH KIDS THAT GET AWAY WITH MURDER.
SAY, AIN'T VICTOR THE GUY DATING YOUR DAUGHTER, LIZ?
NOT ANYMORE.
DON'T YOU THINK THAT'S UP TO HER?
WHA...?
POLICE

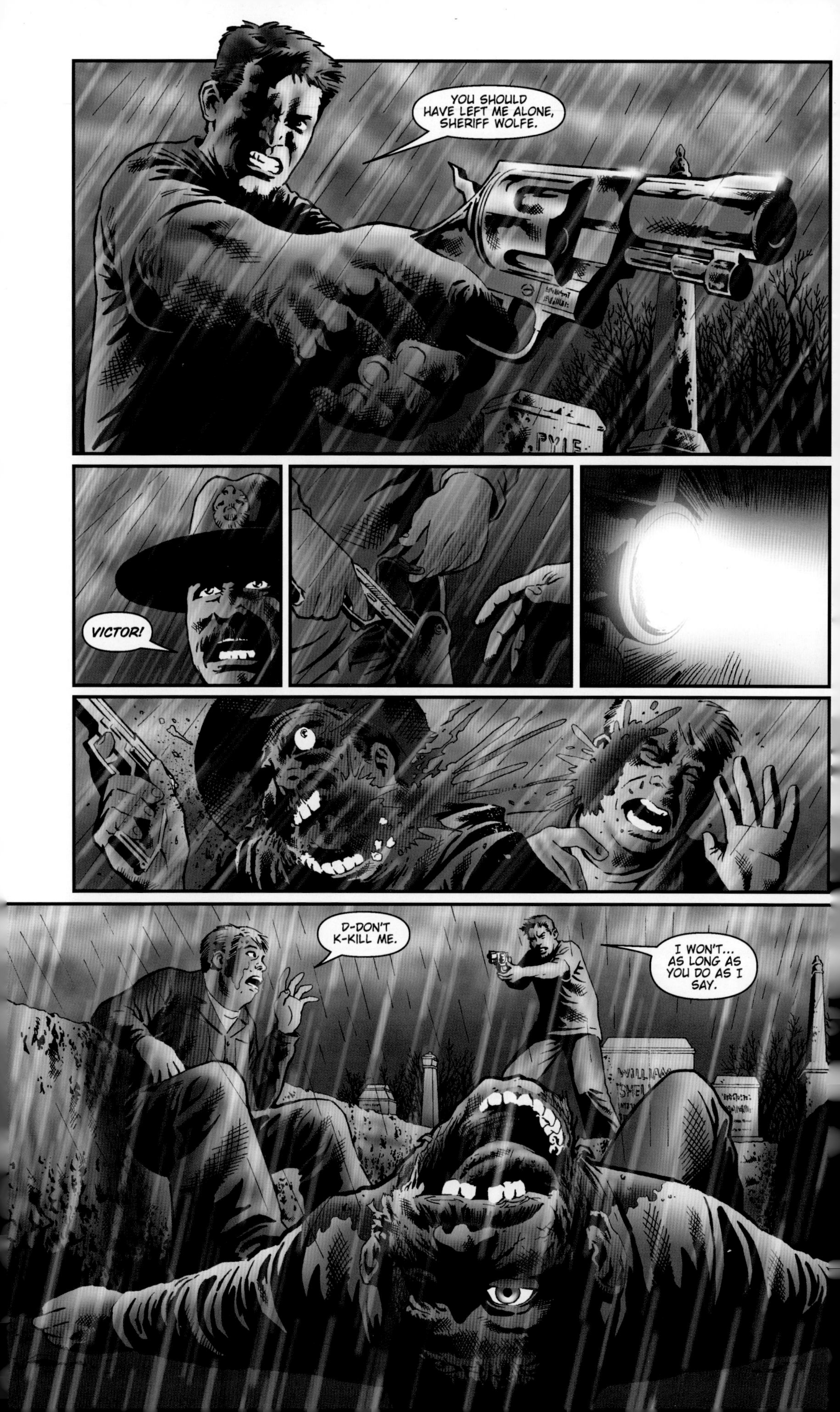

YOU SHOULD HAVE LEFT ME ALONE, SHERIFF WOLFE.
PYLE
VICTOR!
D-DON'T K-KILL ME.
I WON'T... AS LONG AS YOU DO AS I SAY.

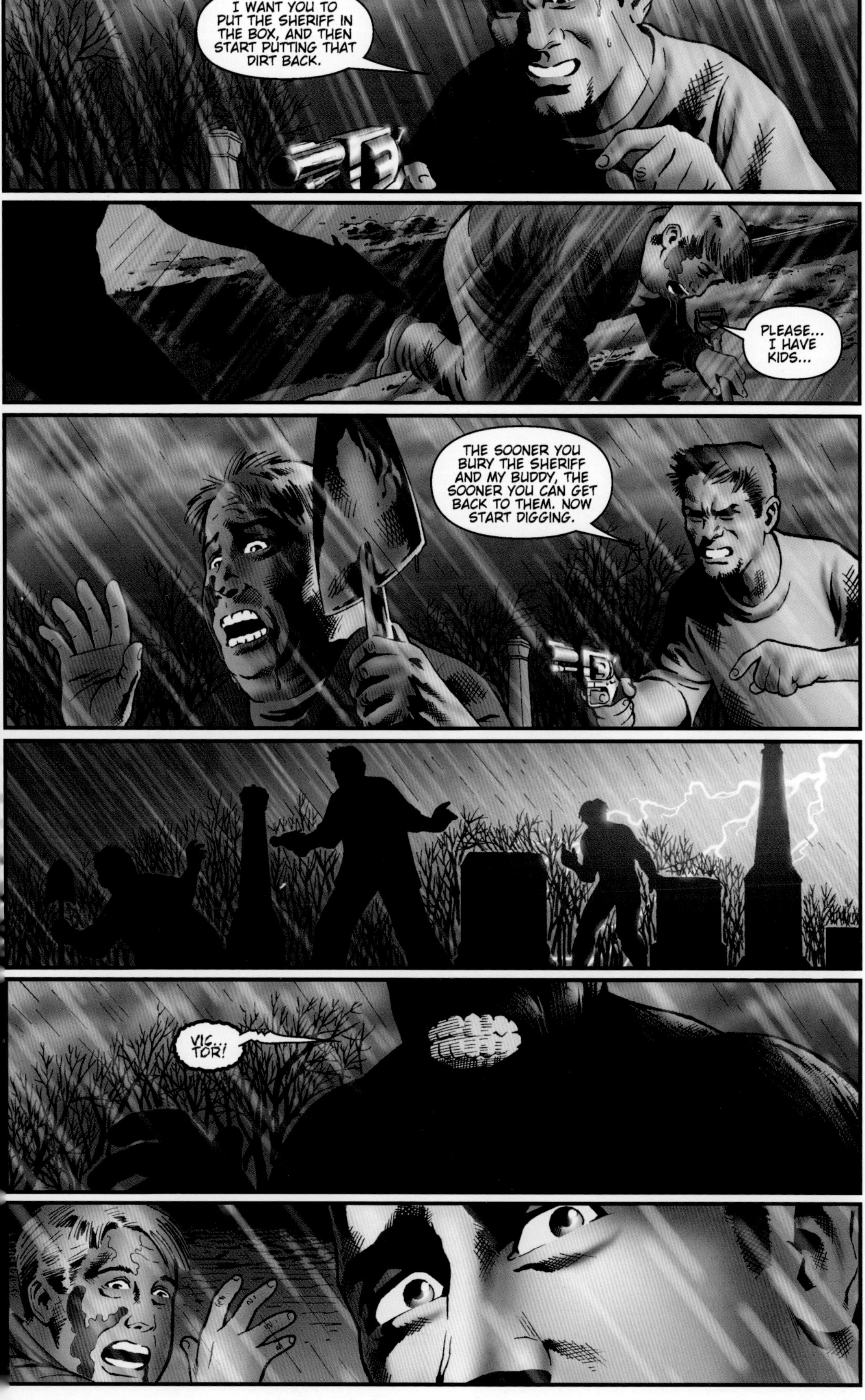
I WANT YOU TO PUT THE SHERIFF IN THE BOX, AND THEN START PUTTING THAT DIRT BACK.
PLEASE... I HAVE KIDS...
THE SOONER YOU BURY THE SHERIFF AND MY BUDDY, THE SOONER YOU CAN GET BACK TO THEM. NOW START DIGGING.
VIC... TOR!

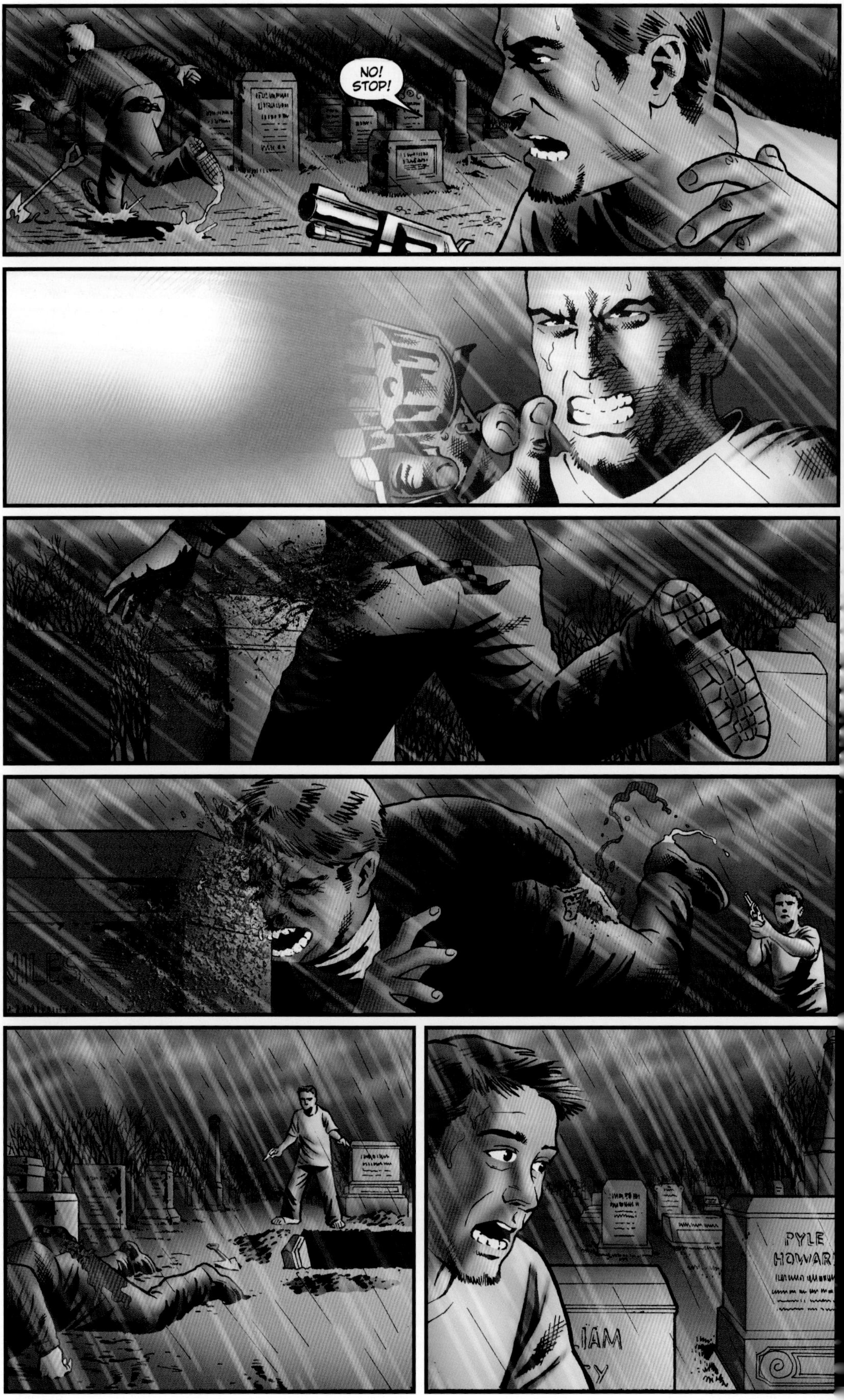
NO! STOP!
PYLE

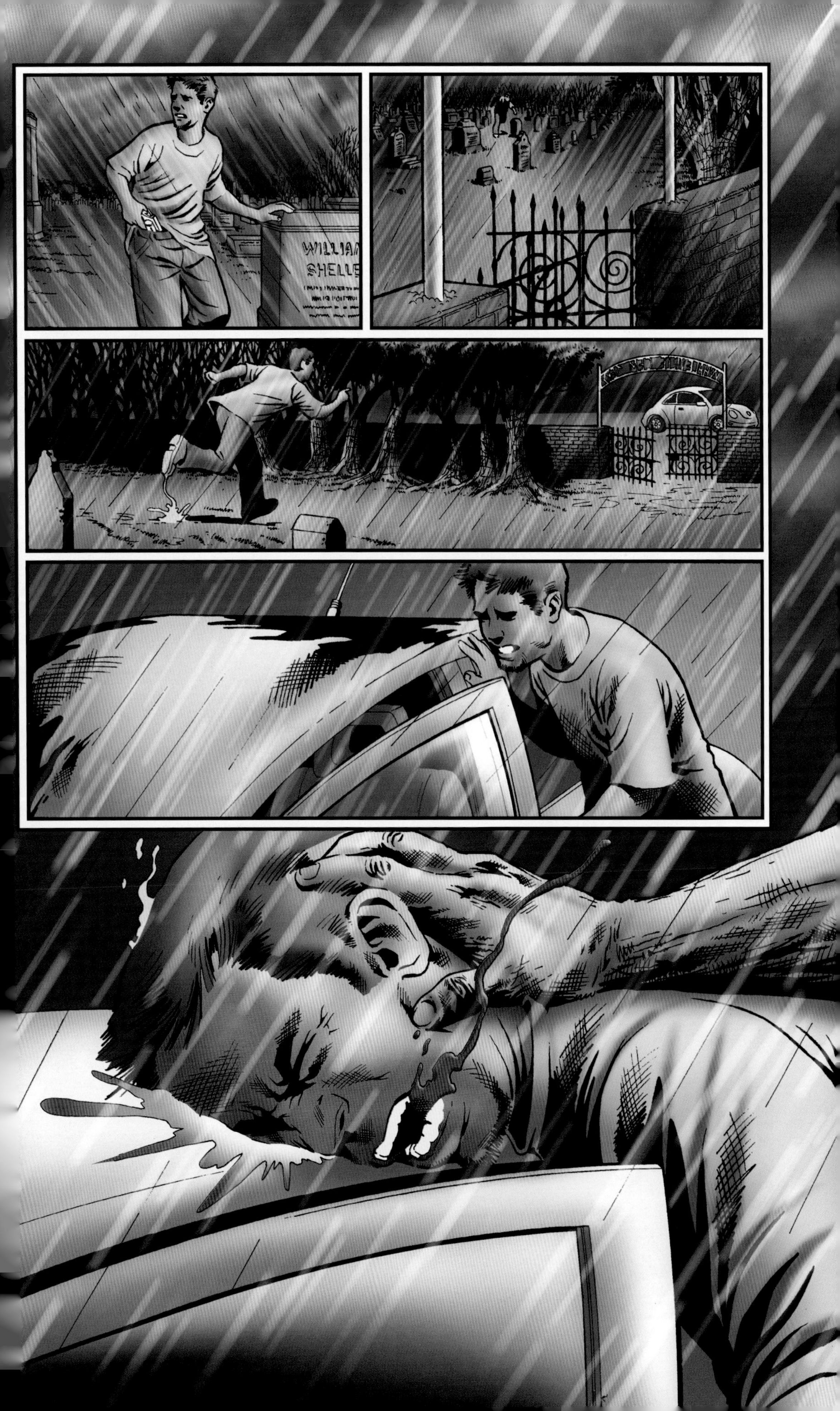

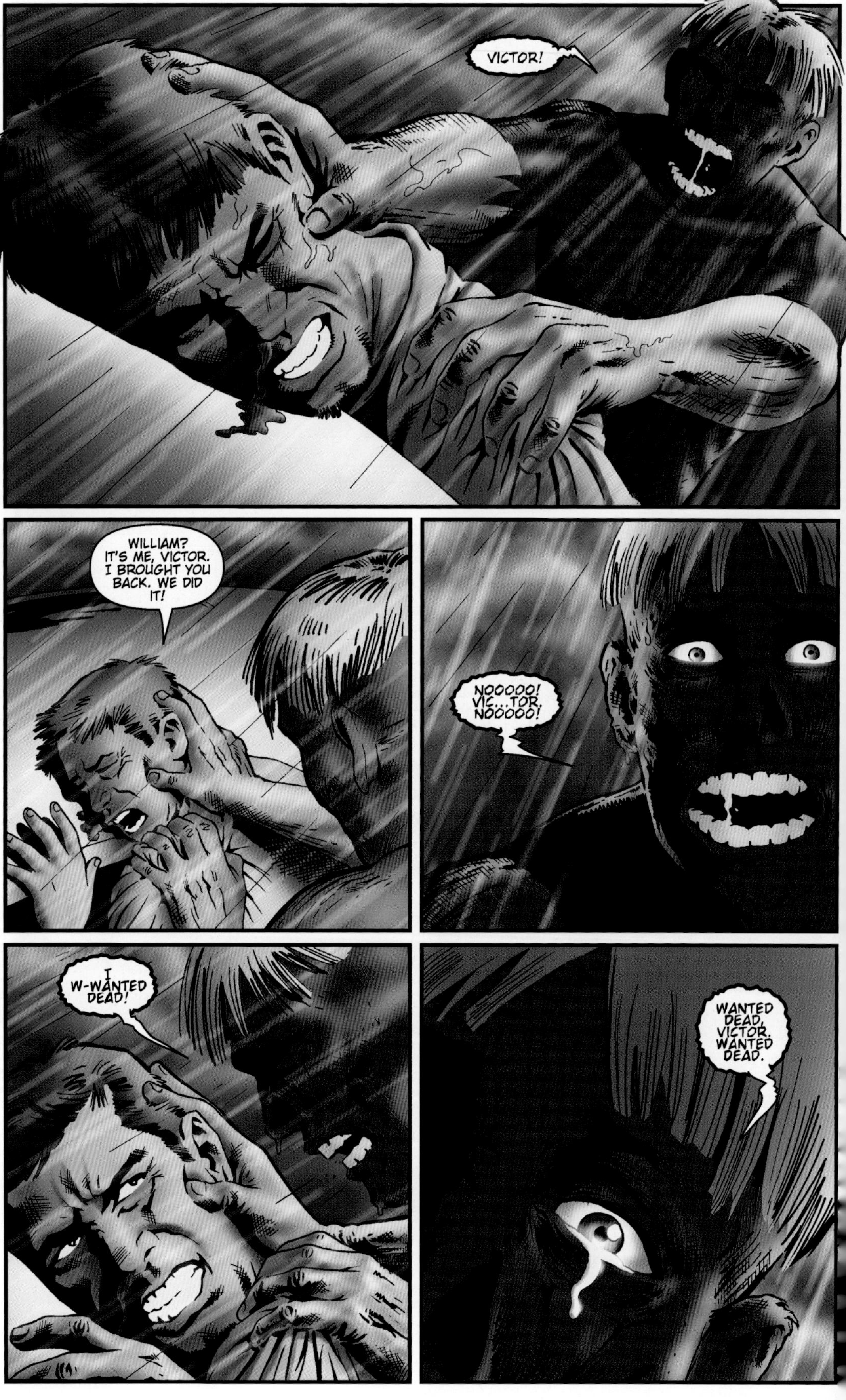
VICTOR!
WILLIAM? IT'S ME, VICTOR. I BROUGHT YOU BACK. WE DID IT!
NOOOOO! VIC...TOR. NOOOOO!
I W-WANTED DEAD!
WANTED DEAD, VICTOR. WANTED DEAD.

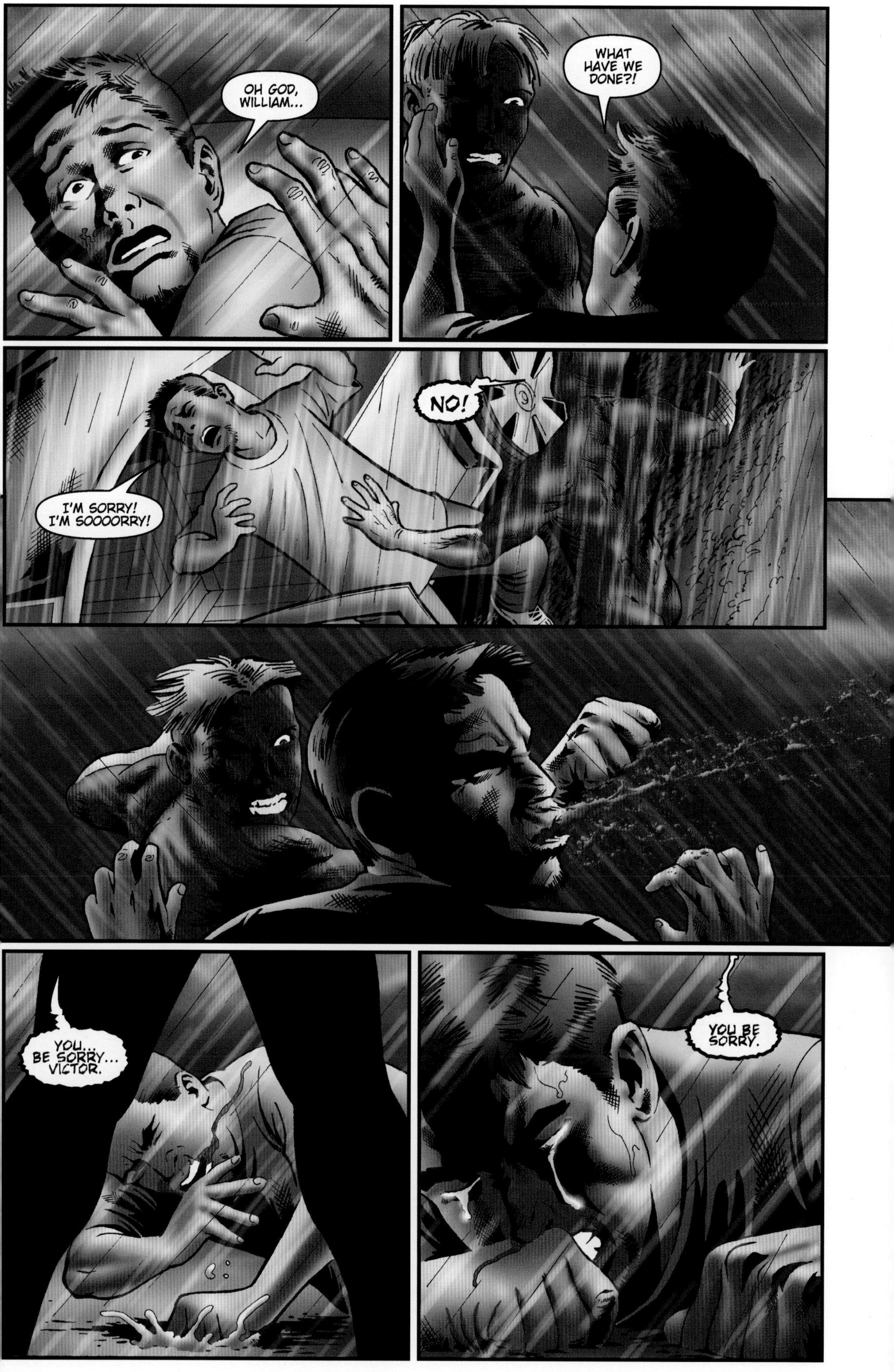
OH GOD, WILLIAM...
WHAT HAVE WE DONE?!
NO!
I'M SORRY! I'M SOOOORRY!
YOU... BE SORRY... VICTOR.
YOU BE SORRY.

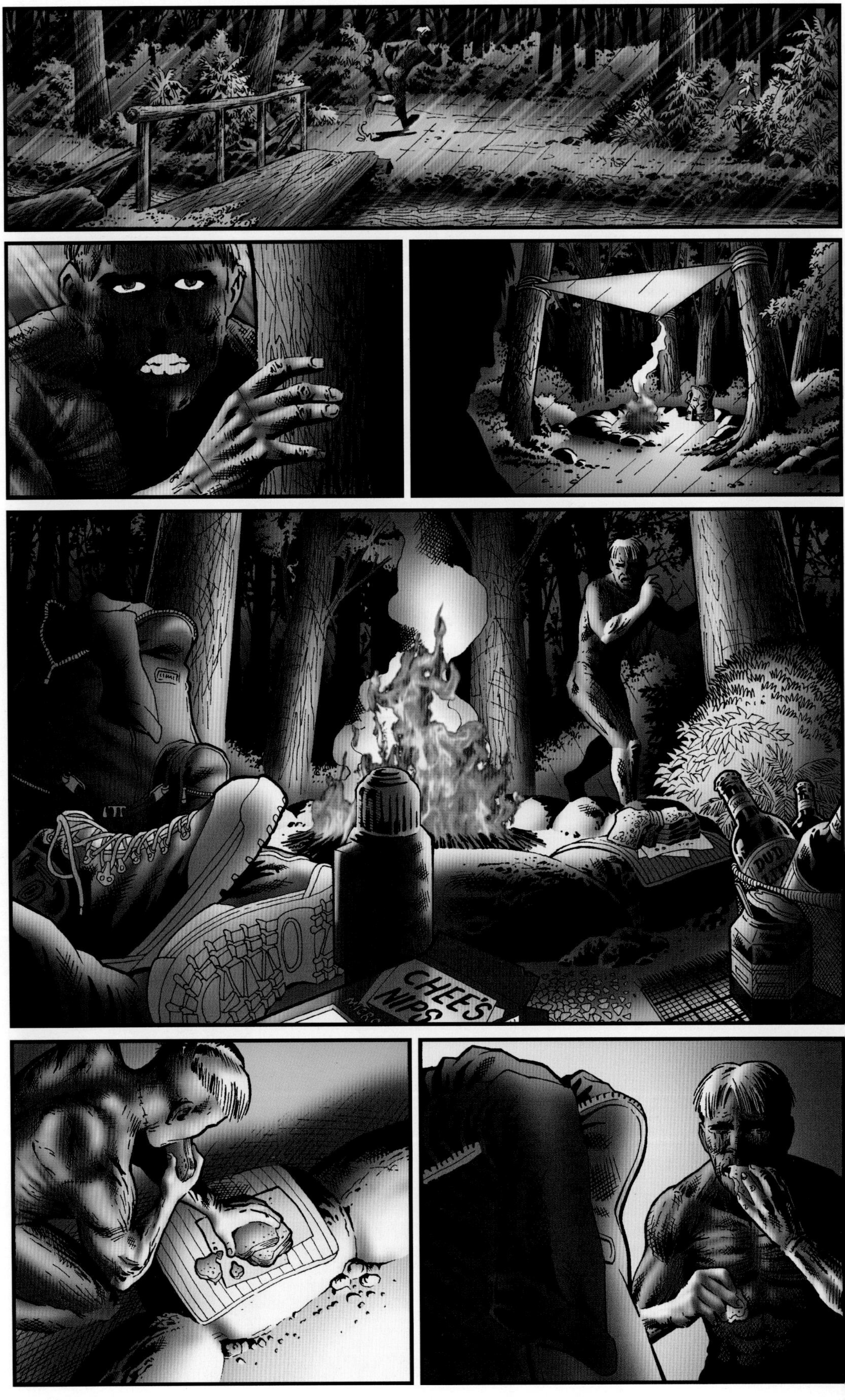
CHEE'S NIPS

I'D COMPLAIN ABOUT YOU TAKING MY CLOTHES...

...BUT I PREFER THAT TO FINDING A NAKED MAN BY THE FIRE.

NOW, NOW, DON'T BE AFRAID. YOU'RE SAFE HERE.

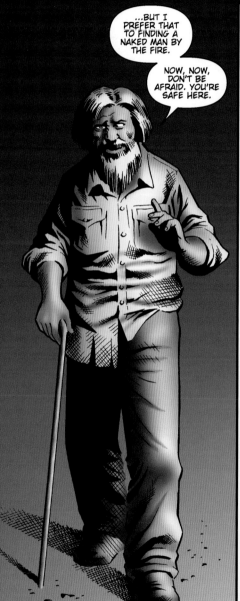

SIT, SIT! I NEVER SEE ANYBODY BACK HERE 'CEPT FOR THEM KIDS, THEM FOOTBALL PUNKS, BUT I AIN'T SEEN THEM RECENTLY.

SIT?

YES, SIT! YOU SAT DOWN BEFORE, HAVEN'T YOU?

SO, WHAT'S YOUR NAME... IF YOU DON'T MIND ME ASKIN'?

NO. NAME.

NO NAME? OF COURSE YOU HAVE A NAME. WHAT IS IT PEOPLE CALL YOU?

WILLIAM.

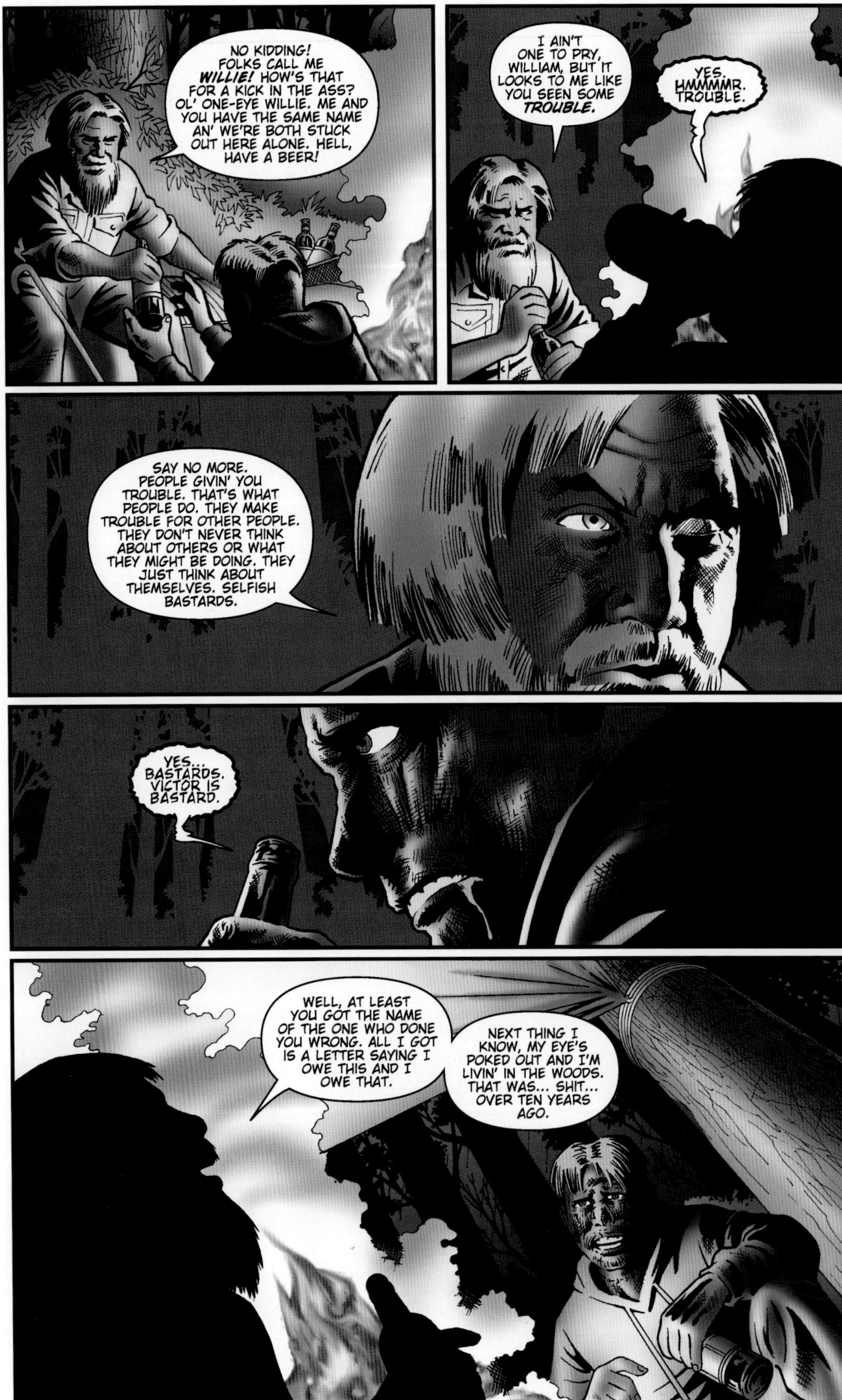
NO KIDDING! FOLKS CALL ME WILLIE! HOW'S THAT FOR A KICK IN THE ASS? OL' ONE-EYE WILLIE. ME AND YOU HAVE THE SAME NAME AN' WE'RE BOTH STUCK OUT HERE ALONE. HELL, HAVE A BEER!
I AIN'T ONE TO PRY, WILLIAM, BUT IT LOOKS TO ME LIKE YOU SEEN SOME TROUBLE.
YES. HMMMMR. TROUBLE.
SAY NO MORE. PEOPLE GIVIN' YOU TROUBLE. THAT'S WHAT PEOPLE DO. THEY MAKE TROUBLE FOR OTHER PEOPLE. THEY DON'T NEVER THINK ABOUT OTHERS OR WHAT THEY MIGHT BE DOING. THEY JUST THINK ABOUT THEMSELVES. SELFISH BASTARDS.
YES... BASTARDS. VICTOR IS BASTARD.
WELL, AT LEAST YOU GOT THE NAME OF THE ONE WHO DONE YOU WRONG. ALL I GOT IS A LETTER SAYING I OWE THIS AND I OWE THAT.
NEXT THING I KNOW, MY EYE'S POKED OUT AND I'M LIVIN' IN THE WOODS. THAT WAS... SHIT... OVER TEN YEARS AGO.

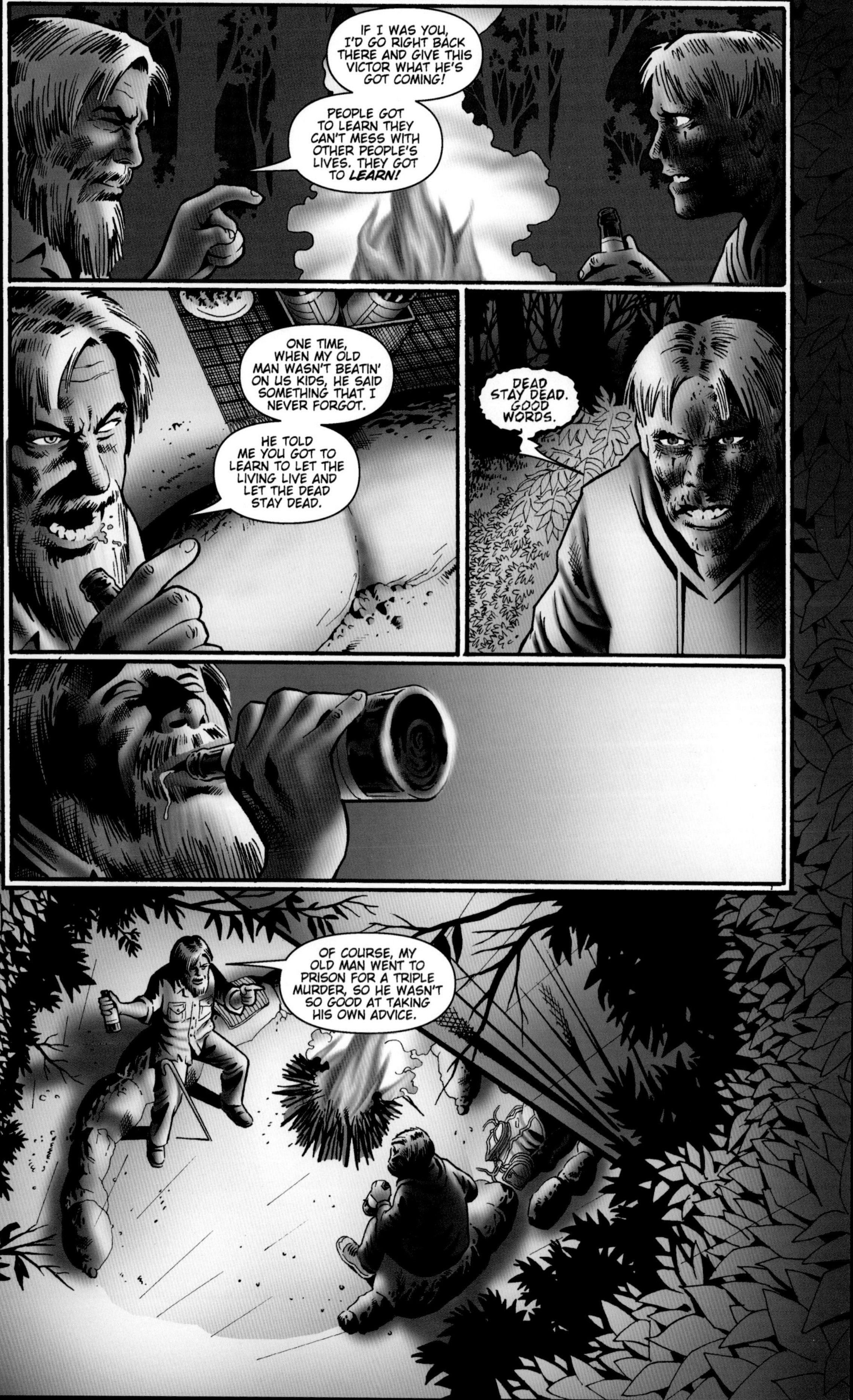
IF I WAS YOU, I'D GO RIGHT BACK THERE AND GIVE THIS VICTOR WHAT HE'S GOT COMING!
PEOPLE GOT TO LEARN THEY CAN'T MESS WITH OTHER PEOPLE'S LIVES. THEY GOT TO LEARN!
ONE TIME, WHEN MY OLD MAN WASN'T BEATIN' ON US KIDS, HE SAID SOMETHING THAT I NEVER FORGOT.
HE TOLD ME YOU GOT TO LEARN TO LET THE LIVING LIVE AND LET THE DEAD STAY DEAD.
DEAD STAY DEAD. GOOD WORDS.
OF COURSE, MY OLD MAN WENT TO PRISON FOR A TRIPLE MURDER, SO HE WASN'T SO GOOD AT TAKING HIS OWN ADVICE.

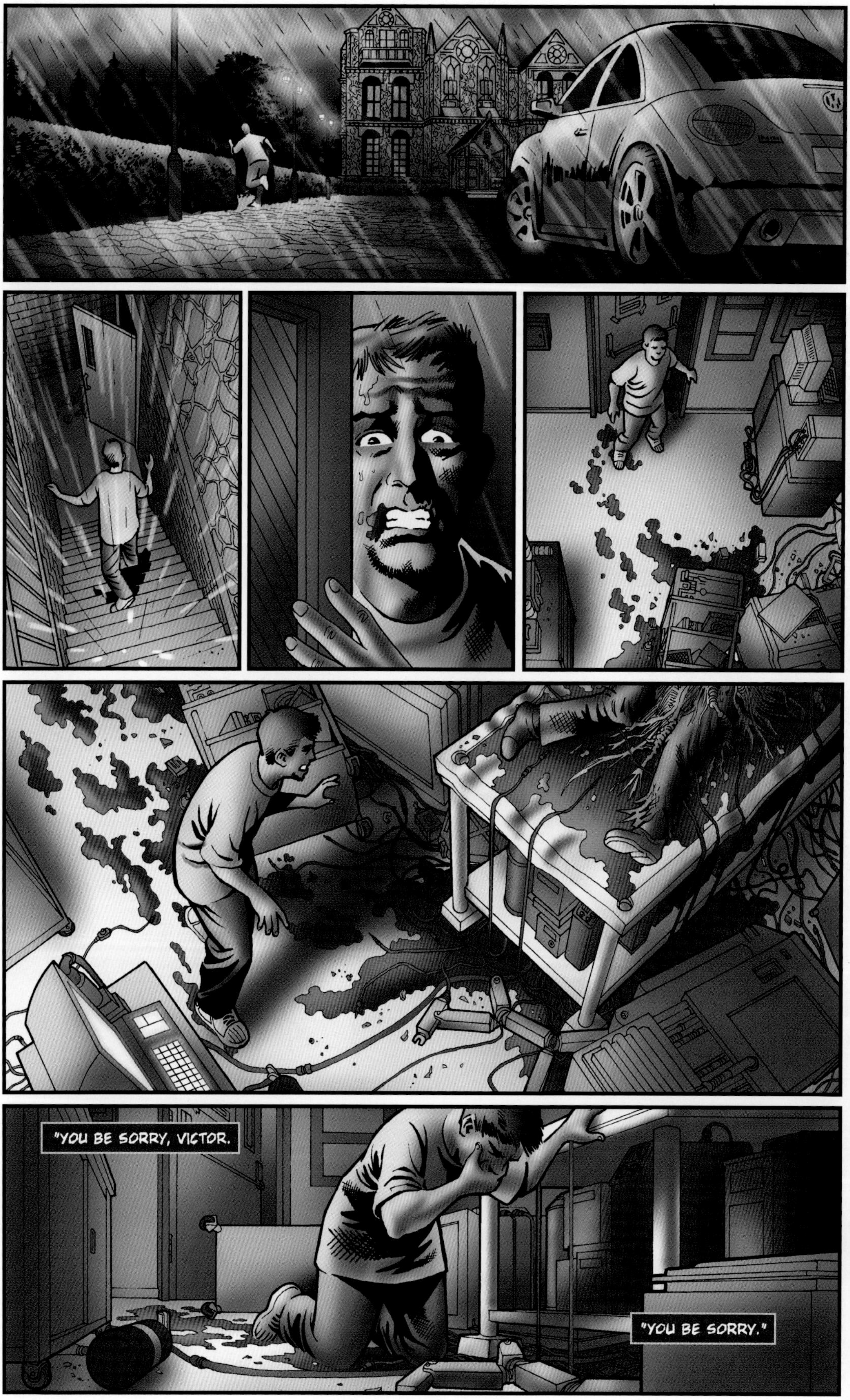
"YOU BE SORRY, VICTOR.
"YOU BE SORRY."

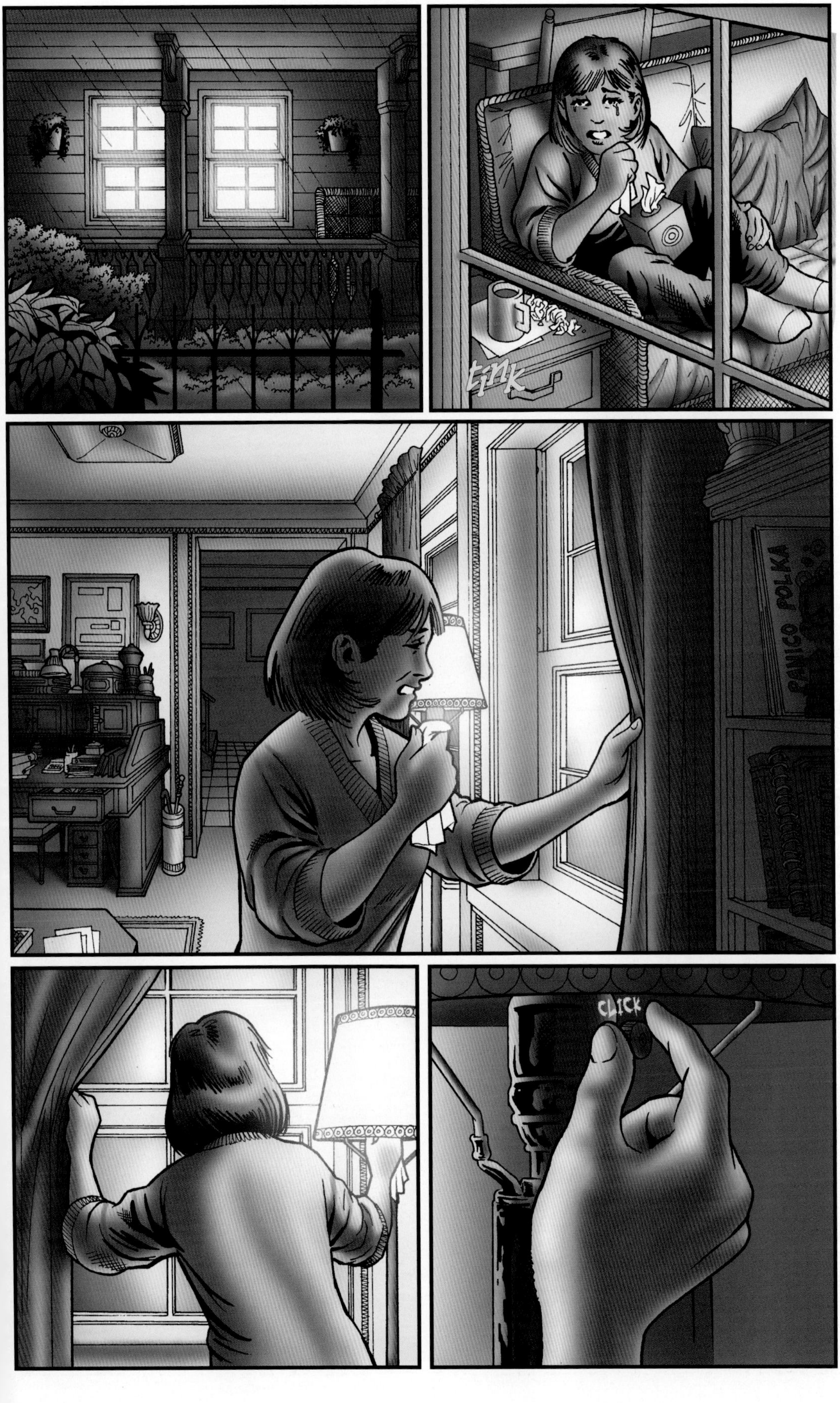
tink
PANICO POLKA
CLICK

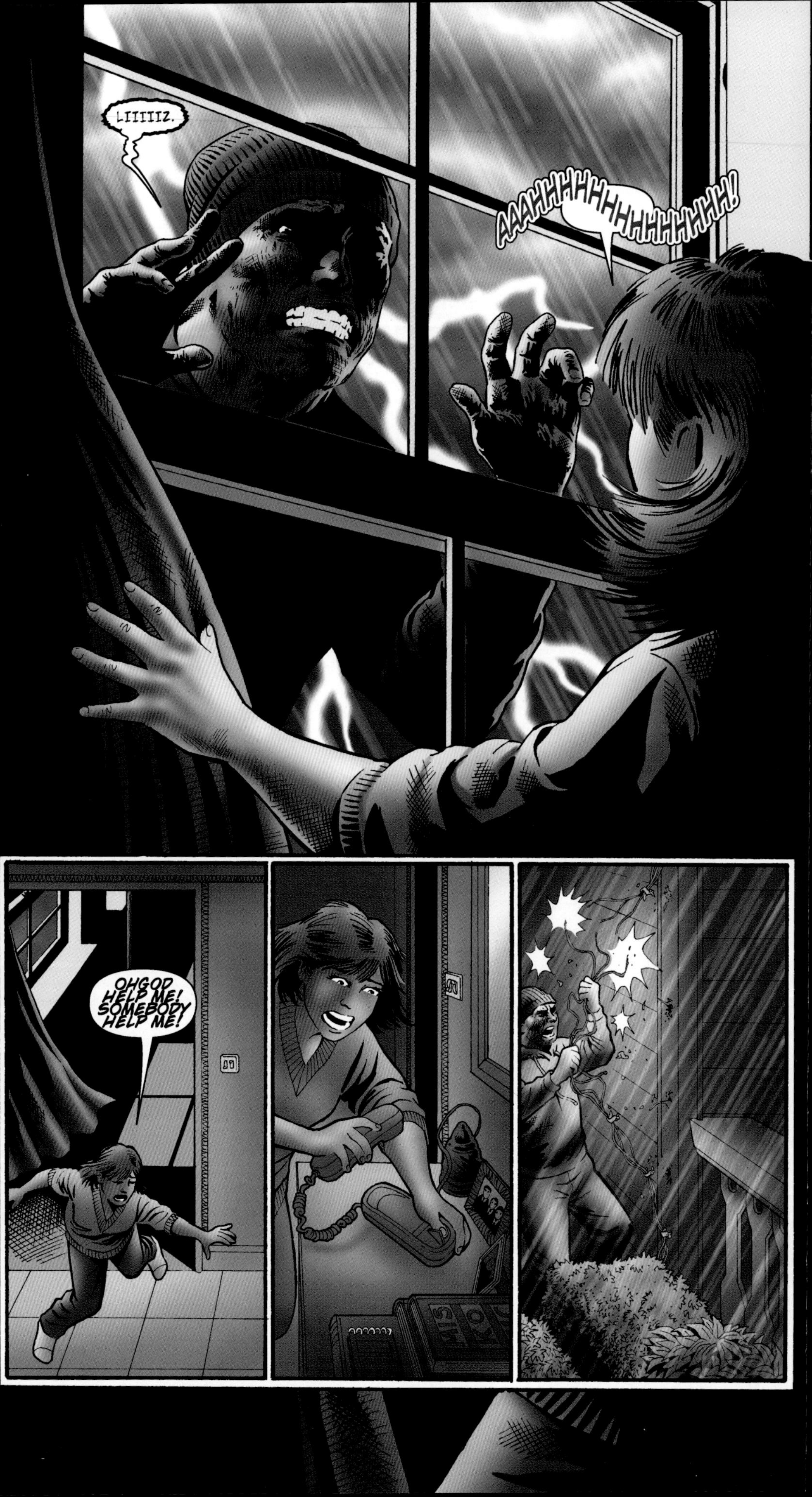
LIIIIIZ.
AAAHHHHHHHHHHHHHH!
OHGOD HELP ME! SOMEBODY HELP ME!

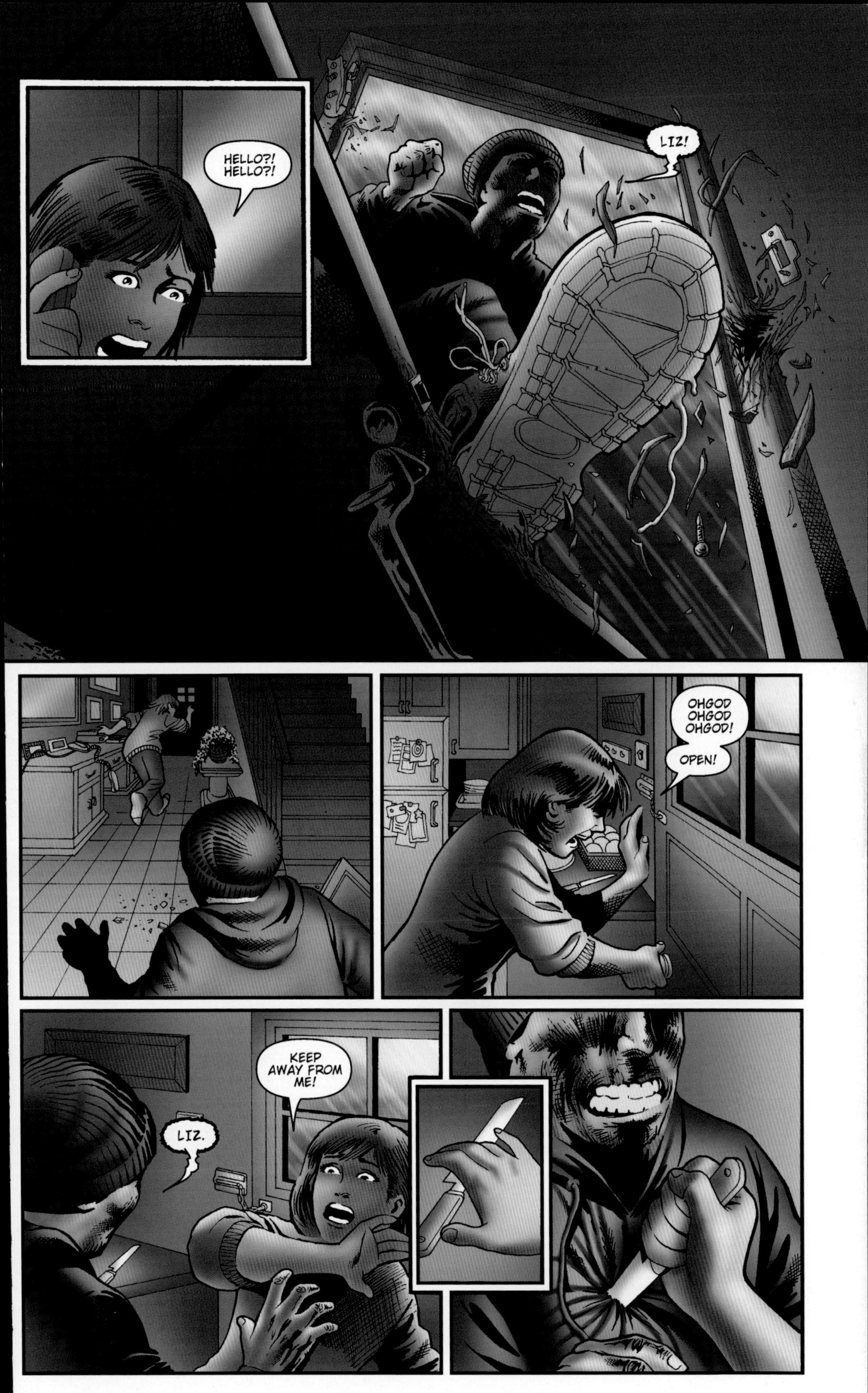

HELLO?!
HELLO?!
LIZ!
OHGOD
OHGOD
OHGOD!
OPEN!
KEEP
AWAY FROM
ME!
LIZ.

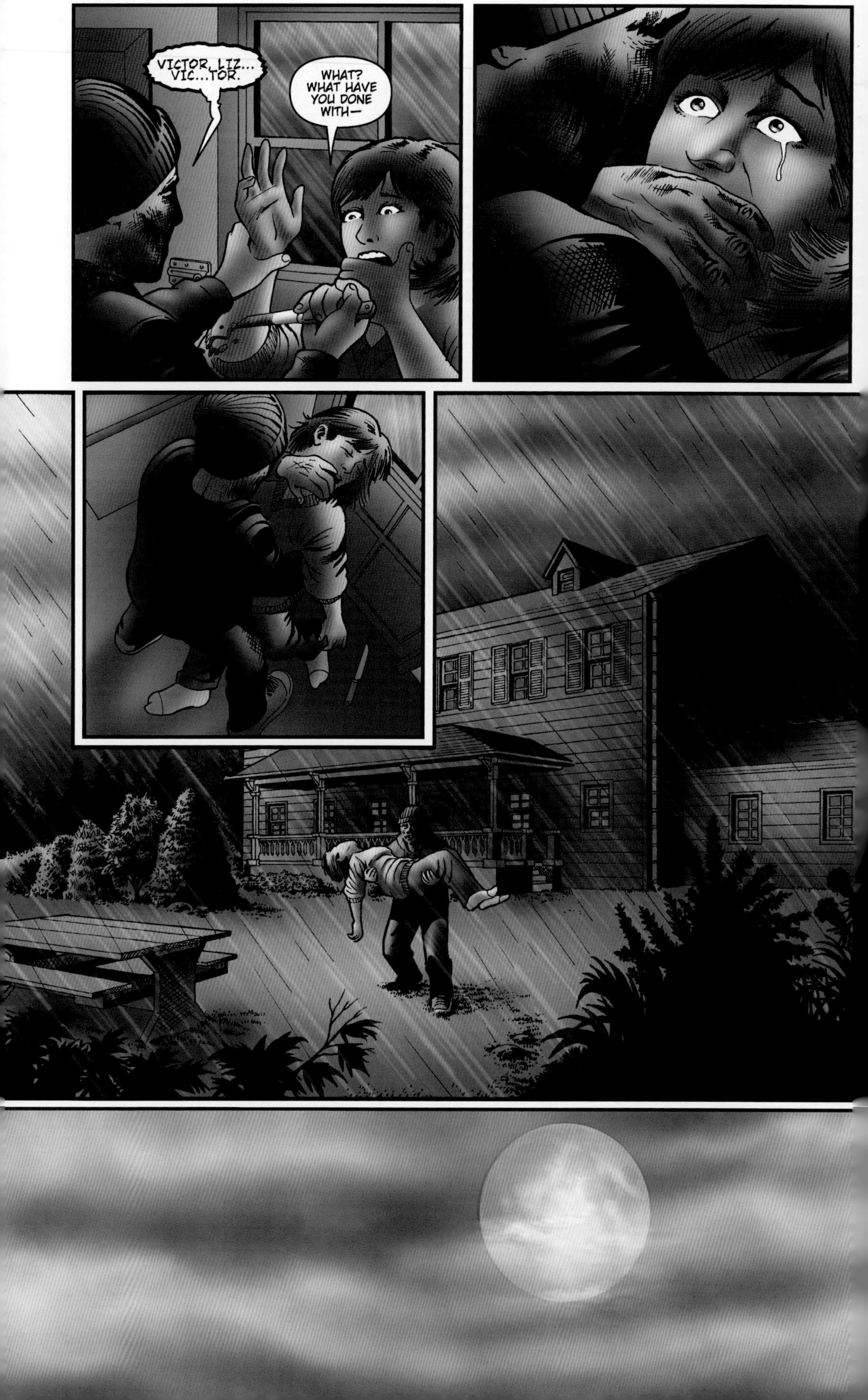
VICTOR, LIZ... VIC...TOR.
WHAT? WHAT HAVE YOU DONE WITH—

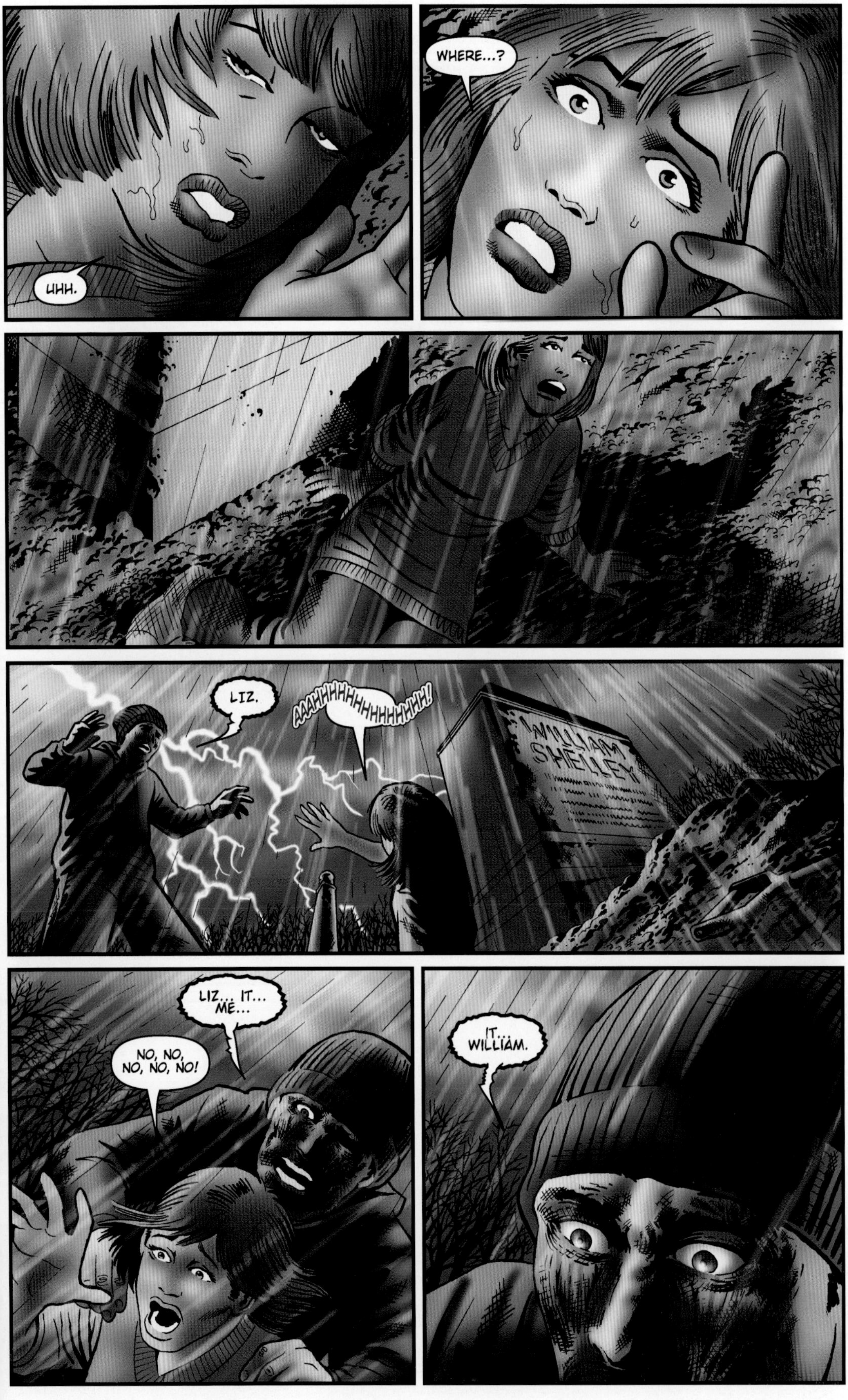
UHH.
WHERE...?
LIZ.
AAAHHHHHHHHHHHHHH!
WILLIAM SHELLEY
LIZ... IT... ME...
NO, NO, NO, NO, NO!
IT... WILLIAM.

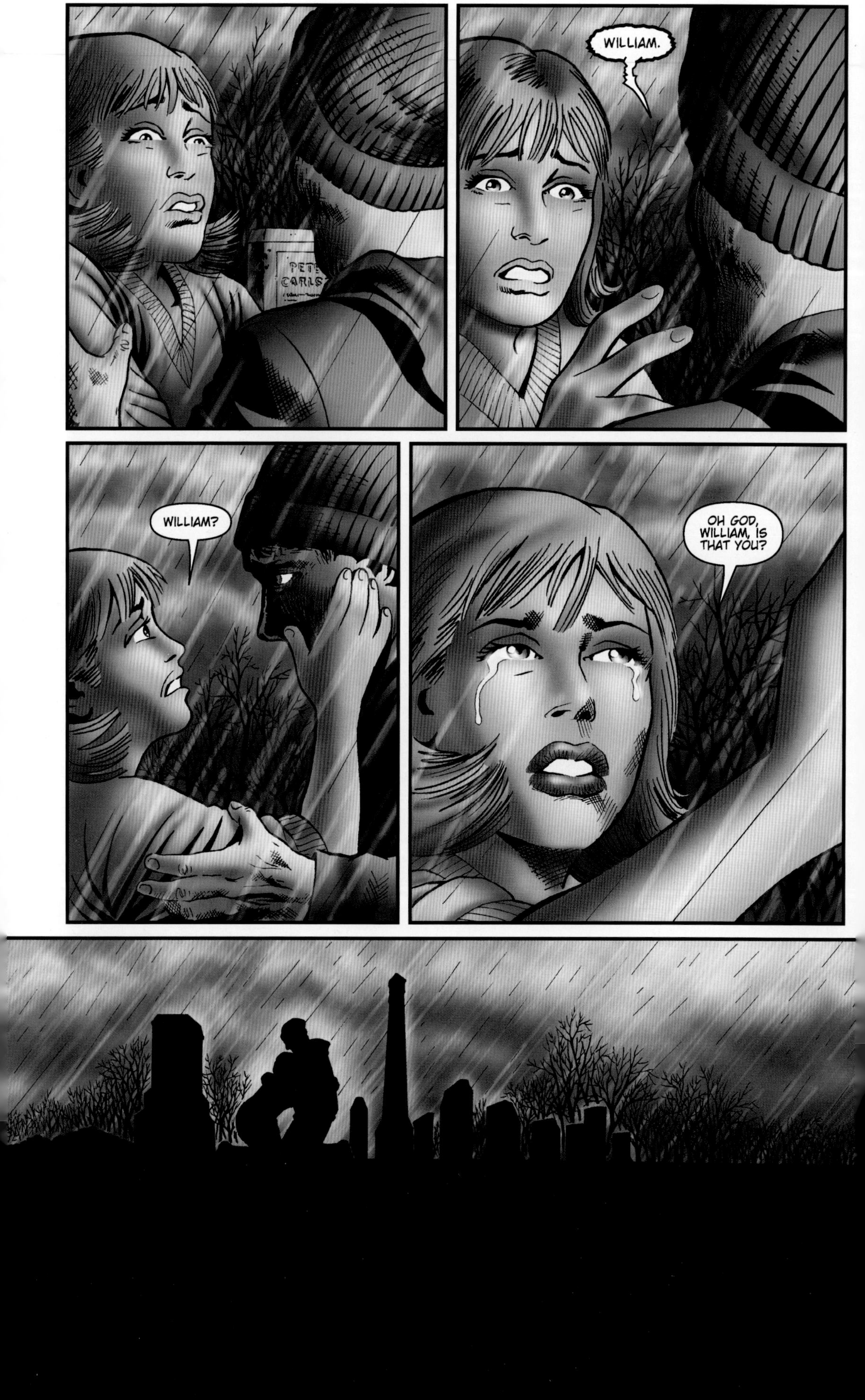
PETE CARLS
WILLIAM.
WILLIAM?
OH GOD, WILLIAM, IS THAT YOU?

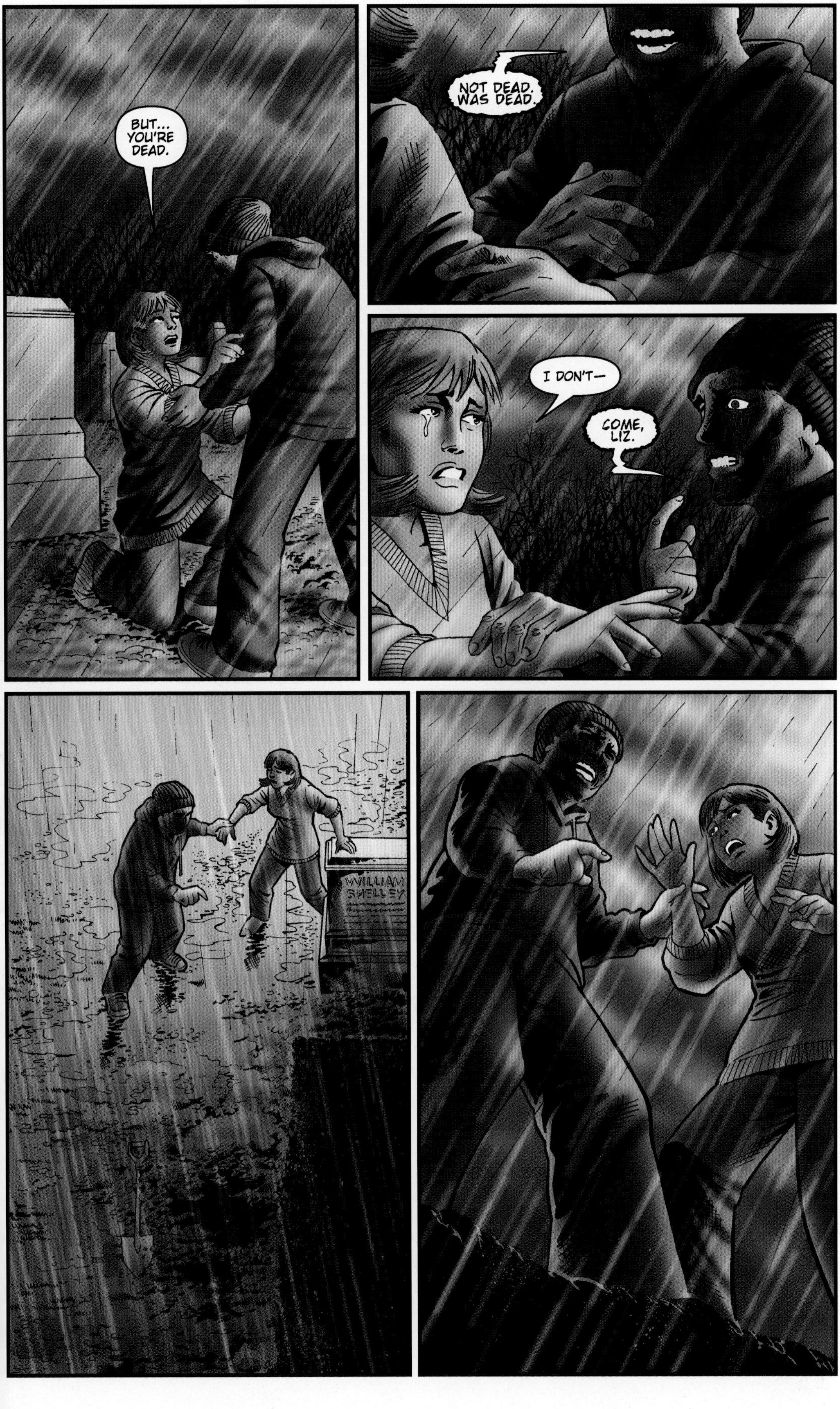
BUT... YOU'RE DEAD.
NOT DEAD. WAS DEAD.
I DON'T—
COME, LIZ.
WILLIAM SHELLEY

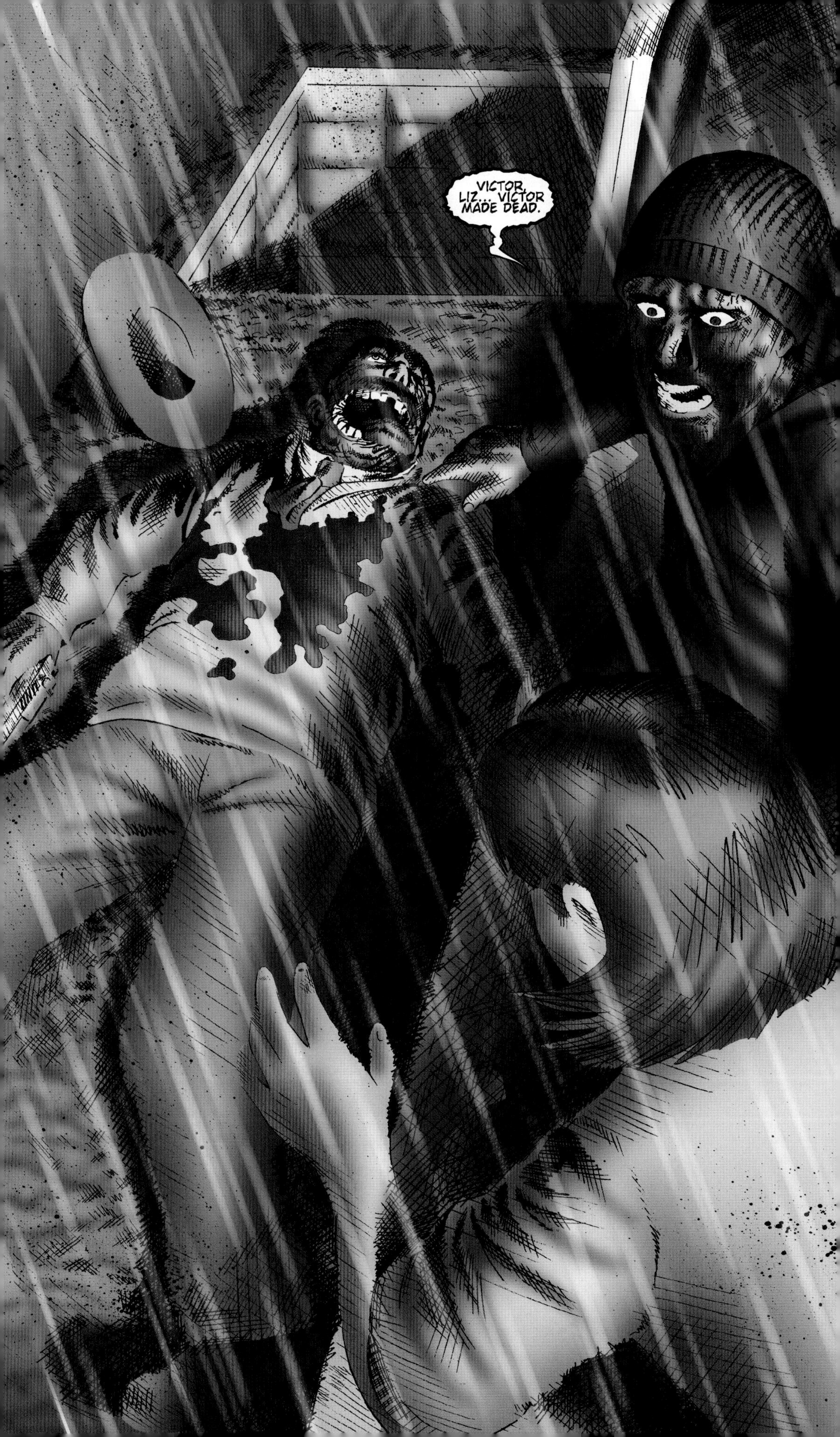
VICTOR, LIZ... VICTOR MADE DEAD.

chapter five

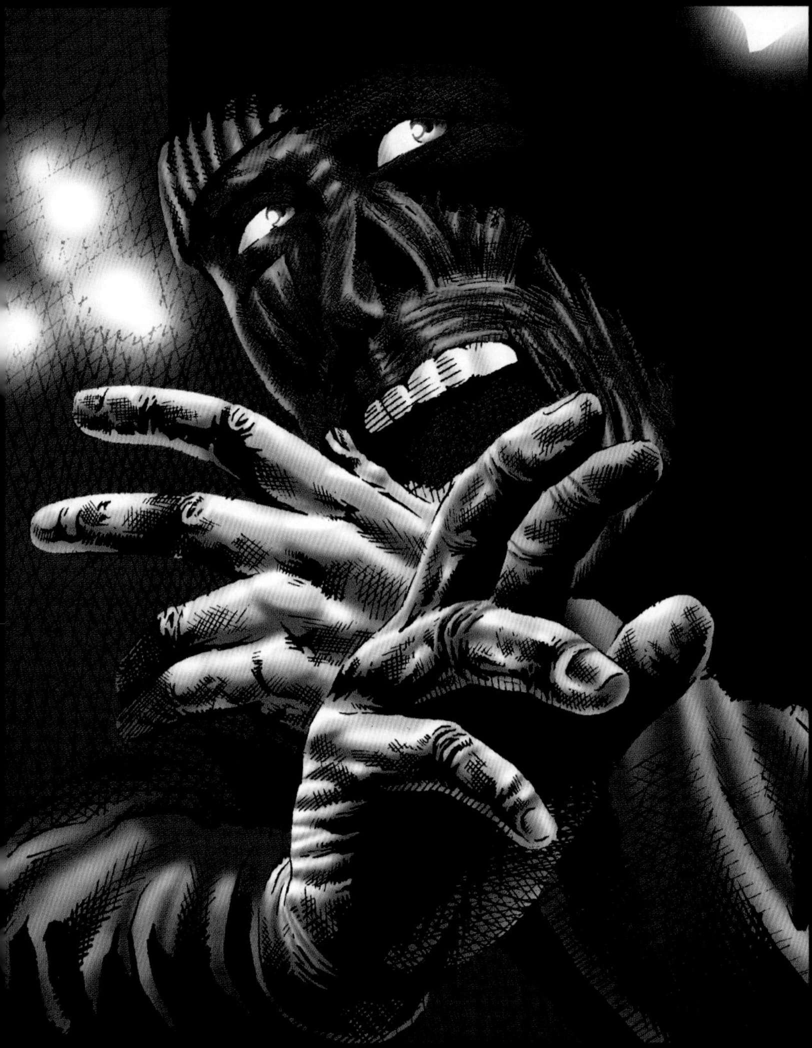

Wake the Dead no.5 mini-series cover by Chee

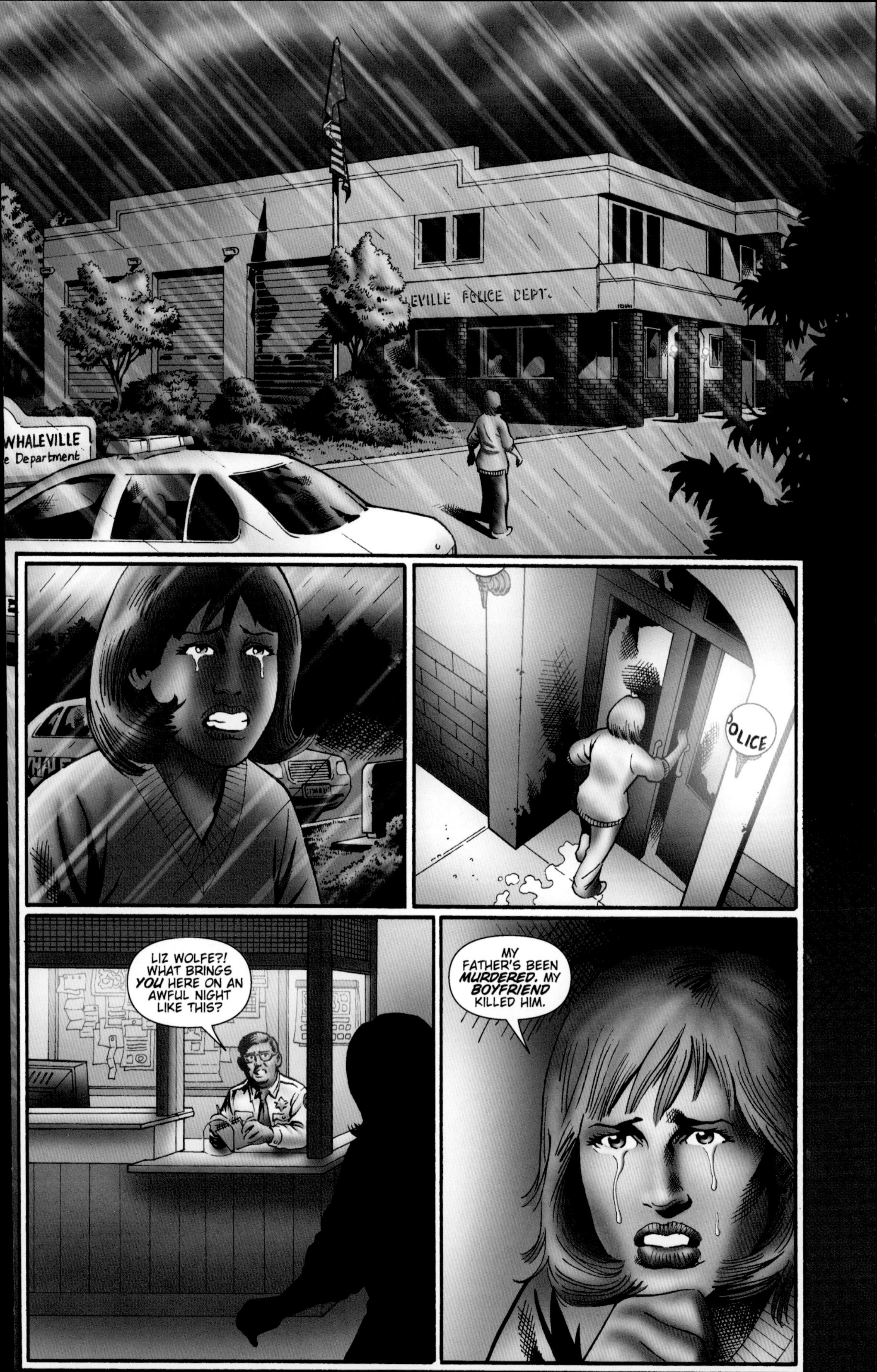

WHALEVILLE
e Department
EVILLE POLICE DEPT.
POLICE
LIZ WOLFE?! WHAT BRINGS *YOU* HERE ON AN AWFUL NIGHT LIKE THIS?
MY FATHER'S BEEN *MURDERED.* MY *BOYFRIEND* KILLED HIM.

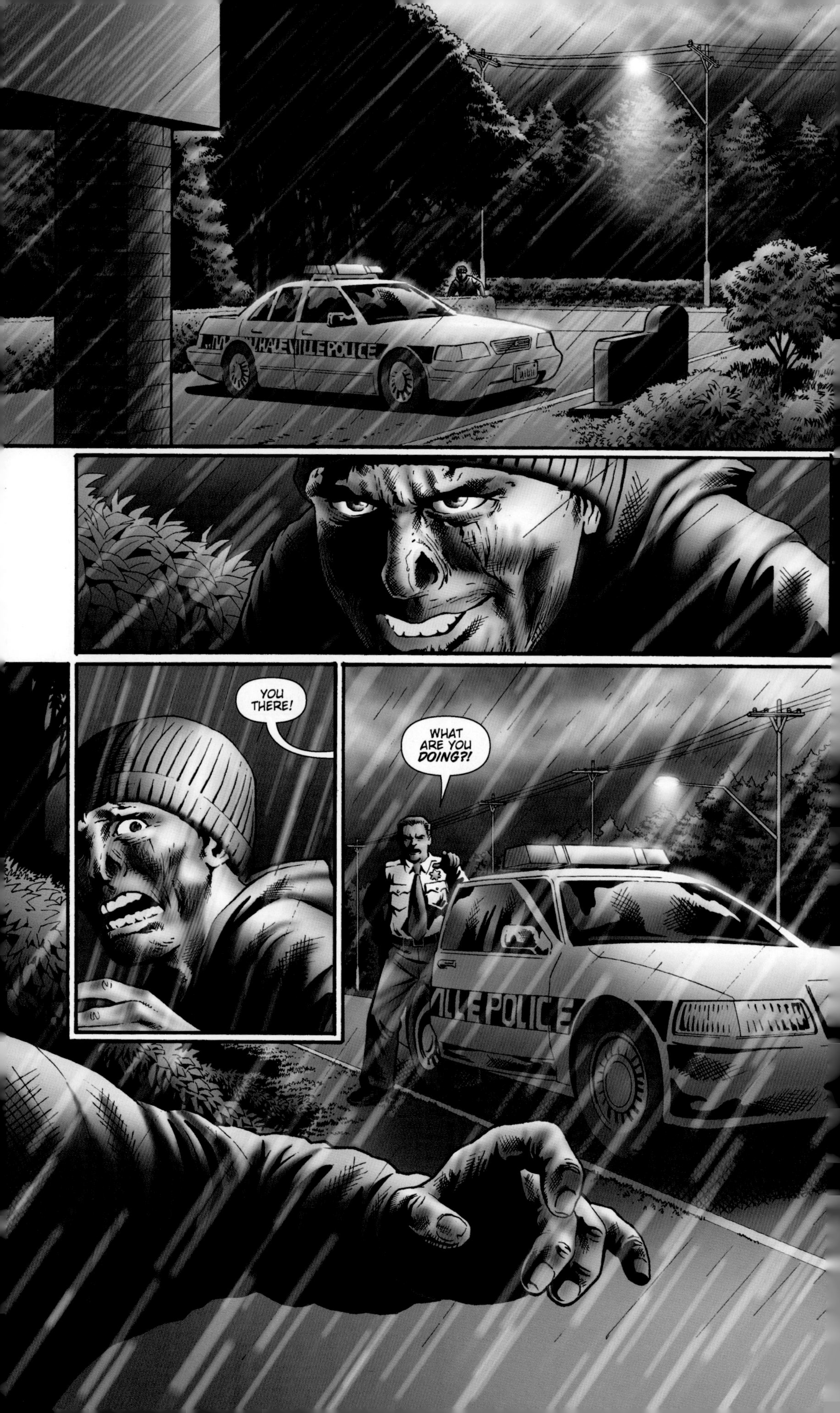

YOU THERE!
WHAT ARE YOU *DOING?!*

STOP! DON'T MOVE!
NUHHH!
GET UP! LET ME SEE YOUR HANDS.
SNAP
AHHHHHHHHHHHHH!

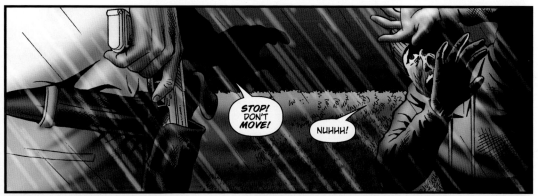

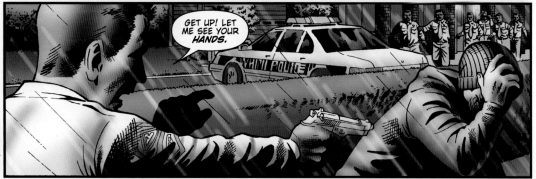

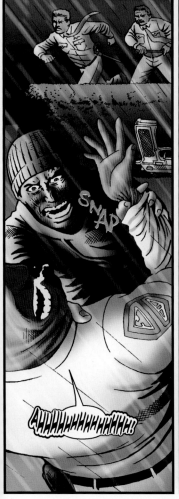

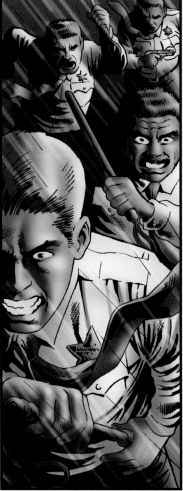

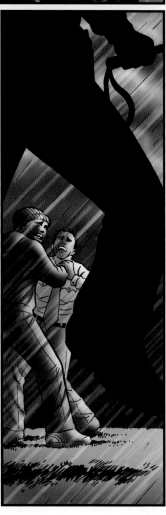

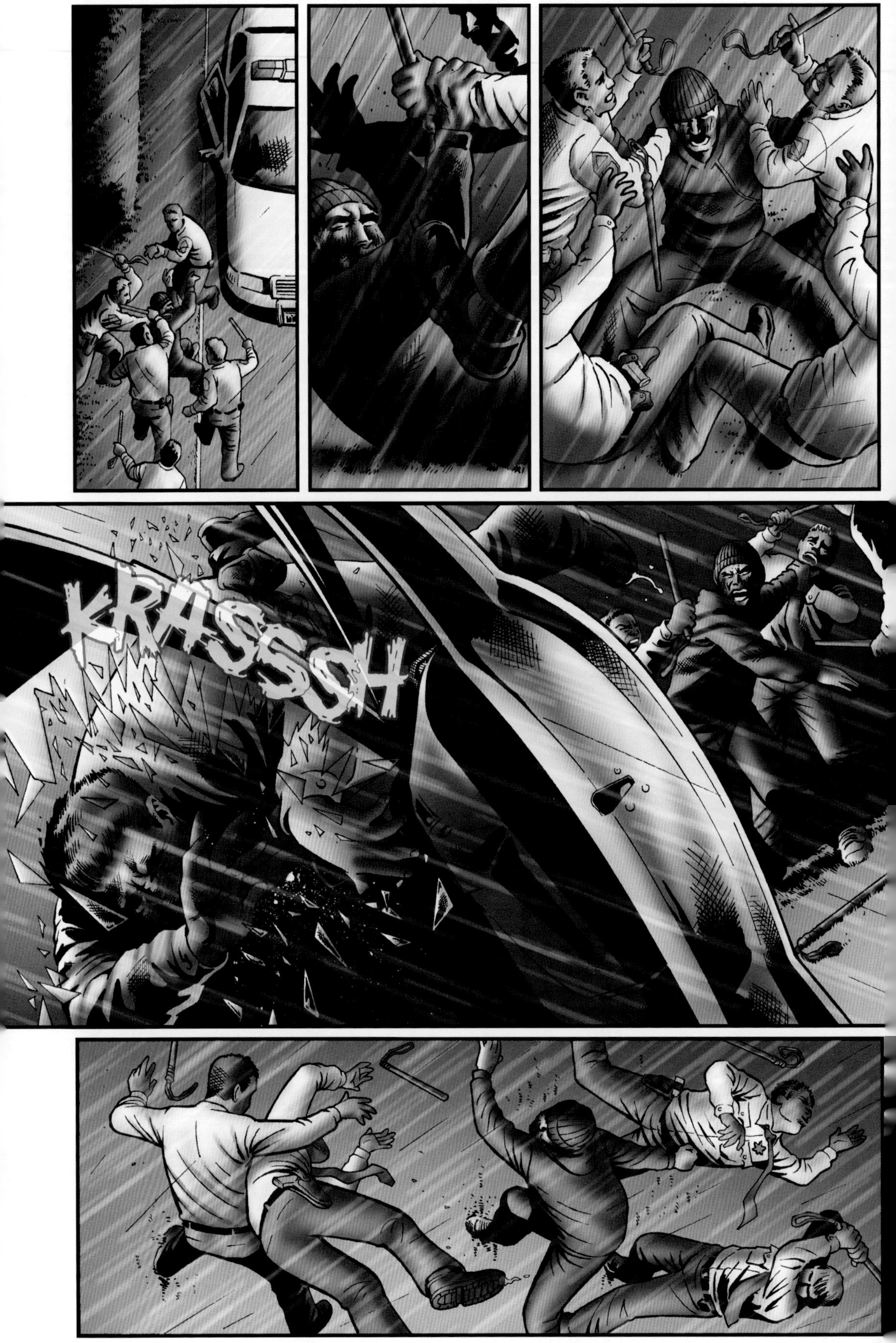
KRASSSH

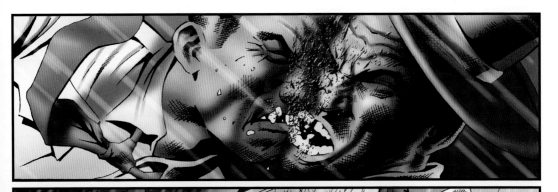

AFTER HIM! DON'T LET HIM GET AWAY!

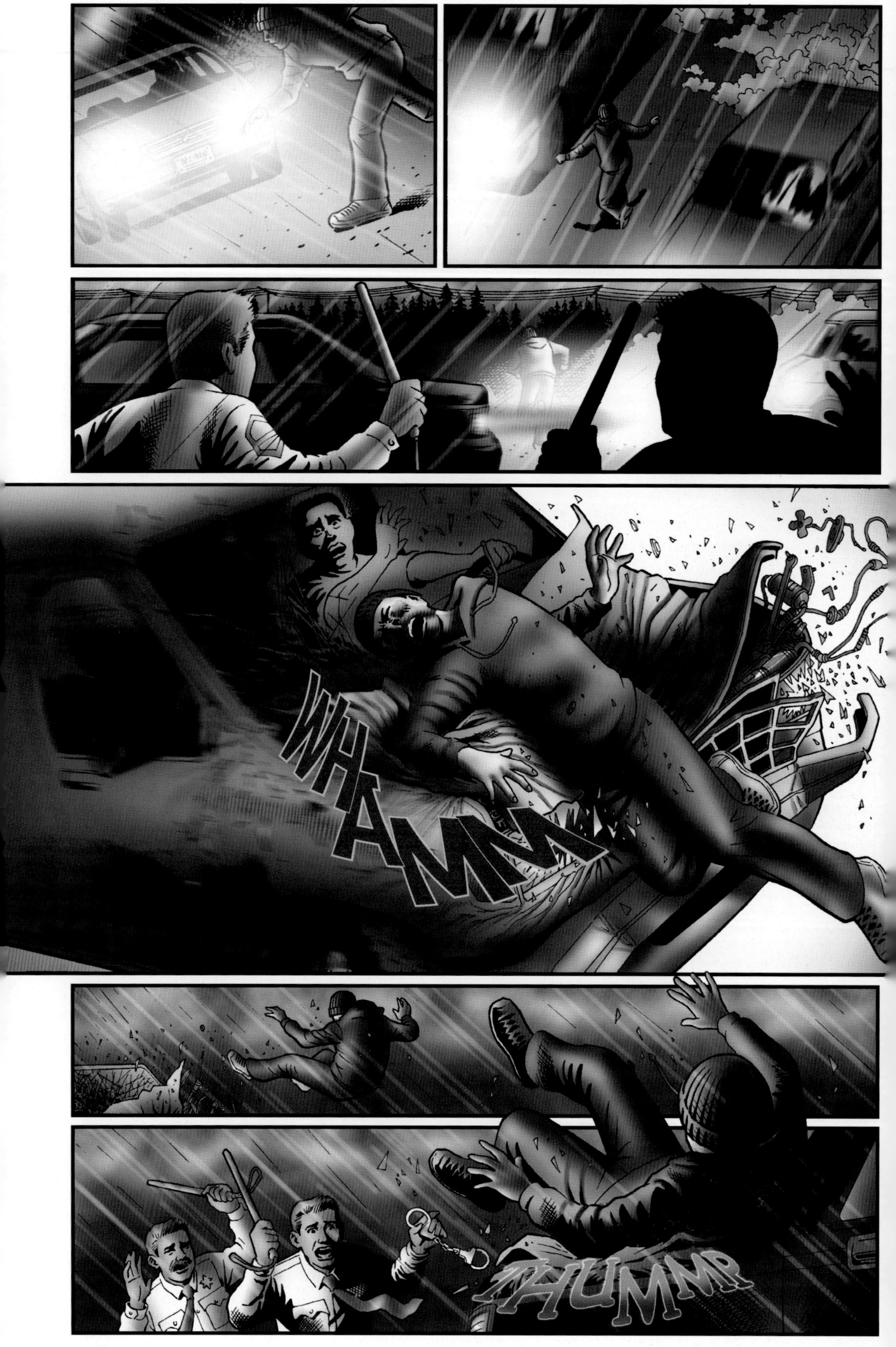
WHAMM
THUMMP

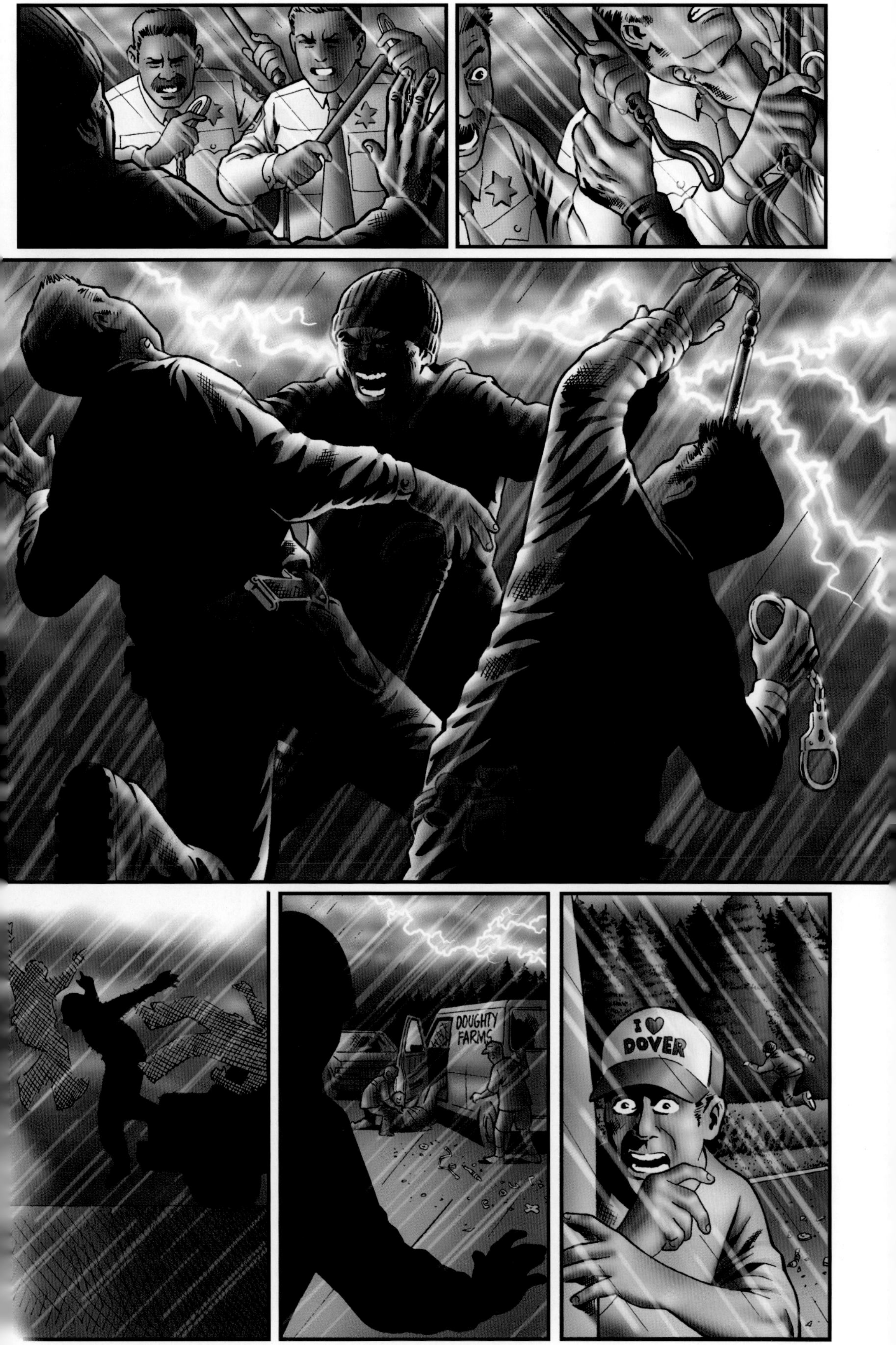
DOUGHTY FARMS
I ♥ DOVER

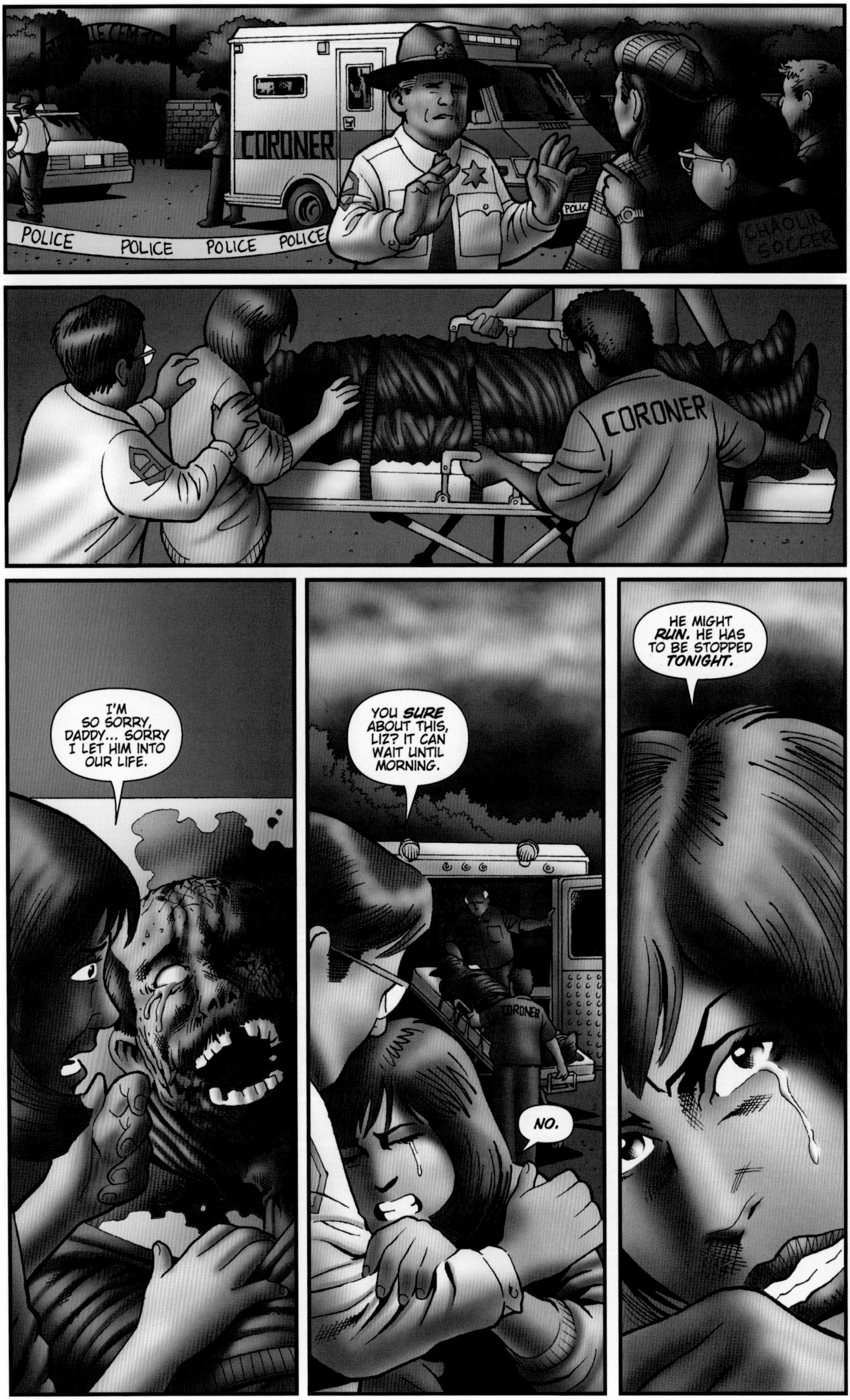
CORONER
POLICE POLICE POLICE POLICE
CHAOLIN SOCCER
CORONER
I'M SO SORRY, DADDY... SORRY I LET HIM INTO OUR LIFE.
YOU *SURE* ABOUT THIS, LIZ? IT CAN WAIT UNTIL MORNING.
CORONER
NO.
HE MIGHT *RUN.* HE HAS TO BE STOPPED *TONIGHT.*

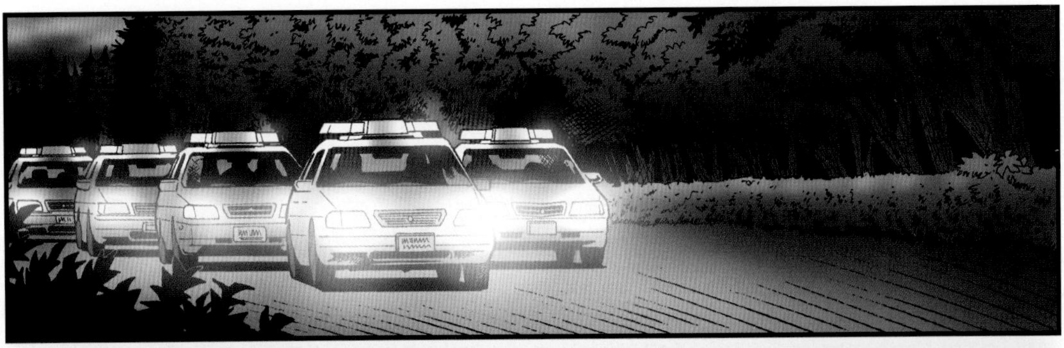

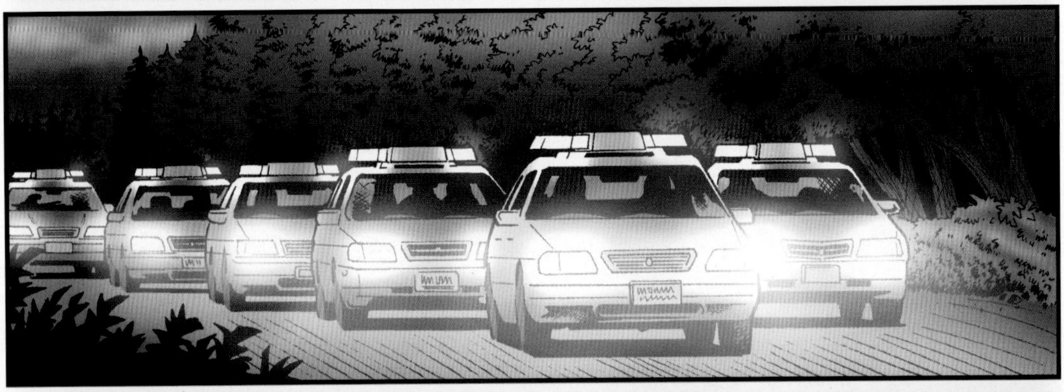

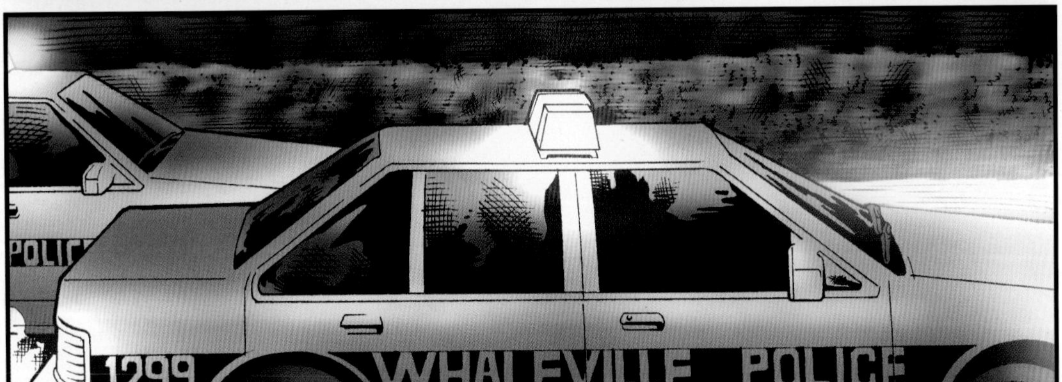
1299
WHALEVILLE POLICE

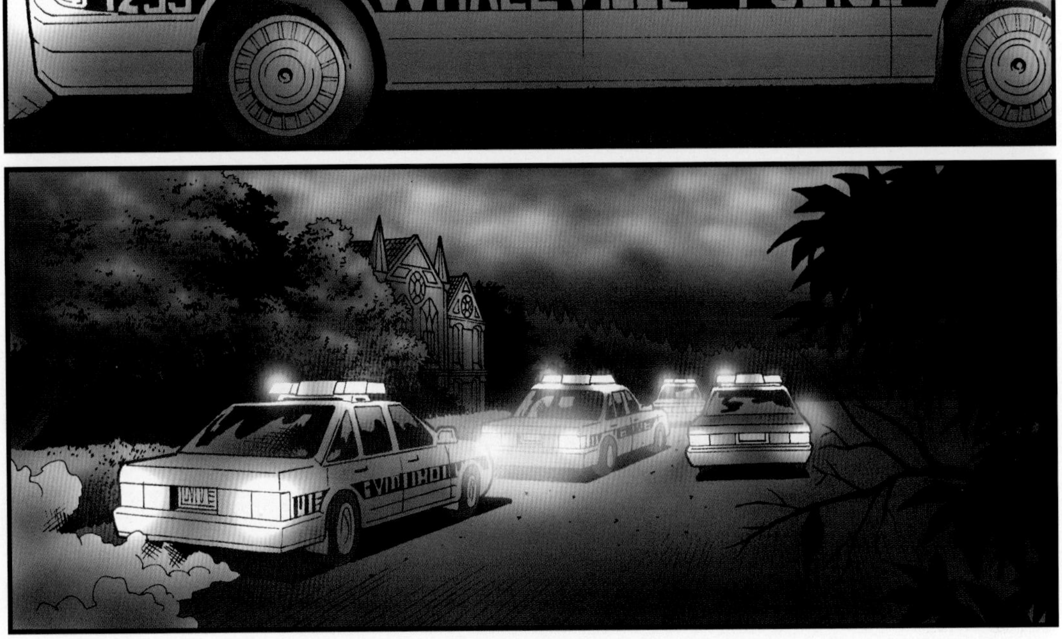

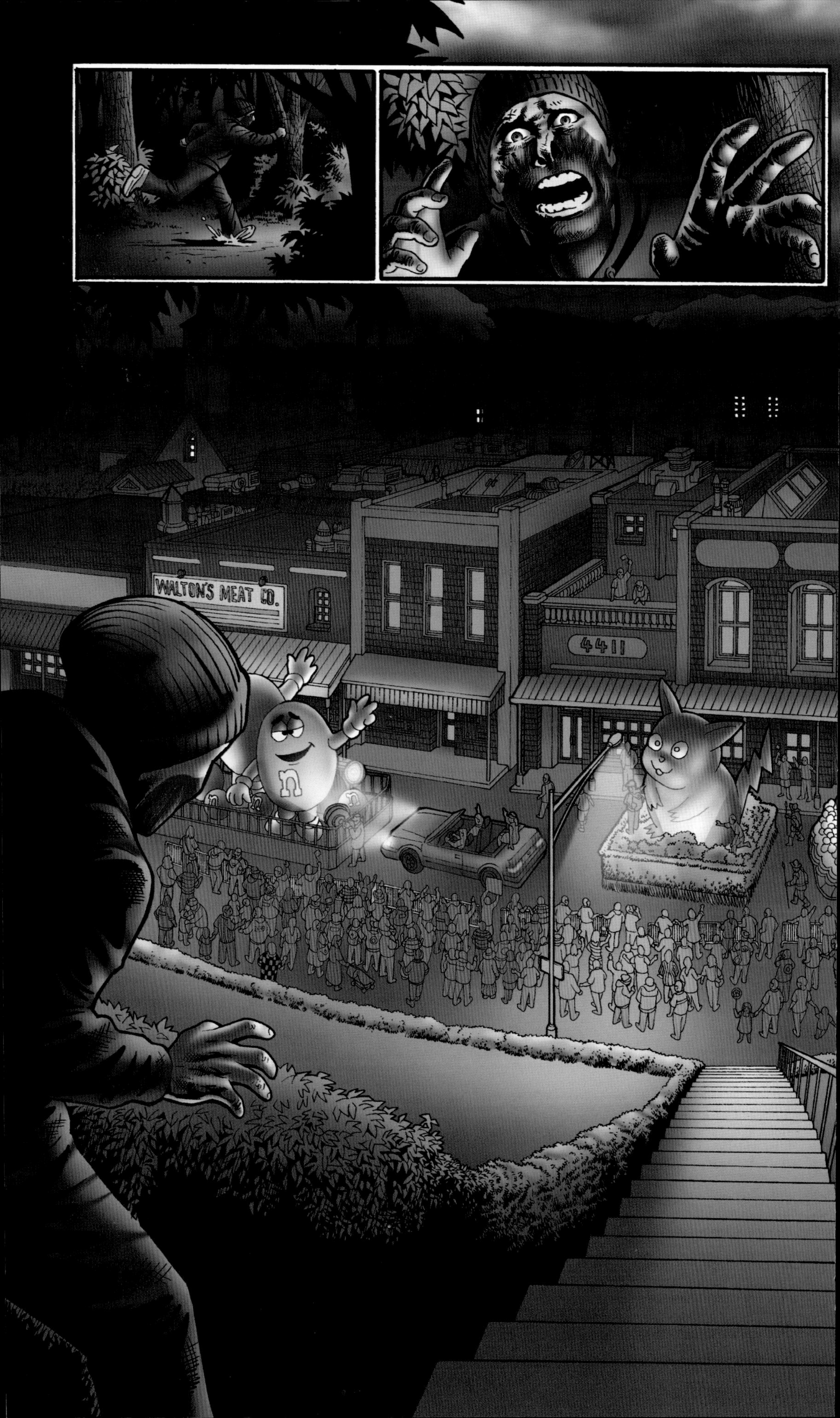
WALTON'S MEAT CO.
4411

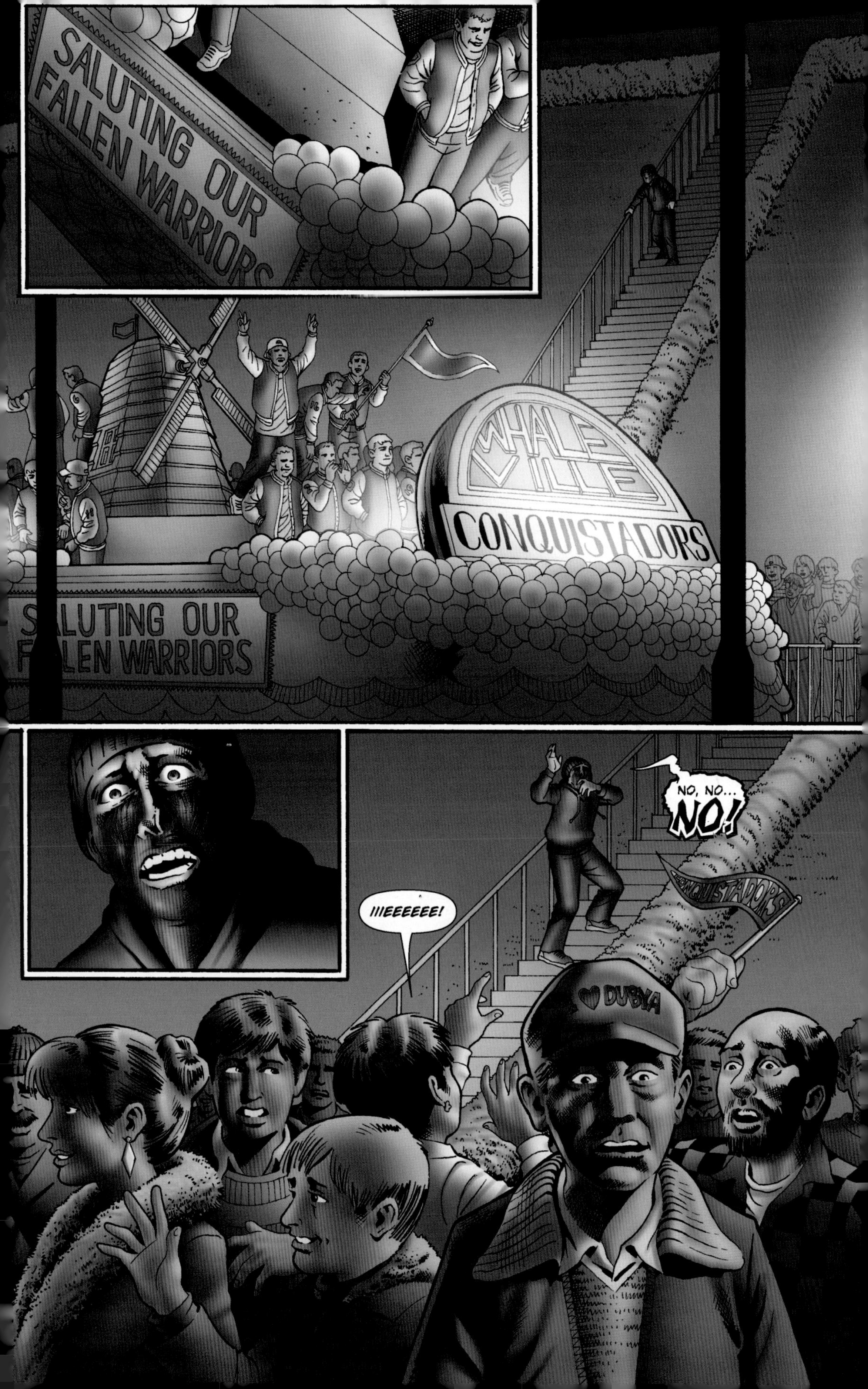
SALUTING OUR FALLEN WARRIORS
WHALE VILLE
CONQUISTADORS
SALUTING OUR FALLEN WARRIORS
NO, NO... NO!
CONQUISTADORS
IIIEEEEEE!
I ♥ DUBYA

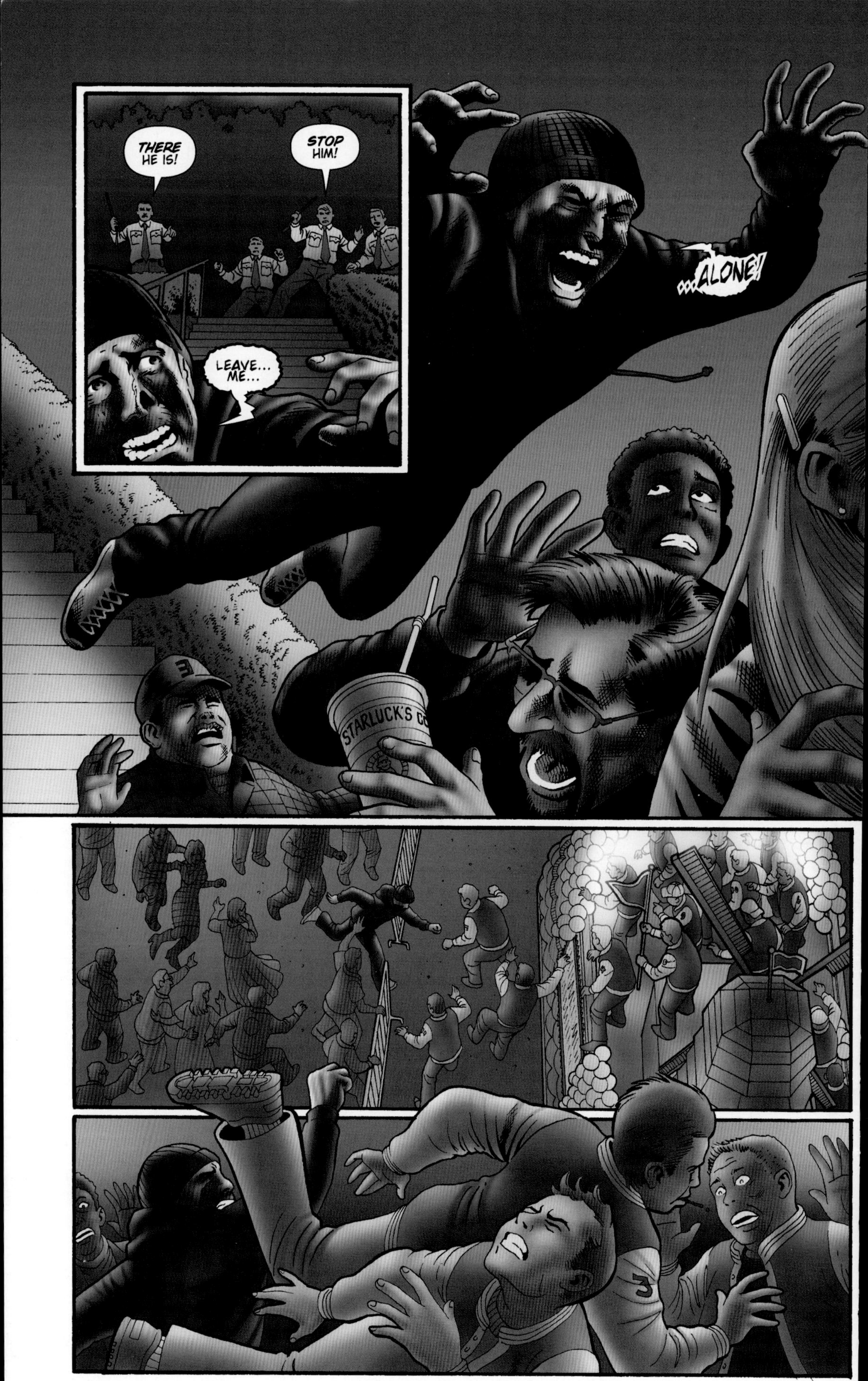

THERE HE IS!
STOP HIM!
LEAVE... ME...
...ALONE!
STARLUCK'S CO

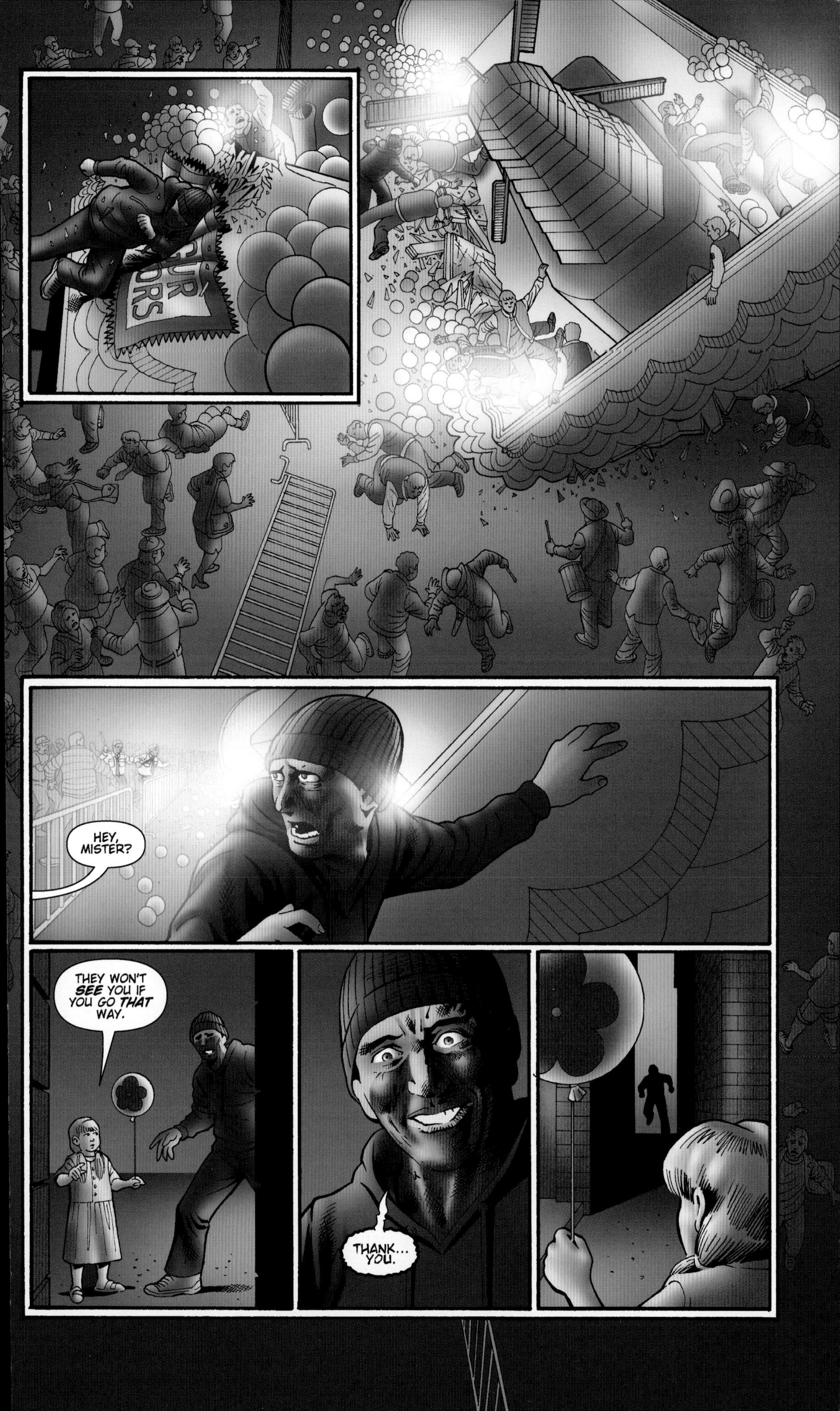

HEY, MISTER?
THEY WON'T SEE YOU IF YOU GO THAT WAY.
THANK... YOU.

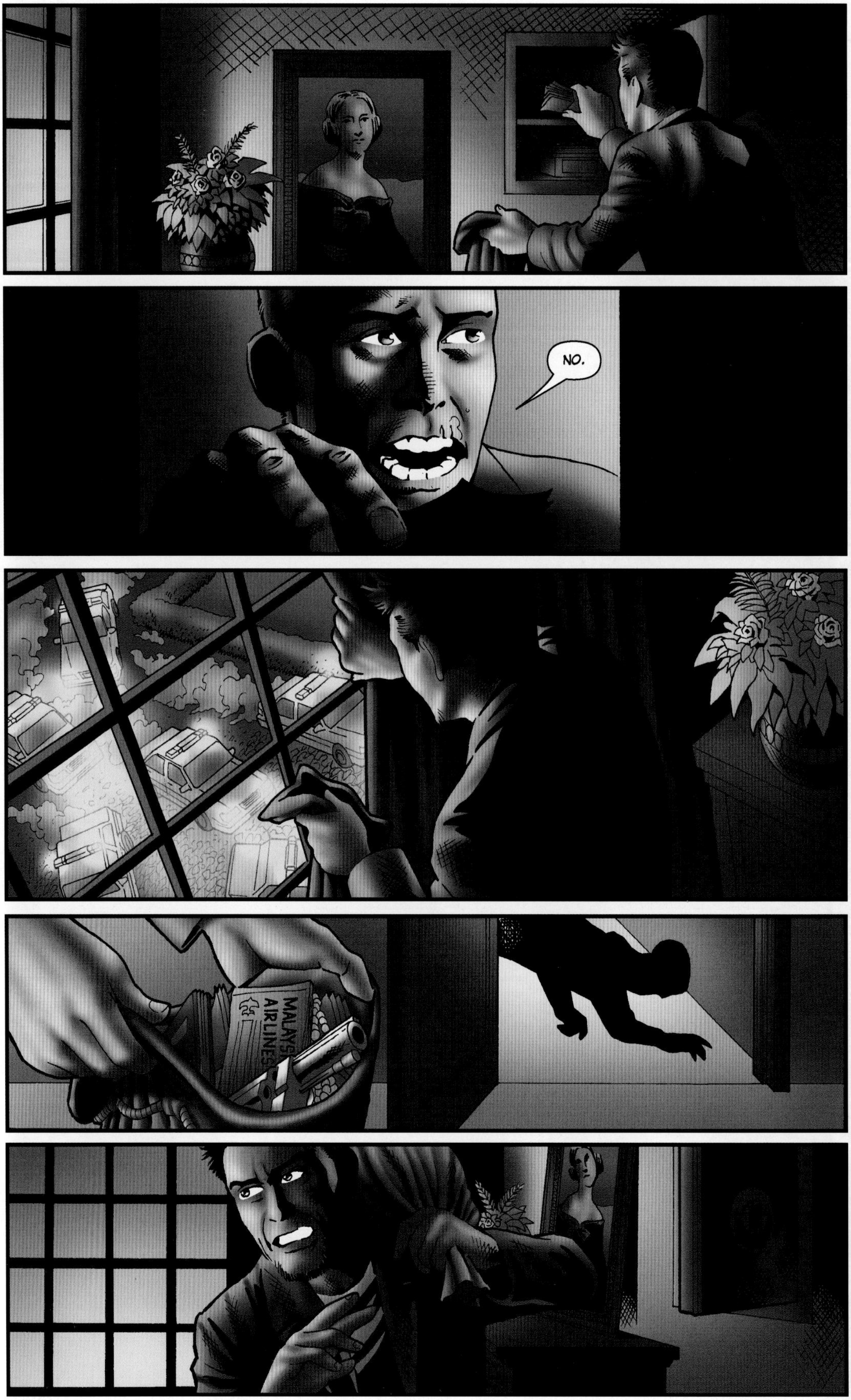
NO.
MALAYSI
AIRLINES

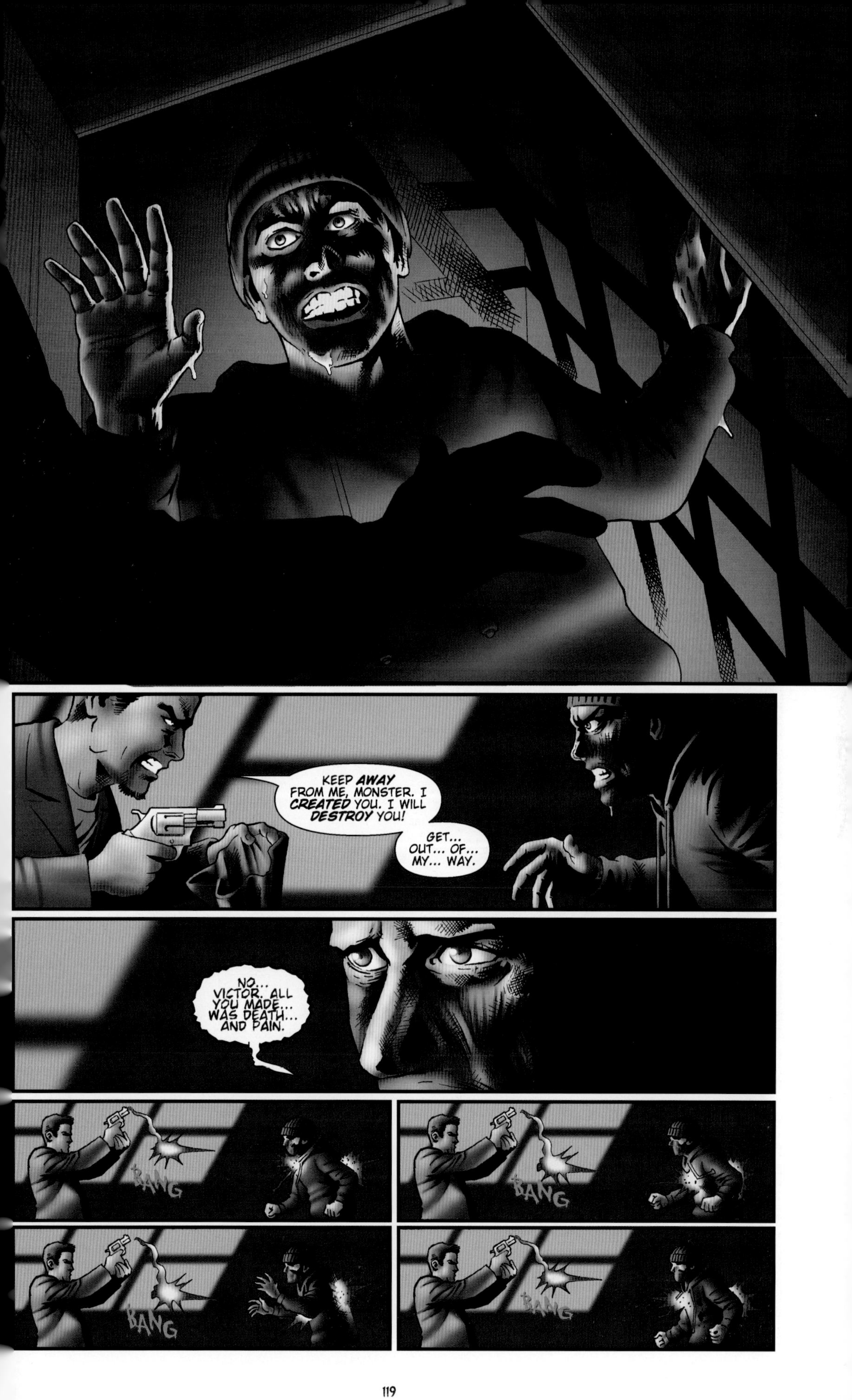
KEEP AWAY FROM ME, MONSTER. I CREATED YOU. I WILL DESTROY YOU!
GET... OUT... OF... MY... WAY.
NO... VICTOR. ALL YOU MADE... WAS DEATH... AND PAIN.
BANG
BANG
BANG
BANG

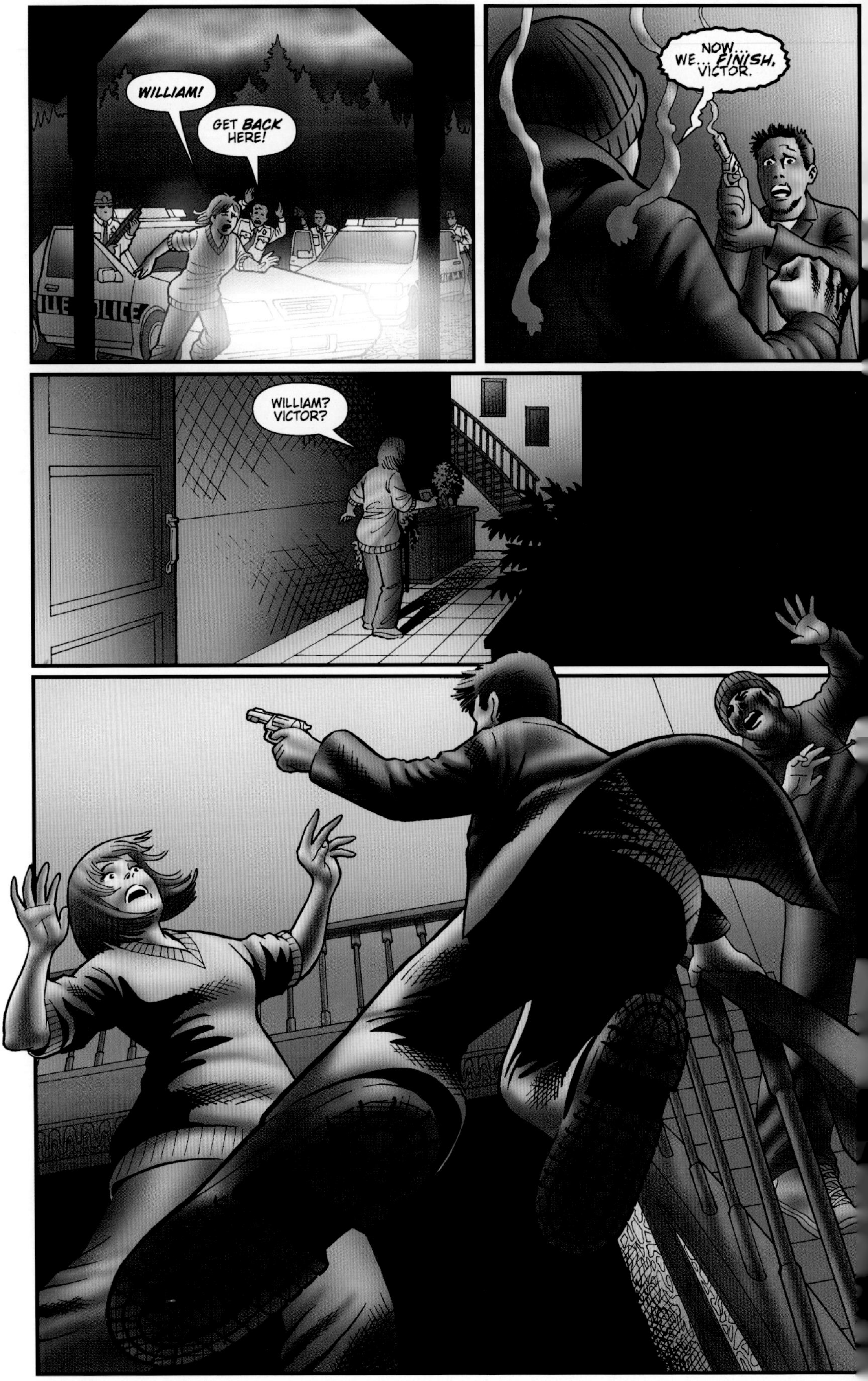
WILLIAM!
GET BACK HERE!
POLICE
NOW... WE... FINISH, VICTOR.
WILLIAM? VICTOR?

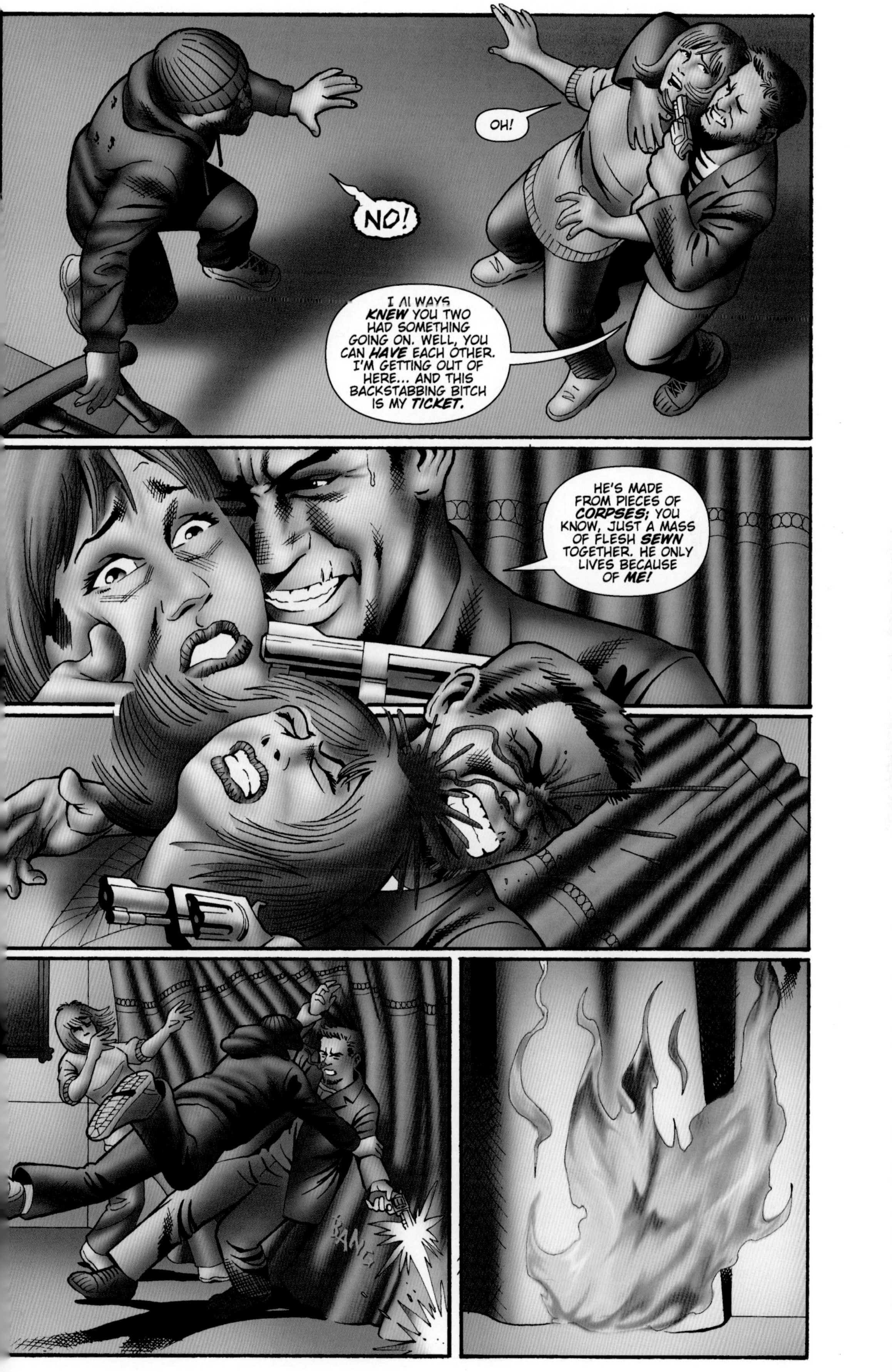
OH!
NO!
I ALWAYS **KNEW** YOU TWO HAD SOMETHING GOING ON. WELL, YOU CAN **HAVE** EACH OTHER. I'M GETTING OUT OF HERE... AND THIS BACKSTABBING BITCH IS MY ***TICKET.***
HE'S MADE FROM PIECES OF **CORPSES;** YOU KNOW, JUST A MASS OF FLESH **SEWN** TOGETHER. HE ONLY LIVES BECAUSE OF **ME!**
BANG

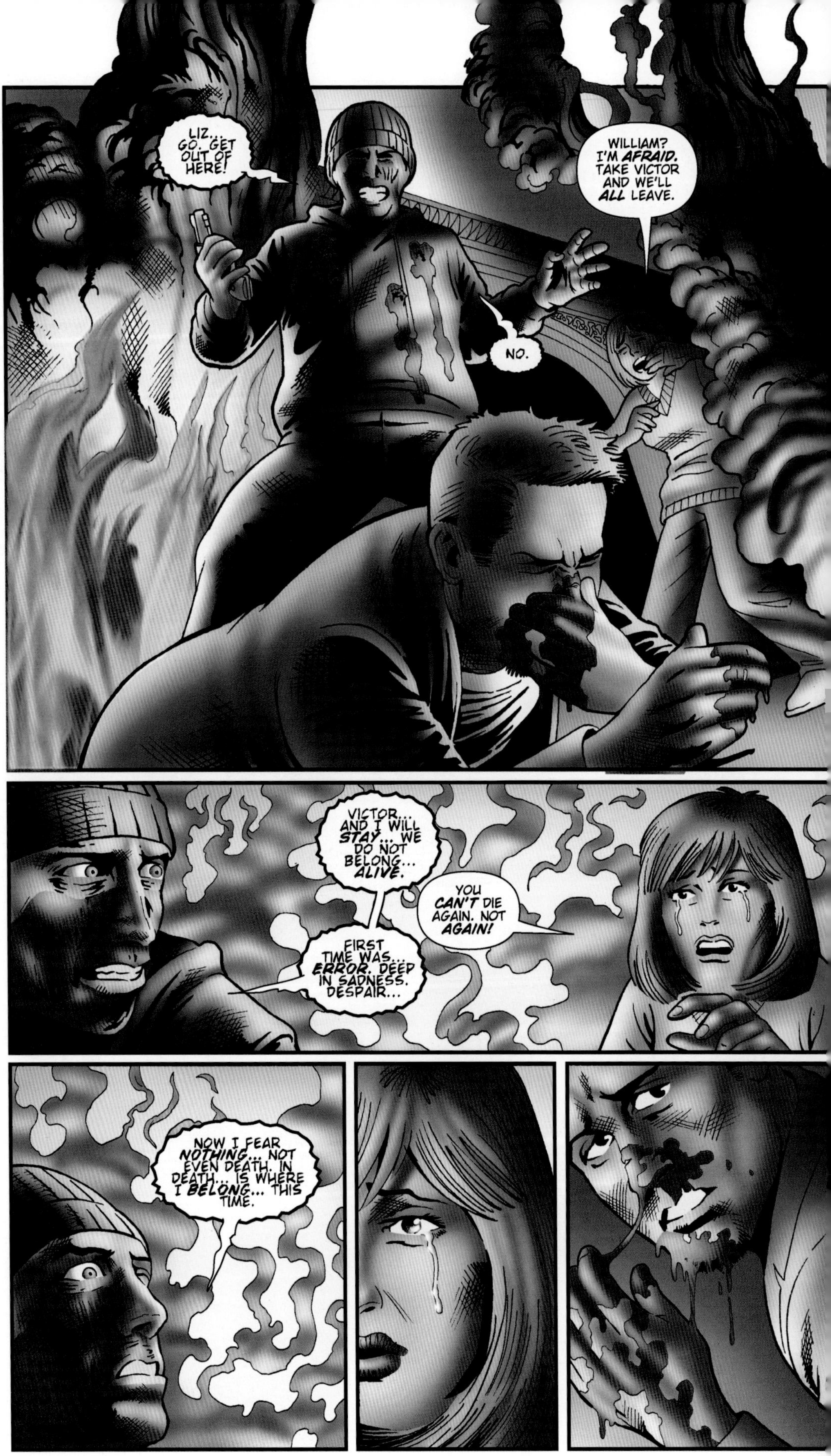
LIZ... GO. GET OUT OF HERE!
WILLIAM? I'M AFRAID. TAKE VICTOR AND WE'LL ALL LEAVE.
NO.
VICTOR... AND I WILL STAY... WE DO NOT BELONG... ALIVE.
FIRST TIME WAS... ERROR. DEEP IN SADNESS. DESPAIR...
YOU CAN'T DIE AGAIN. NOT AGAIN!
NOW I FEAR NOTHING... NOT EVEN DEATH. IN DEATH... IS WHERE I BELONG... THIS TIME.

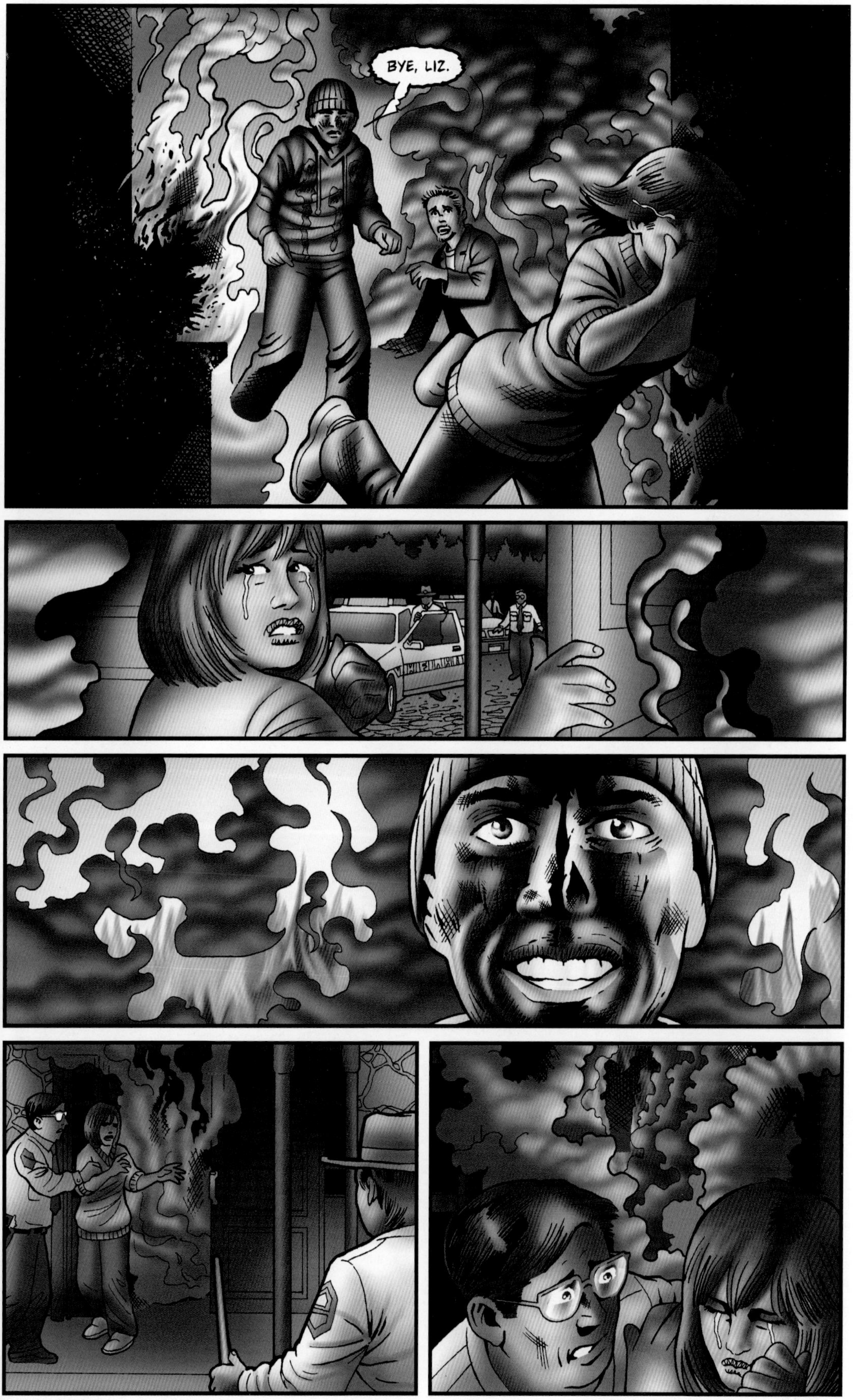
BYE, LIZ.

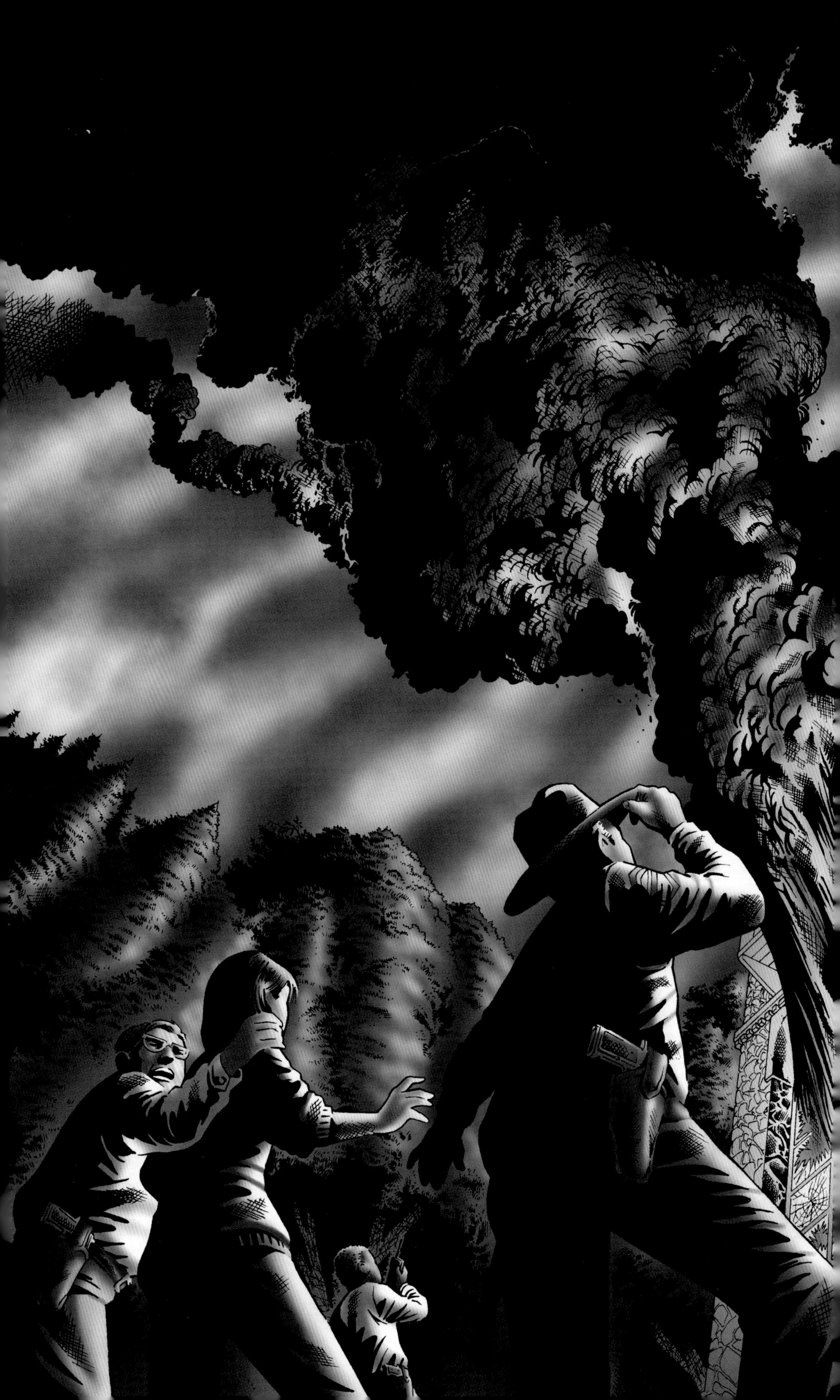

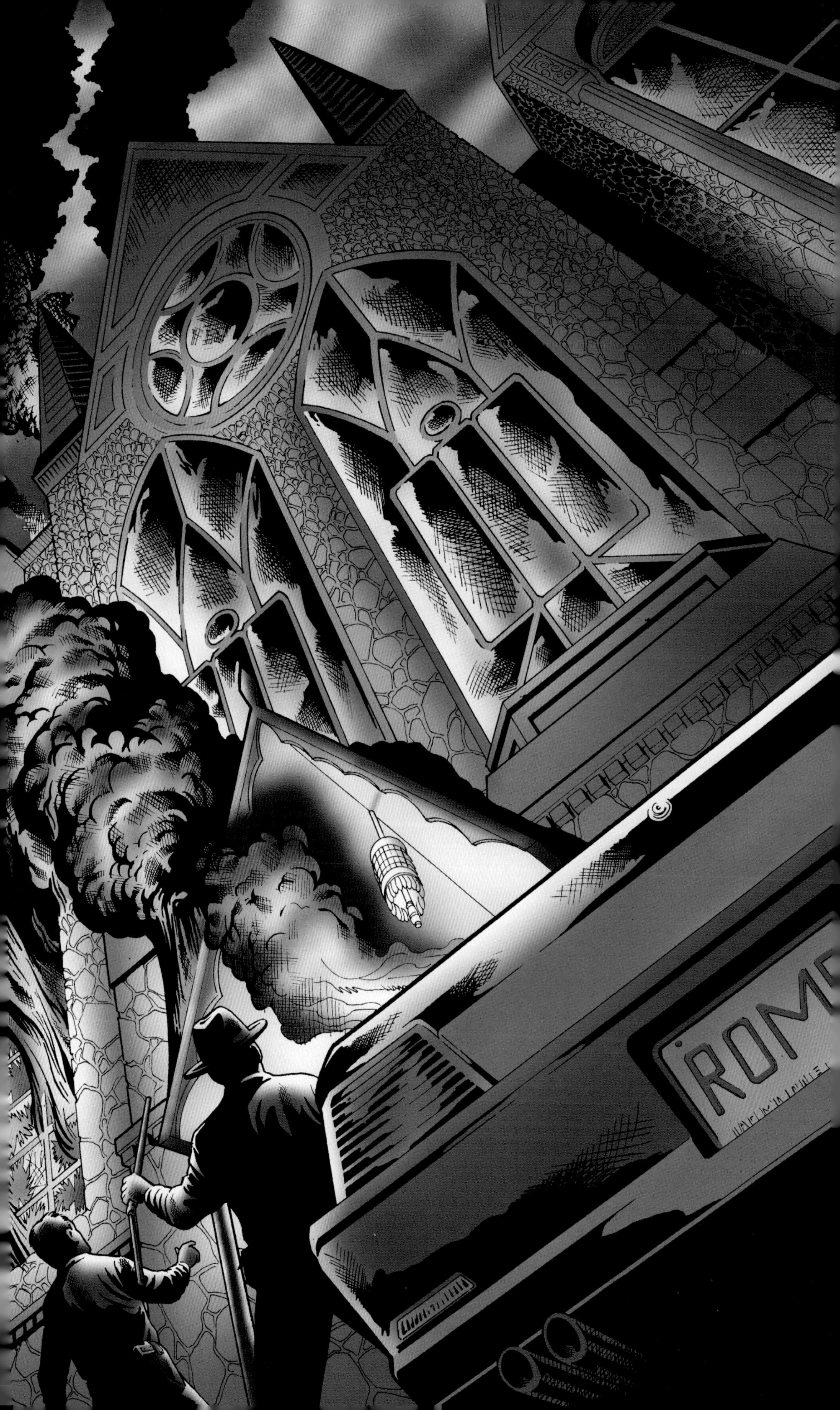
ROM

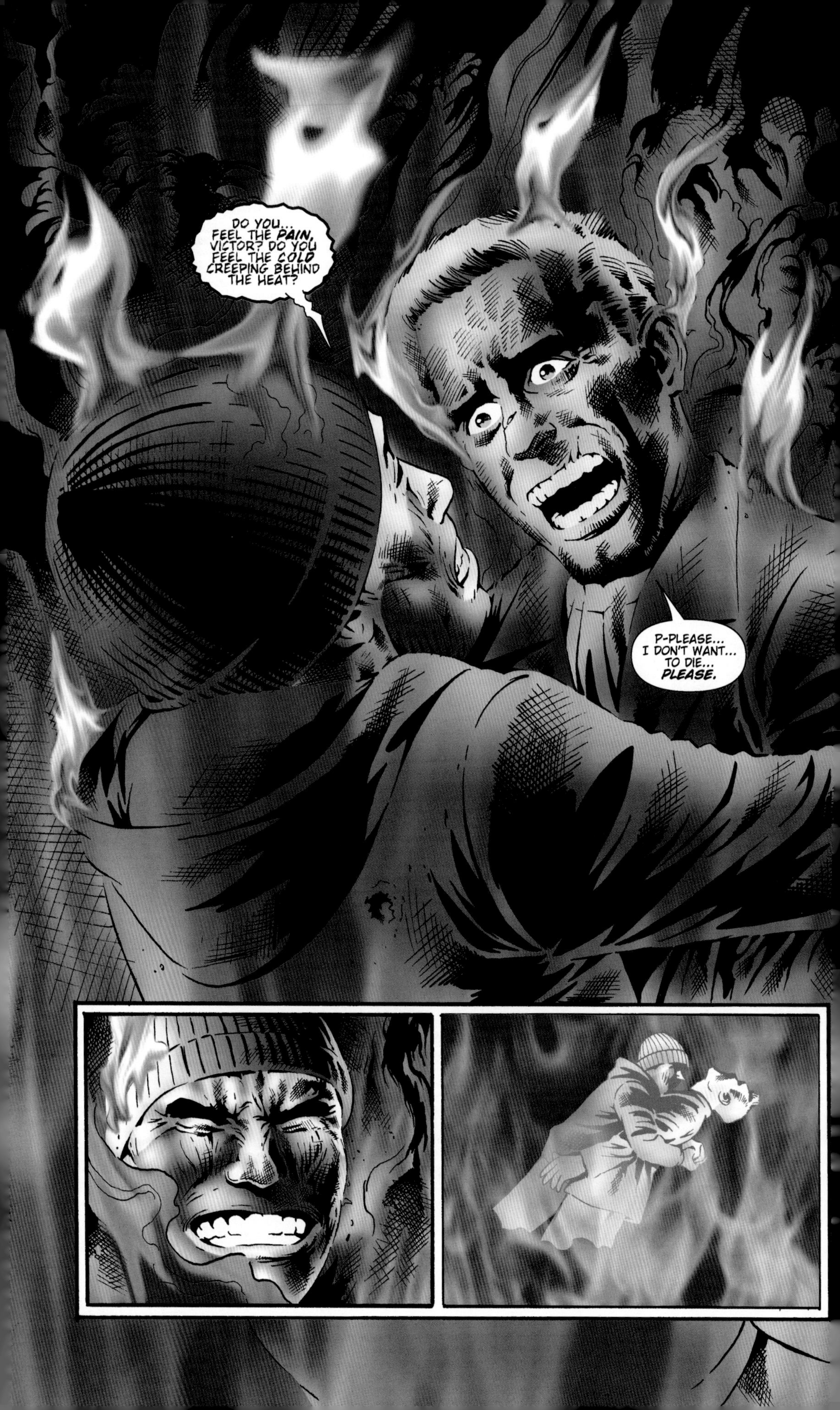
DO YOU... FEEL THE PAIN, VICTOR? DO YOU FEEL THE COLD CREEPING BEHIND THE HEAT?
P-PLEASE... I DON'T WANT... TO DIE... PLEASE.

MORNING.

WHERE IS THE OTHER BODY?

THE ONE IN THE BASEMENT HAS BEEN IDENTIFIED AS *IGGY PRETORIUS*...

NO... THE *OTHER* BODY. I TOLD YOU THERE WAS SOMEONE *IN* THERE WITH *VICTOR*.

CORONER

SORRY, MA'AM. WE ONLY FOUND THE TWO... NOBODY ELSE.

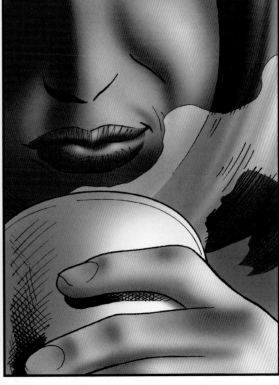

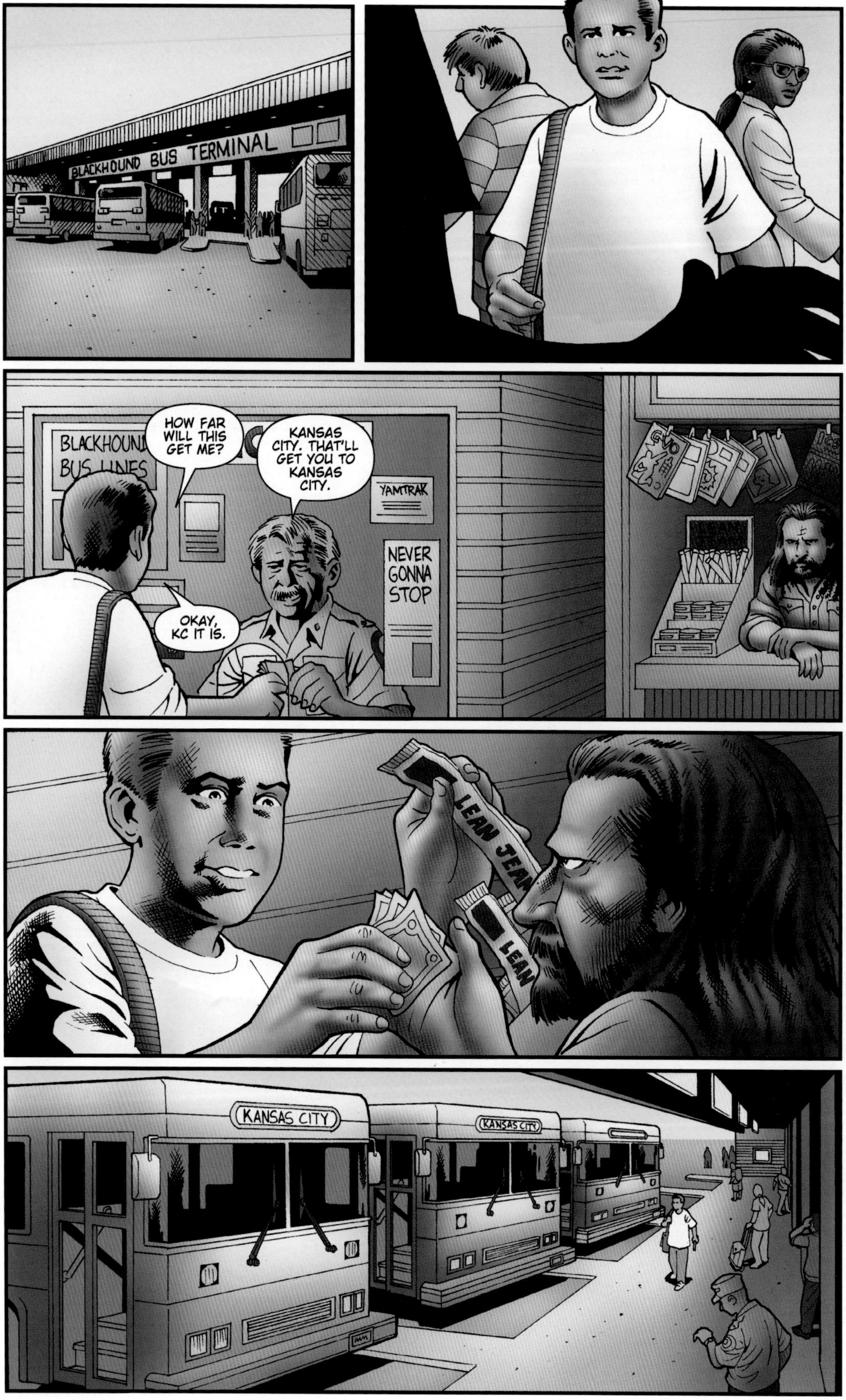
BLACKHOUND BUS TERMINAL
BLACKHOUND BUS LINES
HOW FAR WILL THIS GET ME?
KANSAS CITY. THAT'LL GET YOU TO KANSAS CITY.
YAMTRAK
NEVER GONNA STOP
OKAY, KC IT IS.
LEAN JEAN
LEAN
KANSAS CITY
KANSAS CITY

LOOKS LIKE WE'RE NEIGHBORS. MY NAME'S MATT. YOU WANT SOME JERKY?

THANK YOU.

HEY, NO SWEAT. YOU GOTTA HAVE FRIENDS ON THE ROAD, RIGHT?

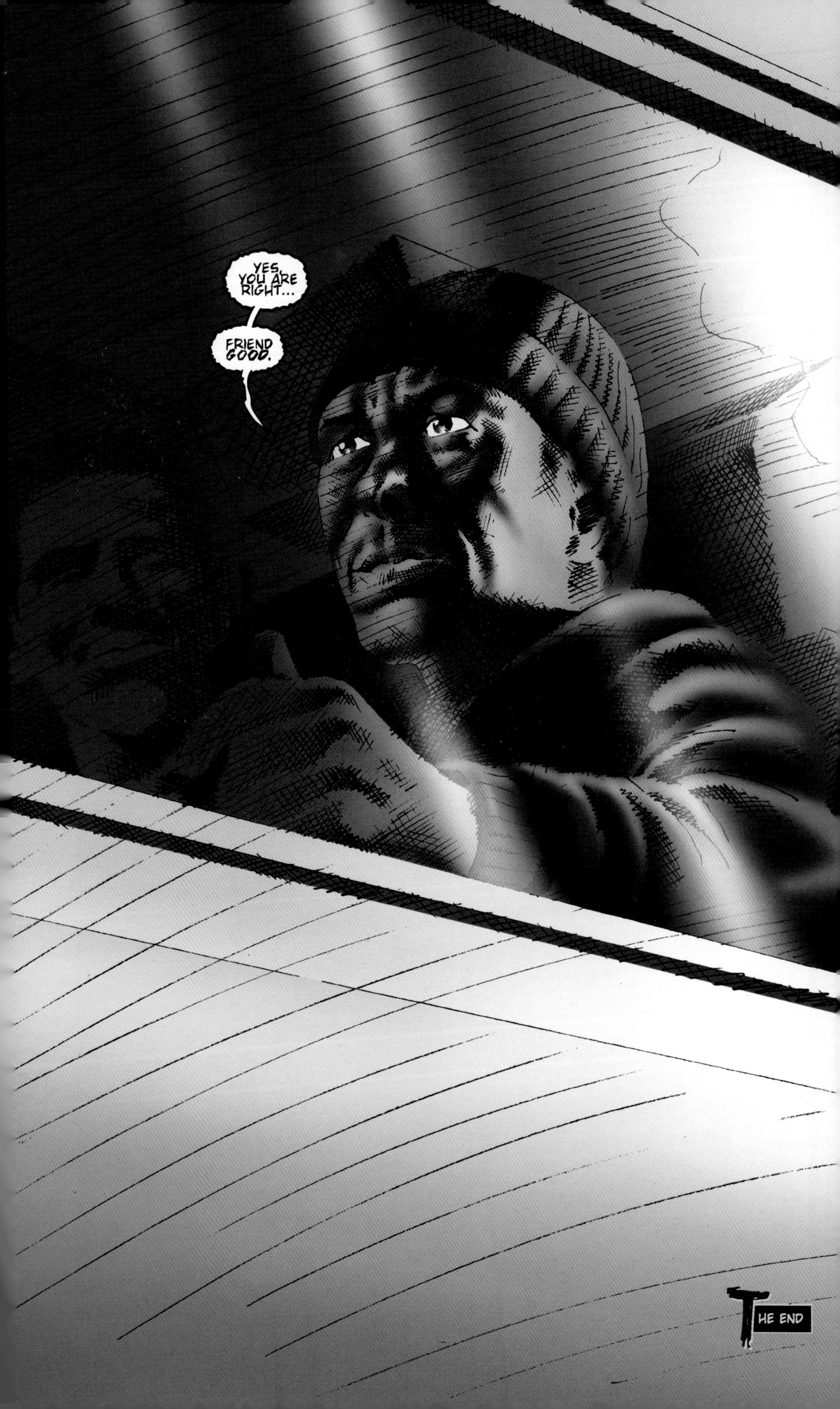
YES, YOU ARE RIGHT...
FRIEND GOOD.
THE END